Investing in
Employee Health

Richard P. Sloan
Jessie C. Gruman
John P. Allegrante

Investing in Employee Health

*A Guide to
Effective Health Promotion
in the Workplace*

 Jossey-Bass Publishers
San Francisco • London • 1987

INVESTING IN EMPLOYEE HEALTH
A Guide to Effective Health Promotion in the Workplace
  by Richard P. Sloan, Jessie C. Gruman, and John P. Allegrante

Copyright © 1987 by: Jossey-Bass Inc., Publishers
                     433 California Street
                     San Francisco, California 94104
                              &
                     Jossey-Bass Limited
                     28 Banner Street
                     London EC1Y 8QE

Library of Congress Cataloging-in-Publication Data

Sloan, Richard P.
   Investing in employee health.

   (A Publication in the Jossey-Bass management series,
the Jossey-Bass social and behavioral science series,
and the Jossey-Bass health series)
   Bibliography: p.
   Includes index.
   1. Industrial hygiene. 2. Health promotion.
I. Gruman, Jessie C. II. Allegrante, John P. (John
Philip), date. III. Title. IV. Series:
Jossey-Bass management series. V. Series: The Jossey-
Bass social and behavioral science series.
VI. Series: Jossey-Bass health series. [DNLM: 1. Health
Promotion—methods. 2. Occupational Health Services—
organization & administration—United States.
WA 412 S634i]
RC969.H43S55   1987   658.3'82   87-45506
ISBN 1-55542-065-6

Manufactured in the United States of America

The paper in this book meets the guidelines for
permanence and durability of the Committee on
Production Guidelines for Book Longevity of the
Council on Library Resources.

Credits are on page 307.

JACKET DESIGN BY WILLI BAUM

FIRST EDITION

Code 8736

A publication in
The Jossey-Bass Management Series
The Jossey-Bass Social and Behavioral Science Series
and
The Jossey-Bass Health Series

For C.P.E.R.,
Ellie and Larry,
and Andrea and Jason

Contents

Figures and Tables   xiii

Preface   xv

The Authors   xxiii

Part One: Health Promotion in the Workplace

1. Health Promotion as Preventive Maintenance   1

   The Myth of Resiliency • Risk Factors and Disease • Workplace Health Promotion and the Organization • Conclusion

2. Origins of Health Promotion and Applications in
   the Workplace   16

   The Historical Context of Health Promotion • Contemporary Views of Health: Risk Factors • What Is Health Promotion? • Workplace Health Promotion • Why Health Promotion in the Workplace? • Conclusion

3. Health Promotion in Perspective: Relationship to
    Organizational Goals   37

    Assumptions Underlying Workplace Health Promotion • Im-
    plications of a Broader View of Health Promotion • Conclu-
    sion

4. Making the Case to Top Management   55

    Health Promotion and the "Bottom Line" • Benefits of
    Workplace Health Promotion • The Time Course of Bene-
    fits and Its Effect on Evaluation • Case Examples of Work-
    place Health Promotion Programs • What Do These Cases
    Demonstrate? • Conclusion

    Part Two: Designing the Health Promotion Program

5. Analyzing the Organization's Health Needs and
    Resources   78

    How Organizations Conduct Health Analyses: Case Exam-
    ples • Workplace Health Promotion Organizational Analysis:
    An Outline • Some Qualifications • Conclusion

6. Planning: Developing the Mission, Business Plan,
    and Budget   102

    The Mission Statement • Developing a Business Plan • The
    Business Plan • Budget • Conclusion

7. Evaluation: Assessing Program Effectiveness from
    the Outset   123

    Why Programs Can Fail • The Levels of Evaluation • Choos-
    ing an Evaluation Design • Conclusion

8. Dealing with Ethical Issues and Other Problems   142

    Conflicting Loyalties: For Whom Do I Work? • Blaming the
    Victim • Can Coercion Be Justified? • Minimizing Unin-
    tended Consequences • Conclusion

Part Three: Putting Health Promotion into Practice

9. Tools of the Health Promotion Manager   156

    Print Materials • Audio-Visual Materials • Management and
    Authority • Committees • Microcomputer Software • Health
    Promotion Events • Lectures/Talks • Workshops/Skills
    Training • Ongoing Programs • Self-Help/Support Groups •
    Referral • Screening for Early Detection of Disease • Health
    Risk Appraisals • Conclusion

10. Running the Program: Internal Organization,
    Marketing, and Selection of Vendors   186

    Organization of the Program • Establishing a Health Promo-
    tion Committee • Using Existing Divisions Within the Orga-
    nization • Marketing • Selection of Vendors and Consultants
    • Conclusion

11. Helping Individuals Change Their Behavior   206

    Health Promotion Goals for Individuals • Recognizing That
    Behavior Influences Health • Personalizing the Link Between
    Behavior and Health • Creating a Plan • Initiating Behavior
    Change • A Healthy Lifestyle • Conclusion

12. Changing the Organization's Health-Related
    Policies   217

    The Role of the Health Promotion Manager • Policies Regu-
    lating Health-Related Behavior • Passive Influence of Health-
    Related Behavior • Policy Change in the Smaller Company •
    Conclusion

13. Beyond the Individual: Health Promotion
    Through Organizational Change   233

    The Effect of Organizational Factors on Employee Health •
    The Concept of Organizational "Climate" • Organizational
    Climate and Health Outcomes • Organizational Interventions
    and Health: Case Studies • Conclusion

14. Conclusion: Observations on the Healthy
    Workplace   251

    Why Workplace Health Promotion Programs Are Likely to
    Grow in Importance • Organizations as Interdependent Sys-
    tems

    Resource A: Alternative Strategies for Managing
    Health Care Costs   259

    Benefit Redesign • Mechanisms to Reduce Use of the Health
    Care System • Increasing the Efficiency of Health Care Pro-
    viders • Health Maintenance Organizations

    Resource B: Publications for Health Promotion
    Professionals   264

    Resource C: Organizations Providing Health
    Promotion Information   270

    Resource D: Sample Employee Health and
    Attitude Survey   275

    Resource E: Health Risk Appraisals   279

    Which Type of HRA?

    References   287

    Index   297

Figures and Tables

Chapter Two

Figure 1. Pictorial Representation of the Changing
Contribution of Chronic and Infectious
Conditions to Total Mortality in the
United States 1900–1970   18
Figure 2. Interaction of Factors Affecting Health   21
Table 1. Percentage of Total Deaths and Risk
Factors for Ten Leading Causes of
Death in the United States in 1983   22

Chapter Three

Figure 1. Workplace Health Promotion   39
Figure 2. A Social-Psychological Model of
Workplace Health Promotion   41
Figure 3. The Broader Focus of Workplace
Health Promotion   48

Chapter Four

Figure 1. The Relationship of Health Promotion
Objectives over Time   61

Chapter Five

Table 1.   The Major Diagnostic Categories for
            Medicare, 1983   86

Chapter Six

Figure 1.   The Business Plan   104

Chapter Seven

Figure 1.   Categories of Program Failure   127
Figure 2.   Three Levels of Program Evaluation   129
Figure 3.   Participation in a Stress Management
            Program   135
Figure 4.   Participation in a Stress Management
            Program Offered in Two Buildings   138

Chapter Twelve

Table 1.   Continuum of the Reliance of Workplace
            Health Promotion Programs on Individual
            Motivation   218

Chapter Thirteen

Table 1.   Continuum of the Reliance of Workplace
            Health Promotion Programs on Individual
            Motivation (amended)   236
Figure 1.   A Social-Psychological Model of
            Workplace Health Promotion   239
Figure 2.   The Relationship Among Job Demands,
            Control, and Strain   240

Preface

From 1979 to 1984, health insurance benefit payments in the United States increased 66.4 percent, from $6.5 billion to $10.9 billion. During the same five-year period, the cost of health insurance premiums increased 75 percent, from $73.9 billion to $129.8 billion. In 1950, national health expenditures represented 4.4 percent of the gross national product. By 1985, they represented 10.7 percent of the GNP. Even during 1986, when the consumer price index increased by only 1.1 percent, medical care costs rose at a rate of 7.7 percent. The U.S. Department of Health and Human Services has reported that acute health conditions such as infectious diseases, respiratory conditions, and injuries accounted for more than 333 million workdays lost in 1985. These figures do not include workdays lost because of chronic disease such as cancer or heart disease.

Who pays for these disease-related costs? A substantial fraction comes from employers. According to the U.S. Chamber of Commerce, employers paid $2,560 per employee in 1985 for health-related costs, an amount that constituted 11.8 percent of payroll. Employer contributions to health insurance have risen steadily, from $68.8 billion in 1981 to $104.6 billion in 1985. Employer contributions to Medicare have risen at a similar rate, from $2.3 billion in 1970 to a projected $23.5 billion in 1985.

As the late Senator Everett Dirksen of Illinois once said: "A billion here and a billion there—pretty soon you're talking about real money."

This rapid increase in the cost of health care and in employer health care expenses in the United States has been paralleled roughly by a steady increase in the public's interest in greater participation in matters of health. Evidence of this interest abounds: the emergence of exercise as a major leisure-time activity, increased concerns about fat and salt content of foods, the prominence of stress as a concern in the workplace and elsewhere, and so forth.

During the past decade, these two concerns have converged to produce interest in a field unknown until recently: workplace health promotion. Some of the largest American companies, as well as some of the smallest, have attempted to capitalize on individuals' increasing concern about their health as a way of addressing the high cost of health care. As employers have become interested in health promotion as a better way to manage their health care costs, a number of books and articles have appeared on the topic. Most of these books and many of the articles have served the useful purpose of presenting general information on health promotion in the workplace. In our view, however, virtually all of the writing on the topic has been directed largely at occupational medicine specialists and social scientists, thus limiting its value to people in organizations who are attempting to establish and maintain health promotion programs. A second and related limitation has been the tendency of these works to focus on the techniques of health behavior change in the abstract, without fully considering the practicalities of the workplace. We believe that to be optimally effective, people in charge of workplace health promotion need a solid grounding in basic behavioral science and also need to recognize the organizational realities that can influence their efforts. It is to these ends that this book has been written.

In a sense, then, *Investing in Employee Health* is a "how to do it" book for the *health promotion manager*—that person in the organization assigned the responsibility of coordinating the development, implementation, and evaluation of workplace health promotion programs. This book offers the program manager the most current information available on programs as well as a conceptual framework to guide program development. Throughout the book, case material from actual programs is presented; the focus is on the actual workplace, the constraints it imposes, and the advantages it offers.

Who is the health promotion manager? In our experience, the health promotion manager may be attached to any of a number of areas within the organization: personnel, benefits, medical, employee assistance, finance, health and safety, human resources development, education and training, or others. In a small company, one in which a single individual may wear many of these hats, the health promotion manager may have other unrelated responsibilities. This book is written primarily for the person in the organization—large or small—who will manage the health promotion program. (Note: When we use the pronoun *you*, we are talking specifically to this person.)

This book will also be useful to others within the organization. Because we examine the potential benefits, financial and otherwise, of a workplace health promotion program and explore *how* such a program relates to the rest of the organization, *Investing in Employee Health* will be of value to upper-level executives who confront the problem of managing health care costs. We believe that the book should be read by such executives *before* they embark on a program and assign a manager to it.

Finally, as social scientists with interests and experience in the diverse fields of social and organizational psychology, health education, and behavioral medicine, we have drawn on relevant current literature to illuminate the process of workplace health promotion both from the perspective of the individual employees who may participate and from that of the organization for which they work. For this reason, we believe that *Investing in Employee Health* will be of value to both graduate and advanced undergraduate students in organizational and health psychology, health education, behavioral medicine, occupational medicine and nursing, social work, and even business.

Although we have described *Investing in Employee Health* as a "how to do it" book, strictly speaking, this is only partially correct. The book is really designed to take a "how to *think about it* so that you can do it" approach. Accordingly, we raise issues throughout the book that may appear to be well beyond the concerns of the health promotion manager, more appropriate for higher executives of the organization. For example, in Chapter Thirteen, we discuss the relationship between such organizational characteristics as remuneration systems and health outcomes. Clearly, the responsibilities of most health promotion managers in the United States do not extend to determination of remuneration. Yet we believe that for this book to serve its purpose, it must consider health promotion in its largest context and in this way help to transcend some common misunderstandings and conceptual limitations regarding the nature of the field.

Workplace health promotion requires as much knowledge about the *workplace* as it does about *health*. As we discuss in Chapter Three, the *goals* of workplace health promotion—for example, reductions in health care costs and absenteeism—may result from organizational activities only loosely related to health promotion. It is for reasons such as these that we believe it essential to inform all of those involved in workplace health promotion of its fullest potential, even if acting on that potential is well beyond one's authority. It is important to know what *can* be done, even if at present it is not possible to do it.

The issue of organizational size merits specific attention. Because such large organizations as Johnson & Johnson and AT&T have developed extensive and highly regarded programs, there is a tendency among those in small or moderate-sized companies to regard workplace health promotion as a luxury reserved for the "big boys." Nothing could be further from the truth. Small companies, just as large ones, can and have created inventive, popular, and successful workplace health promotion programs. For example, we cite the case of a company with only thirty-five employees. Examples from small and mid-sized companies are also provided.

In Part One of the book, we present a general introduction and orientation. Chapter One introduces workplace health promotion using an analogy of preventive maintenance for physical equipment. Chapter Two provides a more detailed review of workplace health promotion, including its brief history and the forces that have influenced its current form. In this chapter, we discuss the relationship of health promotion to the traditional approach of medicine, examining similarities and differences. In Chapter Three, we present a broader view of the field based on the individual psychology of people in the workplace. Chapter Four has been written specifically to help program managers deal with the considerable skepticism that often characterizes top management views of workplace health promotion. As the chapter demonstrates, noteworthy cases can be cited of organizations that have implemented programs whose successes can be measured in financial as well as other terms. We hope that this material can be used to persuade reluctant executives that workplace health promotion, when carefully planned and developed, is worth the investment.

Part Two provides the details of program design: analysis, planning, and evaluation. The chapters in this section can be used to guide the reader through the initial stages of the process that culminates in implementation. Chapter Five addresses organizational analysis and emphasizes the need for all organizations, large and small, to conduct a systematic examination of the need for a health promotion program before embarking on one. We believe that the analysis must examine organizational resources as well. Once these and other relevant data have been collected, data interpretation and program planning can begin. These processes are the subject of Chapter Six. The natural counterpart to organizational analysis and planning, program evaluation, is the topic of Chapter Seven. Part Two concludes with a chapter examining the ethical issues and other problems raised by workplace health promotion programs. The issues raised in this chapter merit serious attention, but relatively little has been written about them. We believe that program managers must consider potential ethical conflicts that may arise in the course of their work.

We devote Part Three to some of what we call the "nuts and bolts" of health promotion in the workplace: development and implementation. Chapter Nine provides a detailed examination of the "tools" of health promotion at work. In Chapter Ten, some central responsibilities of the program manager are considered, and Chapters Eleven, Twelve, and Thirteen comprise an organized series addressing three different levels of programs: individual change, policy change, and organization change. Chapter Eleven focuses on what has become the traditional mechanism of health promotion in the workplace: encouraging individuals to change their health behaviors by offering such programs as personal stress management, weight control, and smoking cessation. Chapter Twelve treats a variant of this approach, mandating health behavior change through policies that, for example, require the use of seat belts when driving on company time. In Chapter Thirteen, we present what may be regarded as the most controversial topic in the book: how organizations can have a significant impact on health care costs and outcomes by focusing on aspects of the organization such as managerial style or workload. Thus, these three chapters present workplace health promotion programs in the context of decreasing dependence on the motivation of individual employees to make health behavior changes. In Chapter Fourteen, we provide some concluding comments and look forward.

Finally, we have included several Resources at the end of the book that provide program managers with sources of useful reference material. In recognition that health promotion in the workplace is only one of many cost-management strategies, Resource A is devoted to a brief presentation of alternative strategies. Resource B provides an extensive list of publications of interest to health promotion managers. In Resource C, we list sources of current health statistics from organizations that can provide helpful literature, films, videotapes, and other material and organizations that specialize in workplace health promotion. Because effective workplace health promotion programs require collection of information regarding employee health habits and program preferences, in Resource D we provide a sample employee survey. Health risk appraisals are discussed in considerable detail in Resource E.

We believe that the development of a successful workplace health promotion program requires a conceptual understanding of the nature and processes of health promotion and their place in the real workplace. Simply knowing the "tools of the trade" with little or no appreciation of the nature of the undertaking involved is not sufficient for success. One also must develop an understanding of the factors that influence health and health-related behaviors, especially as they operate in the work setting. *Investing in Employee Health,* we believe, can provide both.

A number of our colleagues, students, and professionals provided encouragement and assistance in this undertaking. Among those to whom we are especially indebted for their kind support are Joseph Warren, Dorothea Johnson, Veronica Gilligan, Thomas Consul, Marie Lauer, Kyle Cavanaugh, and Molly McCauley, all of the Total Life Concept Program at AT&T; Richard Bellingham and Barry Cohen, Possibilities, Inc.; John L. Michela, Teachers College, Columbia University; Clarence E. Pearson, National Center for Health Education; and Joanne Shovlin, State University of New York, College at New Paltz.

We also want to acknowledge and thank the following individuals whose careful professional review of the manuscript during varying stages of the writing proved enormously valuable: Andrew J. J. Brennan, Metropolitan Life Insurance Company; Gail E. Lufkin, Blue Cross & Blue Shield of Alabama; James L. Malfetti, Teachers College, Columbia University; Peter Messeri, School of Public Health, Columbia University, and Lawrence W. Green, Center for Health Promotion, Research and Development, University of Texas Health Sciences Center at Houston.

In addition to these individuals, we are grateful in particular to the State University of New York, College at New Paltz, the Behavioral Medicine Program at the Columbia-Presbyterian Medical Center, AT&T, the American Cancer Society,

Teachers College of Columbia University, and the W. K. Kellogg
Foundation for providing us with the institutional supports that
permitted us to collaborate on this project. Finally, no effort
such as this would have been possible without the encouragement and support of our families, whose love and enduring support of our work has been more helpful than they realize.

New York City   Richard P. Sloan
July 1987   Jessie C. Gruman
                                                        John P. Allegrante

The Authors

Richard P. Sloan is coordinator of the Behavioral Medicine Program at the Columbia-Presbyterian Medical Center in New York. He is also associate professor of psychology in the Department of Psychology at the State University of New York, College at New Paltz. After receiving his B.S. degree (1970) in biology from Union College in Schenectady, New York, Sloan completed his M.A. (1974) and Ph.D. (1977) degrees in psychology at the Graduate Faculty of Political and Social Science, the New School for Social Research, in New York City. He has studied behavioral medicine at the Harvard School of Medicine, and he is a New York State licensed psychologist and is certified in the practice of biofeedback.

Sloan's areas of interest fall into two distinct but related categories: working with organizations in the areas of stress management and workplace health promotion, and behavioral cardiology. In regard to the former, he has worked with numerous companies and organizations around the country, in Canada, and in Europe. His published work is in the areas of management, health, and medicine and their interaction. In the area of behavioral cardiology, his research interests include the relationship between psychological stress, cardiac arrhythmias, and sudden cardiac death and more basic work examining factors that contribute to the relationship between psychologically stressful events and the performance of the heart.

Sloan has served as an adviser to the New York Academy of Medicine, the National Science Foundation, and the New York Association for the Blind. He is a frequent speaker for the American Management Association and is a member of the American Psychological Association, the New York Academy of Sciences, the American Psychosomatic Society, and the Society of Behavioral Medicine.

Jessie C. Gruman is the director of adult education for the national organization of the American Cancer Society. In this capacity, she is responsible for the public implementation of cancer risk reduction and early detection health education based on current research in changing health behavior. She received her B.A. degree in English from Vassar College in 1975, her M.A. degree in social psychology from the New School for Social Research in 1981, and her Ph.D. degree in social and organizational psychology from Teachers College, Columbia University, in 1984.

Prior to joining the American Cancer Society, Gruman served as the manager of AT&T Communications' comprehensive health promotion program, at AT&T's corporate headquarters in Basking Ridge, New Jersey. At both the American Cancer Society and at AT&T, the main emphasis of her work has been on the application of behavioral research to health behavior change programs. She has worked in the areas of cancer and heart disease risk reduction, back care, and substance abuse with these and other organizations. Gruman's research interests are the building of general models for the transfer of technology from behavioral health research to practice as well as health policy development and implementation.

Gruman has served as an adviser to the National Cancer Institute, the U.S. Centers for Disease Control, and the New York State Department of Substance Abuse. She is a member of the American Psychological Association, the Society of Behavioral Medicine, and Sigma Xi. She has been a visiting professor at Teachers College, Columbia University, and Fordham University.

John P. Allegrante is associate professor and chairman of the Department of Health Education and is director of the Center for Health Promotion at Teachers College, the graduate school of education at Columbia University. He has been a member of the faculty there since 1979. He also holds an appointment in the Faculty of Medicine as associate professor of Clinical Public Health in the Columbia University School of Public Health.

In 1985, Allegrante was awarded the W. K. Kellogg Foundation National Fellowship. He completed his B.A. degree at the State University of New York College at Cortland in 1974. He received his M.S. degree in health education in 1976 and his Ph.D. degree in health education in 1979 at the University of Illinois.

Allegrante's principal interests include research in community cardiovascular health education program development and evaluation, ethical issues in health promotion and disease prevention, and health and social policy. He is the author or co-author of numerous published papers and reports and has presented more than fifty papers and speeches at national and regional conferences.

He is a member of the American Public Health Association, American School Health Association, and Association for the Advancement of Health Education and is a fellow of both the Society for Public Health Education and the New York Academy of Medicine. Allegrante has been a consultant and adviser to several major private and government agencies, including the National Center for Health Education, the National Institutes of Health, and several agencies of the U.S. Public Health Service. He serves on the editorial boards of several journals.

Investing in
Employee Health

1

Health Promotion as Preventive Maintenance

Companies spend millions of dollars each year in preventive maintenance on machines. We see no earthly reason why we can't make the same commitment to our people.
        —Peter Thigpen, president of Levi Strauss USA
                                    [1984, p. 2]

What would you think if your vice-presidents approved the purchase of a large, complex, and expensive piece of equipment but failed to provide for periodic servicing and preventive maintenance? At the very least, you would probably raise serious questions about their foresight. Given the cost of today's equipment, even for standard office equipment, it is essential to commit resources to regular servicing. Only through periodic maintenance is it possible to maximize the output and lifetime of the equipment and minimize the "down time" required when it fails, either temporarily or permanently.

Failure to provide preventive maintenance for physical equipment can lead to catastrophe. Indeed, an entire industry has been spawned by the failure to maintain buildings properly and periodically. According to New York architect and engineer

Walter Melvin, both office and residential building management are spending vast sums of money to make major repairs on facades and roofs to cure problems that easily could have been prevented with regular and far less costly maintenance. The burgeoning and highly profitable waterproofing industry provides additional evidence of the consequences of failure to provide preventive maintenance for facilities. How could such a situation evolve? The rationale, as might be imagined, is financial. To defer maintenance to save money was seen as fiscally prudent. After all, it is obviously less costly to spend no money than to spend some money for prevention. However, as the deterioration of facilities around the country demonstrates, these "savings" are largely illusory and exist only in the very short run.

In the corporate sector, some notable cases illustrate the value of periodic preventive maintenance programs for equipment. United Parcel Service (UPS), for example, has a computer-directed maintenance program that ensures that each of its vehicles receives regular examination and maintenance. The justification for this program derives directly from the nature of UPS's business: It is a service organization that cannot afford late delivery of packages because of vehicle failure. Note that this policy is based on more than the economics of prevention versus replacement. Not only is it more costly to replace an entire vehicle than to maintain its "health" periodically but it is also immeasurably more costly to lose customers because of unnecessary and preventable equipment failure. The validity of this viewpoint is not confined to the service industry.

The corporation's need to be responsible to stockholders makes it rather difficult to uncover instances of management's failure to provide essential maintenance services for physical equipment. Municipal services, owing to their public nature, provide us with many examples. One of the most celebrated consequences of the failure to provide for preventive maintenance for physical facilities is the case of the New York City Transit Authority, which, during the 1970s fiscal crisis, decided to "save money" by maintaining the level of service while "deferring" maintenance. According to the *Strategic Plan* 1985-1989 written by the Metropolitan Transit Authority and the

New York City Transit Authority, rather than cut back on the delivery of service during this time, maintenance was to be deferred—that is, either delayed or suspended altogether. "In an effort to cut expenditures without visibly sacrificing service, the Transit Authority reduced the size of its maintenance workforce during the late 1970s. For example, while total hours worked by all Authority workers fell 12.3 percent between 1973 and 1979, the hours worked by the employees responsible for maintaining the Transit Authority's subway cars fell 33 percent, nearly three times the overall rate" (*Metropolitan Transit Authority*, 1984, p. 17). As a result of this "money-saving" policy, the transit system deteriorated greatly. Although it is difficult to quantify the costs to the system (not to mention the city and its residents) of this policy, one consequence can be seen in the need to purchase new subway cars. Given proper maintenance, subway cars can last for thirty to thirty-five years. Without proper maintenance, their life expectancy is reduced considerably. As a direct result, the need for new capital expenditures, to replace dysfunctional cars, arises much sooner than it should. To summarize, in the words of the *Strategic Plan,* "the 1970s taught us that deferred maintenance is no maintenance and that undercapitalization mortgages the future" (p. 21).

Problems of this sort also arise in the corporate world. The story's moral is as pertinent to private enterprise as it is to public administration: The "savings" that derive from such a policy are illusory. And worse, an organization with a policy that ignores preventive maintenance for physical equipment and facilities in the name of savings deludes itself. The real costs of these delusions eventually become apparent. For this reason, most companies endorse the expenditure of relatively small amounts of money now to reduce the likelihood of considerably greater future expenses. An "ounce of prevention" does appear to be worth a "pound of cure."

Yet when we consider the most expensive, complex, and important "equipment" in any organization—its people—we discover that no preventive maintenance policy exists at all. Organizations generally have no policies or programs designed to prevent the "breakdown" of employees due to illness or injury.

Although no figures exist to compare the amount of money organizations spend on the maintenance of equipment and their analogous expenditures for human resources, the only very recent popularity of health promotion programs in the workplace suggests that this kind of preventive investment in people has been relatively uncommon. In fact, until recently, it was unheard of. The organizational resources traditionally devoted to employees are spent on selection and training, as well as on the benefits programs. To be sure, most companies provide conventional health insurance benefits, often at great expense, to ensure that employees will receive proper medical attention when necessary. But this approach deals with illness only after it occurs. Similarly, organizations provide vacation time for employees. However, when an employee is "out of service" during a vacation, no specific attention is paid to necessary repair or prevention of future problems. Would an organization with considerable investment in physical equipment, for example, United Parcel Service, settle for this kind of policy for equipment maintenance? Quite obviously, the answer is "no." Those companies that would answer "yes" are more likely no longer around.

But why should organizations devote precious and limited resources to promoting the health of employees in the same way that they endorse preventive maintenance for equipment? Although there are obvious differences between human and physical resources in any organization, there are also important similarities. Both are essential to the optimal functioning of any company. Both are costly. And both operate optimally under certain conditions and less than optimally under others.

Human resources professionals with knowledge of the history of their profession might detect a note of irony here in our implicitly asking that people be treated more like machines, at least in this regard. The irony arises from the fact that in many ways, the human resources movement developed precisely as a protest against the prevailing school of management in the early part of this century: Frederick Taylor's "scientific management" position. Scientific management essentially held that organizations should not distinguish between their two classes of resources: (1) physical equipment such as machinery and facilities and (2) people. According to this viewpoint, management's goal was to study work scientifically and rationally determine the most efficient way to perform each task in the organization to improve performance. Through the lens of efficiency, the distinction between people and equipment faded: People, like machines, could improve their performance by the elimination of wasteful actions and the simultaneous adoption of efficient ones. Henry Ford's assembly line provides an excellent example of the implementation of this perspective.

Largely as a reaction to "scientific management," the human relations movement arose in industry. Pioneered by such people as Elton Mayo, this movement held that there was more to management than the mere focus on the technological aspects of work. What Taylor's position lacked was a recognition that in many important ways, people were different from machines; principally, people, unlike machines, have feelings about work and have relationships with one another. The human relations movement was driven by the recognition that people's behavior in organizations is largely a function of the feelings and attitudes they have about their work and their coworkers, including supervisors.

Current views of the human resources profession are far more consistent with the human relations movement than with its scientific management predecessor. So, one may properly ask, "Why are we asking for a return to the treatment of people like machines?" Our answer is that in some ways in contemporary industry, machines receive better treatment than people do.

Consider the airline industry. According to Jack Barker of the Federal Aviation Administration, "the whole idea of airplane maintenance is to know the useful life of every part and replace it *before* it fails" (in Ibold, 1986, p. 7D). On the basis of an extensive engineering analysis of the expected life of parts and systems, the airlines have developed a five-tiered maintenance schedule that calls for periodic inspection and replacement of these components, irrespective of their apparent physical condition. For example, at the "service check" conducted after 75 to 300 flying hours, 13 to 40 person-hours are devoted to inspection and replacement. After 700 to 1,500 flying hours, depending on the type of aircraft, the "letter check" requiring 300 to 1,000 hours of work is performed. To perform this preventive maintenance, aircraft regularly are taken out of service, but it is understood that periodic, predictable, and time-limited removal from service, as a business policy, is vastly superior to unexpected and indefinite down time. Although it is true that people are also regularly "taken out of service"—we work only about eight hours per day and we receive annual vacations—little effort is made to provide them with "periodic service and maintenance."

In the computer industry, we find that large systems may be shut down as frequently as once per week for maintenance and service. During this down time, the system is examined for malfunctions. Moreover, computer systems are provided with special environments and conditions in which they operate. Large systems are housed in specially air-conditioned rooms to control temperature and humidity. Special care is taken to ensure continuity of electrical service. In general, physical equipment is cared for in a way that attempts to minimize the likelihood of breakdown and preserve its "health." Rarely do we find that people receive such treatment.

To be sure, we also can demonstrate that machines receive poorer treatment than people. Much equipment, for example, runs twenty-four hours a day with no breaks for meals or sleep or life at home with a family. Our view, however, is that physical equipment is capable of being so treated because it is much, much simpler than people. It is axiomatic that the more complex a piece of equipment, the more things on it can go wrong. The complexity of people, in both their physical and psychological aspects, is so exquisite and enormous that we should expect to be provided with the best of treatment. Therefore, when we see machines receiving superior treatment, our inclination is to expect that people should receive treatment at least as good. We incline toward the highest, not the lowest, common denominator.

The Myth of Resiliency

A major reason why executives endorse the idea of preventive maintenance for machines but neglect the idea of similar maintenance for people is that, to a large degree, they believe that people are resilient. Unlike machines, people are capable of re-bounding from many circumstances, for instance, illness and injury, that temporarily restrict their functioning. In most cases, employees who become ill eventually recover, either with or without medical attention. Machines that malfunction do not. Nevertheless, what is the cost of employees' absences or, if not absences, reduced productivity while they are recovering? And what is the cost to the organization when an employee does not recover?

Illness and injury produce both direct and indirect costs to organizations. Direct costs include:

- salary to the absent employee
- medical expenses
- rehabilitation costs
- in the case of death, survivor benefits (either paid directly by the company or through rapidly increasing insurance premiums)
- increasingly common workmen's compensation awards, even in the cases of stress-related disabilities

Indirect costs include:

- distress to others and disorganization during the period of absence
- costs of temporary replacement or overtime pay to cover the responsibilities of the missing employee
- training of temporary replacements
- retraining of the employee upon return to the job
- recruiting, selecting, and hiring a permanent replacement when the employee goes on permanent disability or dies
- administrative costs associated with all of the preceding

Costs for each employee are significant. When multiplied by the number of employees in a company, these costs can be enormous. According to the U.S. Chamber of Commerce's most recent survey of employee benefits, American companies were paying an average of $2,560 per employee in 1985 for health care, an increase of approximately 100 percent from 1977. This amount is 11.8 percent of the average company payroll ("Employers Pay $2,600 per Employee for Health Costs," 1986). Employer contributions to health insurance have risen steadily from $68.8 billion in 1981 to $104.6 billion in 1985 (Clearinghouse on Business Coalitions for Health Action, 1986). As a point of reference, this figure is the rough equivalent of the annual revenues of only the world's largest companies. From 1972 to 1982, this increase has averaged 15 percent per year. During the same period, the average rate of increase of total employee compensation was only 10 percent. In addition, employers contribute to the Medicare trust fund. This contribution totaled $23.5 billion in 1985 (Clearinghouse on Business Coalitions for Health Action, 1986) and is increasing at an annual average of 20 percent (Freeland and Schendler, 1984). Business has become the largest private purchaser of health services and products in the United States. (Although this book is about workplace health promotion and its potential to contribute to health care cost management, other strategies are designed to accomplish the same purpose. Interested readers can find a brief discussion of these alternatives in Resource A.)

Moreover, virtually all of these expenses are for the treatment of illness and injury after the fact—almost no resources are devoted to prevention of illness. According to Regina Herzlinger and David Calkins (1986), in 1983, 24 percent of companies' net profits were expended on health insurance but *only* 0.11 percent were spent on health promotion programs. To summarize, "corporate expenses for health care are rising at such a fast rate that, if unchecked, in eight years they will eliminate all profits for the average Fortune '500' company and the largest 250 nonindustrials" (Herzlinger and Schwartz, 1985, p. 69).

Take Chrysler Corporation as an example of how health care costs affect a major corporation's balance sheet. According to Joseph Califano (1983), former United States secretary of health, education, and welfare and now a member of the board of directors of Chrysler, the 1983 direct health care bill for employees, dependents, and retirees exceeded $6,000 per active worker; that is, each Chrysler worker has to produce $6,000 just to pay for direct health care costs *before Chrysler can pay for anything else, including wages.* Thus, health care costs exceed $600 per car sold. Chrysler's biggest single supplier is not a steel company: It is Blue Cross/Blue Shield. The same is true for General Motors. Note that these are Chrysler's direct costs, not the indirect costs mentioned previously.

In addition, illness and injury represent tremendous losses in productivity for companies. And when a valued employee dies or goes on permanent disability, not only does the company bear all of the previously listed costs, but it also has lost its "investment" in that employee.

Risk Factors and Disease

We have learned a great deal recently from several major studies of population-wide health risk factors that contribute to the likelihood of contracting diseases (Allegrante, 1984). The most striking finding (especially from those in cardiovascular disease prevention) is that people may be among their own worst enemies when it comes to health; that is, what we eat, whether we exercise regularly, how much we smoke or drink, and how we manage stress—to name just a few of the major risk factors—have a good deal to do with whether we are likely to achieve our maximum potential life expectancy—and productivity. It stands to reason that it is in the personal best interests of the individuals, as well as in the economic best interests of their employers, to reduce these risks.

The effect of these risk factors on a company's bottom line is significant. For example, people who are 40 percent overweight visit physicians and miss work twice as often as those of average weight, resulting in costs to employers of an extra $1,000 per overweight employee per year (Read, 1986, in American Dietetic Association, 1986). Obesity also increases the risk of back pain, which accounts for 93 million lost workdays per year (Oliver and Kirkpatrick, 1982). Back problems cost American industry an estimated $14 billion per year, and the frequency of musculoskeletal injuries in general is expected to increase as the workforce ages (Keyserling and Chaffin, 1986). Disease and lost productivity due to smoking amount to $65 billion annually (Berkman, 1986). Losses in productivity due to alcohol and drug abuse cost $30.1 billion (this figure does not include costs associated with medical treatment or replacement, temporarily or permanently, of the employee). Employees with substance abuse problems have four times the number of accidents and have five times the number of compensation claims as the average employee (Quayle, 1983). A 1985 Harris poll estimated that 550 million workdays are lost each year due to pain of some sort and that headache and back pain were the most troublesome ("A Catalog of Pain," 1985). Work accidents in 1985 resulted in 40 million lost workdays and a total cost of $37.3 billion (National Safety Council, 1986). Phrased in another way, the average number of lost workdays in 1985 for a company of 100 employees was 39. Estimates of the costs to an organization of a medically incapacitating event such as a heart attack, cancer, or stroke range from $250,000 to $1 million per event (Bellingham, Johnson, and McCauley, 1985). To be sure, companies do not pay for these expenses directly—they purchase insurance that pays for them. However, the price the organization pays for insurance is directly proportional to the insurance company's costs.

Organizations have become interested in health promotion for a variety of reasons, one of the foremost of which is that it has become clear that many of these costs are, to a large degree, avoidable. The U.S. Center for Disease Control estimates that over 50 percent of all deaths under the age of sixty-five are attributable to unhealthy lifestyles, which is especially significant in light of the changes in causes of mortality since 1900. In 1900, the top three causes of death were pneumonia, influenza, and tuberculosis (that is, infectious diseases); in this decade, the top causes of mortality are heart disease, cancer, and stroke—diseases and conditions that are not infectious and that are significantly influenced by the behavior of people. Today's "risk factors" are the "bacteria" of the turn of the century. If we can develop programs to promote healthier lifestyles, we can help to reduce the high cost of illness in organizations. According to Robert Bertera, health promotion coordinator for the Du Pont Company, "a consensus of medical opinion shows it is more effective to place emphasis on prevention of illness through the practice of good health habits than to rely solely on routine periodic physical examinations" to deal with already existing illnesses.

These figures on the staggeringly high health care costs borne by the nation as a whole and industry in particular, combined with the recognition of the critical importance of individual behavior in increasing risk for disease and disability, have led many companies to introduce programs designed to promote the health of their employees through risk-reducing behavior change. For example, one of the behaviors most closely related to increased risk of disease and need for health care services is cigarette smoking. Economist Marvin Kristein (1983) has estimated that the cost of smoking in an organization amounts to $336 to $601 per person per year. Weis (1981) has estimated the costs to be considerably higher—between $4,000 and $5,000 per smoking employee. New York Telephone estimates that smoking cessation programs yield an annual savings in medical costs (direct costs only) of $645,000 for coronary heart disease and $1.4 million for lung disease. Overall, the annual net gain attributable to New York Telephone's health promotion programs is $2.7 million. The fitness program of the Metropolitan Life Insurance Company's head office in Canada reduced absenteeism rates of participants by an average of one day per year (Brennan, 1983). Campbell Soup estimates that its in-house hypertension screening and treatment program prevents three of four strokes expected per year. An experimental program at Burlington Industries reduced absenteeism due to back pain and injury from 422 days per year to 19 days per year over a four-year period. Illinois Bell, a company with more than 38,000 employees, estimates that it annually saves over $250,000 through its employee assistance program. In addition, off-duty accidents and on-duty accidents decreased by 42.4 percent and 61.4 percent, respectively, as a result of the program (Berry, 1981). In the Dallas Independent School District, participants in a workplace fitness program averaged 1.25 fewer days of absenteeism than nonparticipants. With substitute teachers paid at a rate of $47 per day, this reduction represented a savings of

$149,578 for the 2,546 participants (Blair and others, 1986). A fitness program at the Prudential Insurance Company's southwestern home office produced a 45.7 percent reduction in major medical costs and a 20.1 percent reduction in disability costs relative to the preceding year (Bowne and others, 1984).

These figures represent only a small fraction of the potential of health promotion programs when they are carefully developed and adequately evaluated. We present more detailed examples in Chapter Four. In light of such savings and of the virtually certain steady increase in health care costs of organizations, it is no wonder that interest in health promotion has flourished. In fact, some organizations have taken to using the preventive maintenance metaphor literally. According to Angelica Cantlon, Southern New England Telephone health promotion manager, "we demonstrated to management how much we were paying for maintenance on each of our 1,400 motor vehicle fleet (approximately $400 per vehicle) and asked that at least an equivalent amount be spent on the maintenance of our employees . . ." (1985, p. 53). According to Gregory Scherer of Scherer Brothers Lumber Company of Minneapolis, Minnesota, "instead of tearing down bodies with foods that cause cancer and heart disease, we try to provide food that maintains the human machine and makes people healthier in the workplace" (Tollin, 1980).

"Buns on the Run":
Workplace Health Promotion and the Smaller Company

Reports of successful health promotion programs are newsworthy. Regrettably, the news media tend to report on the successes at the most visible organizations such as AT&T, Johnson & Johnson, and other large corporations. This emphasis on large organizations may seem to imply that workplace health promotion is only for large and well-endowed companies. Nothing could be farther from the truth. According to preliminary findings of a survey conducted by the Department of Health and Human Services, 16.5 percent of companies with 100 to 249 employees currently have physical fitness programs of one sort or another. Among slightly larger companies, those with 250 to 749 employees, 24.7 percent have fitness programs. Even among the smallest of companies, those with only 50 to 99 employees, 9.4 percent have fitness programs. Note that this survey reports only on fitness programs. As we have already suggested, workplace health promotion addresses many other areas as well.

Consider, for example, Northern Telecom, Inc., a moderate-sized company with 580 employees at its Nashville, Tennessee, workplace. Even with so few employees, programs in cancer awareness, stress management, smoking cessation, nutrition, seat belt safety, hypertension screening, and physical fitness are offered. The fitness program is enhanced by a 3,200-square-foot facility with locker rooms. All employees, and family members when accompanied by an employee, can use the facility. Thirty to 35 percent of employees use the facility three or more times per week.

At Hubbard Milling, a Mankato, Minnesota, company with only 150 employees, aerobic dance and jazz exercise programs are offered. All employees are eligible and 60 percent participate. To encourage participation, the company is divided into four teams who compete with one another.

"Team Health," the health promotion program at Union Life Insurance Company, in Little Rock, Arkansas, offers group exercise classes, fitness testing, and health educational materials and seminars to its 150 employees. All employees are eligible and an astonishing 85 percent participate in the testing, which is offered on company time. Ten percent participate in the exercise classes.

The 100 employees at the headquarters of the Provident Indemnity Life Insurance Company of Norristown, Pennsylvania, have a thorough workplace program including classes in aerobic exercise, walking, stress management, hypertension, and weight loss. Smoking is not permitted at the workplace and nonsmokers pay reduced life insurance premiums. To encourage exercise during the cold winter, the company rents the local high school swimming pool after work. Employees and their families are eligible for the program and 97 percent of employees participate in some way.

It is clear, therefore, that small and moderate-sized companies as well as large ones can benefit from health promotion programs in the workplace. In fact, since small companies (compared to the giants of the corporate world) have limited resources, they are often highly innovative in the programs they develop. The larger and more staid corporate giants are not likely to offer running programs called "Buns on the Run," but the Safeway Bakery Division (120 employees) of Clackamas, Oregon, does. The company also attempts to encourage nonsmoking by providing a color TV in the nonsmokers' area of the cafeteria but only a black and white one in the smokers' area. Company management attributes at least part of the reductions in industrial accidents, absenteeism, and employee turnover to its health promotion program.

Workplace Health Promotion and the Organization

Because of the nature of workplace health promotion, program implementation relates to the work of many different functions within the organization. We know of health promotion programs around the country in which the following organizational departments are involved: personnel and human resources, employee and labor relations, safety and health, medical, compensation and benefits, and training and development. The safety and health function of human resource development clearly is related integrally to the concerns and practices of workplace health promotion. Safety and health are major aspects of human resources management because they have a direct effect on the capacity of employees to be productive. For obvious reasons, many of the country's most highly regarded health promotion programs are coordinated by medical departments. But as this book will point out, workplace health promotion programs require expertise beyond the scope of traditional medicine. For example, many programs depend heavily on the training experience of a human resources professional.

Those involved in compensation and benefits also may be involved. The development of, for example, an on-site physical fitness program or smoking cessation program clearly has been perceived as a nonfinancial benefit by employees. As such, it is relevant to the area of compensation and benefits. Similarly, employee and labor relations issues are often raised in the context of the development of health promotion programs because they relate to existing benefits such as health insurance or sick leave policy. As Chapter Eight suggests, the development and implementation of health promotion programs raises ethical issues related to the fate of these benefits. Finally, personnel departments, which typically are involved in all of the preceding organizational functions, often are called on to conduct development activities in which various aspects of work are examined and improved. Workplace health promotion represents just such an activity designed to improve performance on the job, raise the level of morale in the organization, and, equally important, to help manage health care costs.

The topic of organizational location of a workplace health promotion program merits more detailed treatment; Chapter Ten provides a more thorough discussion of this issue.

Conclusion

It has been said that an organization's most precious resource is its people. Clearly, some organizations recognize this more than others. But even those known for their "people management" orientation may often fail to embrace the idea of providing preventive maintenance for people. Physical equipment periodically must be taken out of service and subjected to examination and restoration of vital components to improve its efficiency and extend its life expectancy. In much the same way, the efficiency and life expectancy of an organization's people can be enhanced by such preventive efforts. In both cases, the organization benefits.

The development of a successful workplace health promotion program requires an understanding of the nature and processes of health promotion and their place in the workplace. One also must develop an understanding of the factors that influence health and health-related behaviors, especially as they operate in the work setting.

2

Origins of Health Promotion and Applications in the Workplace

---

Although Parts One and Two of this book provide practical presentations of various aspects of health promotion in the workplace, we believe that it is also important for those involved in these activities to have some general understanding of what workplace health promotion is and how it has evolved. Such an appreciation is desirable for chief executive officers of organizations considering the development of health promotion programs as well as the health promotion manager who will be responsible for program implementation. Our overall goal is to provide information to increase the technical proficiency of workplace health promotion practitioners and also to encourage further development of work in the field. Such further development requires some understanding of basic information regarding the origins and background of this increasingly popular movement in organizations as well as a general introduction to workplace health promotion as it is currently practiced.

The Historical Context of Health Promotion

To understand what workplace health promotion is and how it has evolved, it is important to review briefly the meaning of health and illness in our society. Historically, "health" has been

16

conceptualized primarily in opposition to "illness"; that is, health has long been seen as the absence of disease or pathology. This view arose directly out of nineteenth-century advances in biology and medicine. Louis Pasteur's 1881 discovery that anthrax, a bovine disease, was caused by a specific microorganism represented the first demonstrable proof that disease could be caused by a specific bacterial agent. A year after Pasteur's discovery, the German scientist Robert Koch demonstrated that tuberculosis also was caused by a microorganism, the tuberculin bacillus. The impact of these discoveries cannot be overstated: They resulted in a view of health and disease that, even if currently inadequate, is still widely held. This view has come to be called the "single etiology theory" of disease. Stated simply, the theory holds that each disease is caused by a single agent or pathogenic microorganism: One germ causes one disease. The course of medical research during most of this century has been established by this view that was, until recently, an appropriate and effective way to explain many diseases, especially communicable ones.

In this context, it is instructive to look again at the history of mortality in the United States during this century. Figure 1 shows the leading causes of death in the United States from 1900 through 1977. As we mentioned earlier, in 1900, the three leading causes of death were pneumonia, influenza, and tuberculosis. These infectious diseases plus eight other infectious conditions were responsible for 39 percent of the mortality in 1900. All of these diseases are contracted through contact—that is, infection with a specific virus or bacterium. The medical approach to these diseases focused, as the single etiology theory would lead us to expect, on identifying the disease-producing organisms and, later, on developing vaccines to prevent infection by the disease. This approach has often been referred to as the "magic-bullet" approach to fighting disease. Additional efforts to prevent disease involved successful attempts to eradicate the infectious agent from the environment through broad public health measures.

The discoveries of this era of medicine influenced the general view of health and disease in a number of important

Figure 1.   Pictorial Representation of the Changing Contribution
             of Chronic and Infectious Conditions to Total Mortality
             (Age and Sex-Adjusted) in the United States, 1900–1970.

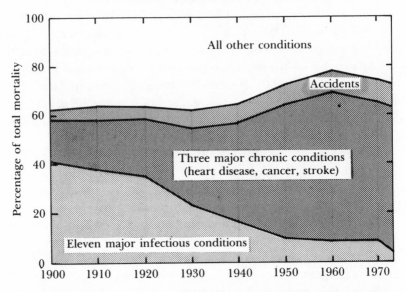

Source: McKinlay, J. B., and McKinlay, S. M. "The Questionable Contribution of Medical Measures to the Decline of Mortality in the United States in the Twentieth Century." *Milbank Memorial Fund Quarterly/ Health & Society*, 1977, *55*, 405–428.

ways. First, these discoveries lent support to the traditional view that conceptualized health as the absence of disease: Either you had tuberculosis or pneumonia or you did not. Thus, the concepts of health and disease were dichotomous and there was no intermediate condition. Second, it was clear why one was either healthy or ill: One was either free of the pathogen or not. Only those who came in contact with the tuberculin bacillus or influenza virus, for example, became ill. Third, medical treatment was directed at the specific agent and its clinical effects. Finally, disease causation was largely a chance occurrence, depending on whether or not one came in contact with the microorganism. Even if one were fortunate enough not to have contracted the disease, the only sure preventive measure one could take was to stay away from others with the disease.

This view of health and disease has had a profound effect on the importance of personal behavior in relation to health status. Because disease and health were seen as dichotomous states distinguished only by the presence or absence of pathogenic microorganisms, concerning oneself with matters of health became reasonable only when one was ill. The sole exception to this view related to attempts to avoid contact with pathogens; however, as we have stated, this was largely a matter of chance and was therefore difficult to accomplish. In the absence of disease—that is, when one was healthy—there was no reason to concern oneself with health, and, in fact, it could have been seen as self-indulgent or narcissistic to do so. Although current thinking in health and medicine has changed dramatically over the past forty or fifty years, this way of thinking still persists among many people.

As our understanding of the human mind and body has increased and the complex relationship among mind, body, and environment has been explicated further, ideas about health have been expanded and reconceptualized. In 1946, the World Health Organization defined health as "a state of complete physical, mental, and social well-being . . . not merely the absence of disease" (Stone, 1979, p. 7). Health became an ideal goal toward which all could strive but which few can attain. Genetic predisposition, the environment, cultural and social norms, accidents, and the aging process drastically limit our ability to approach this goal.

During the past twenty years, the concept of health has expanded still further, becoming more flexible and more useful. Currently, "health" is understood to be a relative rather than an absolute term that describes an "unmeasurable state of a continuously adapting organism" that can, within limits, "be associated with the terms *better* or *worse*" (Stone, 1979, p. 9). According to this definition, health is something that we each possess at all times in some degree or another—it is a position on a continuum. For example, the statement "I am in better health now that I do not smoke" reflects this intrapersonal relationship. At the same time that this concept of health was attaining popularity, publicity about the health effects of personal behavior and the environment was growing. Recall the publicity about the links between smoking and cancer, between DDT and birth defects, and the effects of consumption of red meat, processed food, and pesticides on general health. These discoveries signaled the beginning of the era of personal and individual responsibility in relation to health. Recent research has helped people to begin discerning the direct links between their behavior and their health in a way that the earlier views of health and illness would not have permitted.

Contemporary Views of Health: Risk Factors

Just as the early views of health and disease and the importance (or lack thereof) of personal behavior were closely related to the basic science of the times, so too are the contemporary views of health and disease related to the basic science of this era. This change in the view of health and disease parallels both changes in mortality statistics and the fate of the single etiology theory of disease. Contrast the causes of death in 1900 to those in 1984: Influenza and pneumonia have fallen to sixth place, and the leading causes of death are now heart disease, cancer, stroke, and accidents (U.S. Department of Health and Human Services, 1986). The search for a cause of each of these diseases has not yielded a single, necessary and sufficient agent, be it bacterium, virus, or condition but, instead, an array of different, interacting factors or characteristics with which each disease is significantly associated. These factors are distributed in the population at large but are found more frequently in people who either will develop or currently have one of these diseases. The presence of these factors increases the probability or risk that an individual will develop one of these diseases. Absolutely reliable prediction is not possible, but we can estimate, on the basis of these "risk factors," the relative likelihood of the disease. Implicit in the change from the single etiology view to the risk factor view is the recognition that disease is now thought to be determined by multiple factors. The major factors include biology, environment, lifestyle, and health promoting and restoring systems (medical and health care). Figure 2 depicts the relationship among these factors.

Figure 2. Interaction of Factors Affecting Health.

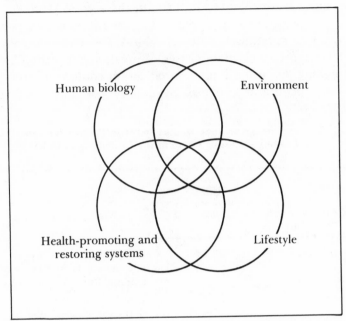

Risk factors are classified as either controllable or uncontrollable. Uncontrollable risk factors are, by definition, not influenced by any purposeful intervention and include such things as age, sex, race, and heredity. For example, men have twice the risk for coronary heart disease (CHD) as women have. Blacks have a greater risk for hypertension than whites have (U.S. Department of Health and Human Services, 1985). A history of early heart disease in an individual's parent increases that person's risk of contracting that disease (Matarazzo, 1985).

Notwithstanding the importance of uncontrollable risk factors, most remarkable about the current ten leading causes of death in the United States is the disproportionately large influence of *controllable* risk factors. So great is this influence that these illnesses have been called "diseases of lifestyle." According to John Knowles (1977), "99 percent of us are born healthy and made sick as a result of personal misbehavior and environmental conditions. The solutions to the problems of ill health in modern American society involve individual responsibility, in

the first instance, and social responsibility through public legis-
lative and private volunteer efforts, in the second instance" (p.
58). For example, Table 1 shows that the first four risk factors
for coronary heart disease are behavioral. The main controllable
risk factors for the leading causes of death in the United States
are smoking, hypertension, elevated serum cholesterol and obesity, and alcohol/drug abuse. Secondary risk factors include

Table 1.   Percentage of Total Deaths and Risk Factors for Ten
            Leading Causes of Death in the United States in 1983.

Cause of Death	Percentage of Total Deaths	Risk Factors
Heart disease	38.1%	Smoking, hypertension, hyper-cholesterolemia, lack of exercise, diabetes mellitus, obesity, stress
Cancer	21.9	Smoking, alcohol, diet, environmental carcinogens, obesity
Stroke	7.8	Hypertension, smoking, hyper-cholesterolemia, stress
Accidents	4.5	Alcohol, failure to use seat belts
Chronic obstructive lung disease	3.3	Smoking
Pneumonia and influenza	2.7	Smoking, alcohol
Diabetes mellitus	1.8	Obesity
Suicide	1.4	Stress, alcohol, drug use
Cirrhosis	1.4	Alcohol
Atherosclerosis	1.3	Smoking, hypercholesterolemia
Other	15.7	
All causes	100.0	

Source: National Center for Health Statistics. "Annual Summary of
Births, Deaths, Marriages, and Divorces: United States, 1983." *NCHS
Monthly Vital Statistics Report,* Sept. 1984.

stress, lack of exercise, and the Type A behavior pattern. Each of these factors has been associated to a varying extent with more than one disease or condition, and each of these factors is, to a large degree, a function of individual behavior and choice. In other words, how one behaves can influence greatly the likelihood of disease. The contrast between this view and the traditional view of health could not be greater.

Personal behavior is important even in cases in which uncontrollable risk factors are present. Such uncontrollable risk factors as age, sex, or race do not necessarily mean that the person will develop a given disease or condition. Their presence simply confers a risk for disease that is greater than that of another person without these risk factors (if both people behave in identical ways in relation to controllable risk factors). In other words, it is possible to compensate for increased uncontrollable risks through behavioral measures designed to reduce controllable risks. Although the risk associated with a family history of heart disease cannot be reduced, the multifactorial nature of heart disease suggests that one's overall risk can be reduced by acting on controllable risk factors (control one's weight, reduce serum cholesterol levels through diet and exercise, reduce Type A behavior, and stop smoking). Through these behavioral changes, the risk for disease may be lower than that for the overweight smoker with Type A behavior who has no family history of heart disease.

What Is Health Promotion?

The idea of health promotion grows out of the contemporary view of health that, as we have seen, is closely connected with the major health problems of our time. Because most of the major health hazards we face can result from any number of factors and because so many of these factors can be controlled or compensated for, health promotion focuses on the actions necessary to reduce risk through changes in risk factor behavior or predisposing environmental conditions. Health promotion, in its broadest sense, can be defined as any effort (1) to *prevent* illness, disease, or premature death through behavioral and organizational change and (2) to increase both the individual and general level of health. When we speak of "health promotion," we are talking about the idea of helping people to move from their current state of health to a greater state of health, which can be accomplished by helping people to compensate for the presence of uncontrollable risk factors and to eliminate controllable ones. *The focus of health promotion, unlike that of traditional medicine, is on the prevention of premature and avoidable disease.*

Health promotion can be approached from two directions. On one side, health promotion efforts can be directed at the sources of risk external to the individual. Eliminating carcinogens from the environment, ensuring that both neighborhoods and worksites are free of harmful substances, guaranteeing that the transportation systems (airplanes, trains, cars) have adequate safety features, and regulating industry to minimize unwanted side-effects of medications and foods are all ways that we, as a nation, have attempted to promote health. Through the funding and operation of city, state, and federal regulatory agencies a certain standard of environmental health and safety is maintained for the public. These broad measures are essentially passive: They do not require that individuals recognize risks and often do not require us to behave differently. Rather, they are an expression of public commitment to the nationally recognized value of a basic right to a clean and safe environment.

The second direction from which the promotion of health may be approached is from the individual level: changing individual behavior in relation to risk factors. Health promotion interventions at this level focus primarily on a known, finite set of controllable risk factors: smoking, hypertension, obesity, elevated cholesterol levels, physical fitness, diet and nutrition, the misuse of drugs and alcohol, and the management of stress. In each of these areas, the specific goal of health promotion is to help people learn and become motivated to make decisions, change their behavior, break habits, and develop new ideas, all on a scale great enough to have both immediate and long-term effects on individual and, eventually, on collective health. This fairly complex objective has been approached using a number of different strategies.

At the most basic level, health promotion can make readily available to people information about the links between their behavior and increased risk of disease, on the assumption that people persist in behaving in ways that are threatening to their health out of ignorance of the consequences of those behaviors. Certainly, public awareness is one of the first steps toward changing overall cultural norms, which then can provide support for changes in individual and collective behavior. Examples of this kind of strategy in health promotion include public service announcements, mandatory cigarette packet warnings, alcohol and pregnancy warnings in bars, and publicity campaigns by nonprofit health organizations such as the American Cancer Society, the American Heart Association, and the American Diabetes Foundation.

The second level of strategy in health promotion involves the presentation of information *plus* the provision of the opportunities that support, enable, and reinforce people to make the recommended changes. This kind of health promotion assumes that, although knowledge of health risks is the primary motivator of behavior change and a necessary factor, people frequently do not know how to change old habits or locate new resources. Therefore, information and resources are made available in a time-limited way. At this level of intervention are events such as National High Blood Pressure Month, during which the American Heart Association sponsors a media blitz and offers numerous free blood pressure screening clinics. Another such event is the annual Great American Smokeout, sponsored by the American Cancer Society each November, which greatly heightens awareness of the dangers of smoking and provides individuals with an "event" through which they can stop smoking. These efforts not only provide information but also heighten motivation for behavior change and provide brief structured opportunities to make this change.

The third kind of strategy in health promotion is distinguished from the first two by its emphasis on encouraging and supporting sustained behavior change through the structure of the intervention. At this level of health promotion, information is provided about health risks and their relation to behavior, convenient opportunities are provided for helping people to make necessary changes, and incentives, financial and otherwise, are often given to encourage long-term behavior change. Interventions of this sort assume that, although the threat of ill health and opportunities to change are important factors, they alone are not sufficient to elicit large-scale behavioral changes in a given population. Therefore, in addition to providing information and opportunities, the barriers to healthy behavior must be reduced by rewarding and supporting health-producing behavior changes. Examples of this type of health promotion include insurance premium rate reduction for ex- or nonsmokers and free smoking cessation clinics that evolve into continuing support groups (sponsored by the American Cancer Society).

At the final level of strategy in health promotion, information is provided about risks, but, more importantly, the behavioral component of the risk reduction becomes mandated through policy, regulation, or law. In such situations, it is considered that certain behaviors are absolutely and directly linked to health risk and that the decision about whether to act in a risk-reducing way is not the individual's prerogative. Rather, it is of public consequence and concern. Such interventions include seat-belt use, the prohibition of driving while intoxicated, laws against the possession and use of certain drugs, and the prohibition of smoking in workplaces, restaurants, and government buildings.

Each of these different strategies for promoting health serves a particular function in the overall health of our communities and our nation; when used in combination, they provide a comprehensive intervention that can encourage individuals and communities of individuals to engage in behavior conducive to promotion of health and prevention of premature disease and disability.

Workplace Health Promotion

What is workplace health promotion, and where does it fit into this broader concept and definition of health promotion? Workplace health promotion is, quite simply, the application of concepts, principles, and general strategies of health promotion to the workplace including its employees and often their families, as well as organizational, managerial, and environmental aspects of work.

Just as health promotion can be approached from two directions, so can workplace health promotion. There exist in most workplaces in the United States certain standards of safety issued by various governmental agencies and overseen by the Occupational Safety and Health Administration. These standards are enforced to ensure that the workplace and the work itself do not cause disease, death, or disability. Thus, it should be the case that most workplaces provide adequate protection of workers against toxic substances, have established emergency procedures, ensure that machinery is safe to operate, and maintain a certain level of hygiene. The task of eliminating the sources of disease and accidents from the environment has long been the domain of occupational medicine and safety departments within an organization.

One source of disease in the workplace that typically does not fall within the territory of either of these internal groups is the stress that an organization itself generates by the way in which it operates. How management styles and practices, policies and goals, and the organization's overall culture contribute to employee health are legitimate but often ignored concerns of workplace health promotion and will be discussed in detail later in the book.

The second approach to health promotion in the workplace is to help individuals improve their health by changing their behavior. The four strategies of general health promotion also are appropriate within the workplace.

Information and Education

At the simplest level are attempts by organizations to provide educational information to their employees regarding health and behavior. Continental Bank, for example, holds monthly health seminars. According to Joseph King of the bank's employee health services, "the topics that seem to attract the largest audiences are those medical issues that relate to many people and have answers that are easily prescribed ... Attractive and stimulating titles made a difference in the number of workers who attended. Titles such as 'Cancer Prevention' were replaced with 'How to Be Fit Without Being Ridiculous' " (King, 1984, p. 60). Simpson Timber Company of Seattle, Washington, also holds successful health seminars offered at lunch time: Topics include nutrition, safe driving, smoking, cancer, and cardiopulmonary resuscitation.

Although most people tend to think of courses or meetings as the only way to serve this function, other activities such as payroll stuffers, newsletters, public address announcements, and periodic health fairs may also be used. Lockheed, for example, makes extensive use of these alternatives:

> Through the use of booklets describing various lifestyle risk factors and a broad-based media campaign, we create a need for greater participation for health education activities. Initially, our approach involves distributing pamphlets on such topics as weight loss, smoking, blood pressure, and stress to employees in all our plant locations. These booklets are conveniently located and available to all workers. We feel this creates a knowledge base and educates employees about the need for change. We then supersede this process with a media campaign of flyers and posters ... When we offer lectures and lifestyle courses, only 10 percent of our workforce participates. But we want to make contact with the remaining 90 percent of our workforce. Our communication methods allow us that very flexibility [Sevelius, 1984, p. 60].

Clearly, many companies regard the delivery of information alone as a highly important activity in health promotion. The way in which that information can be delivered is limited only by one's degree of imagination. Detailed discussion of strategies in workplace health promotion later in the book will provide not only detailed information on existing programs but also practical guidelines and concrete, "hands-on" suggestions for program development in your own organizations.

Information and Opportunity

At the next level of health promotion activities offered in the workplace are programs providing both educational information, again in a variety of ways, and structured opportunities for health-related behavior change. Many organizations, for example, participate in the American Cancer Society's annual Great American Smokeout. This program combines the delivery of information about the health consequences of smoking along with a highly publicized opportunity for smokers to quit for a twenty-four-hour period.

Many other kinds of programs exist in this second level. Campbell Soup Company, for instance, offers, among other things, a workplace hypertension control program. Nurse practitioners conduct the program that provides screening, treatment, and referral. Many other organizations—including large companies (Burlington Industries, General Motors, and Massachusetts Mutual Life Insurance Company), small companies (Plaskolite, Inc., of Columbus, Ohio, and Bodolay-Pratt of Lakeland, Florida), and a union (the United Storeworkers of America)—sponsor similar programs. As is characteristic of any program at this level, not only is information provided to employees but the program also provides opportunities for behavior change.

Many organizations provide screening for diseases other than hypertension—for example, diabetes, glaucoma, breast cancer, colorectal cancer, and hypercholesterolemia. The American Cancer Society offers short-term programs in breast self-examination, either by arranging for a physician to come to the workplace or by training an organization's medical staff to teach this important skill. These services are readily available for workplace implementation, usually free or at low cost, from local community organizations such as the American Lung Association or American Heart Association.

A wide variety of methods of providing both information and time-limited opportunities for health-related behavior change exist at this second level. A more detailed discussion of activities at this level of workplace health promotion appears in Part Two.

Supporting Sustained Behavior Change

At the next level of strategies in workplace health promotion, organizations offer, in addition to information and time-limited structured opportunities for behavior change, programs designed to increase employee motivation to make and sustain these changes. Such programs are often comprehensive and attempt to inform the individuals participating about their own controllable and uncontrollable risk factors and then to encourage change in those areas by a variety of different means.

Comprehensive Programming. Kimberly-Clark Corporation and Sentry Life Insurance Company provide innovative and highly extensive workplace health promotion programs at this level. Kimberly-Clark's "Health Management Program" takes as its objectives (1) increasing the employees' awareness of their health risks and how to reduce these risks (that is, it provides employees with information) and (2) encouraging employees to make changes in their lifestyles by providing structured opportunities to do so. The company offers education, screening, and counseling activities as well as an enviable list of classes in fitness, nutrition, and general health.

Similarly, Sentry Life Insurance offers a comprehensive workplace health promotion program to employees, spouses, dependents, and retirees. An extensive array of educational programs and structured opportunities is offered, focusing on such issues as physical activity and rest, proper nutrition, control of smoking, alcohol, caffeine, and drugs, stress, low-back pain and injury, hypertension, and the proper use of health professionals.

Financial Rewards. Speedcall Corporation offers financial incentives for health behavior change through a voluntary nonsmoking program. With the obvious exception of a prohibition of smoking in high-risk areas such as those containing flammable substances, the company does not restrict smoking. "People are free to smoke during the working hours; those who do not smoke at all during the eight-to-five workday will receive an extra $7.00 gross in the paycheck weekly. If someone 'back-slides' and smokes one week, the person is again eligible the following week to earn the bonus for not smoking. The whole philosophy of the program is that it does not penalize smokers; it only rewards those who do not smoke and provides the necessary incentives—money award and peer pressure. Most of our new employees are nonsmokers" (Glover, 1985, p. 52). The Speedcall example demonstrates the effective use of incentives in a highly sensitive but highly important (from the perspective of health care cost containment and productivity) area: smoking at the workplace. Equally important, Speedcall provides us with an example of how health promotion activities can be implemented successfully in a relatively small company with more limited resources than those of a large organization such as Kimberly-Clark.

Flex Time. Tenneco, Inc.'s "Health and Fitness Program" uses still another incentive: "flex time." To encourage employees to make use of its fitness center, Tenneco permits its employees to have flexible working hours. This policy not only allows employees to organize their individual work schedules but also serves the function of distributing the demand on the fitness center across the entire day.

Environmental and Policy Change

A fourth level of health promotion activities reduces health risks to people in organizations through changes in policies and regulations. Here again, a small company provides us with a good example. Scherer Brothers Lumber Company of Minneapolis, Minnesota, has replaced all candy machines at the workplace with machines dispensing fruit, removed salt from the cafeteria, removed cigarette machines, and replaced caffeinated coffee with decaffeinated coffee in vending machines. These policy changes were accompanied by the dissemination of literature on health and nutrition and the availability of smoking cessation programs.

Although possibly extreme, Westlake Community Hospital in Melrose Park, Illinois, has a policy of refusing to hire employees who smoke cigarettes, pipes, or cigars. New employees are required to sign a statement declaring that they do not smoke, either at work or elsewhere, and that they recognize that not smoking is a continuing condition of their employment. Pacific Bell's smoking policy attempts to accommodate the preferences of nonsmokers and smokers to the greatest extent possible. Among the provisions of the policy are (1) the right of employees to designate their private offices as smoking or nonsmoking areas, (2) prohibition of smoking in conference rooms, classrooms, and auditoriums unless every person in these rooms agrees to permit it, and (3) outright prohibition of smoking in certain public areas.

Policy and regulation of seat-belt use can also advance health promotion. Some companies rely solely on a mandatory seat-belt use policy. Others use a combination of policies and incentives to increase seat-belt use. For example, Pennsylvania-based Berg Electronics, a subsidiary of DuPont, doubled the belt-use rate in private cars used for transportation to and from work through the development of an explicit seat-belt policy. With a similar policy, Teletype Corporation of Arkansas increased belt use from 11 percent to an average of 45 percent in both blue-collar and white-collar workers. Typical policy elements include an across-the-board requirement for seat-belt use in all work-related driving, clearly understood disciplinary measures for failure to comply, periodic monitoring for compliance, and explicit indications that part of a supervisor's responsibility is policy enforcement and associated discipline. Health promotion through policy change or regulation is often accompanied by time-limited campaigns. Although the campaigns are short-lived, the policies remain long afterward.

It should be noted that although we distinguish between these various levels of workplace health promotion activities, in practice, it is common for organizations to combine strategies from each level. The next parts of the book will examine in detail the actual *whats and hows* of workplace health promotion. Before that, we will consider the *whys*.

Why Health Promotion in the Workplace?

Why should health promotion efforts be offered in the workplace as opposed to delivering them through the traditional medical care system? A variety of reasons exist. First, the current system of medical care has not devoted itself enthusiastically to the prevention of disease other than through the development of prophylactic medicine. Instead, it has devoted itself to the treatment of already existing diseases. Of the more than $350 billion spent each year in this country on health care, less than 1 percent is devoted to prevention. In addition, the structure of medicine is such that little incentive and support exist for physicians to embrace prevention: Our insurance reimburses us and pays our physician primarily for the *treatment* rather than for the *prevention* of illness. The incentive structure of the medical industry traps physicians firmly in the task of diagnosis and treatment. Physician training, as well, is directed largely to the detection and cure of pathology, not to determining how to help someone to break a lifelong habit such as leading a sedentary lifestyle, frequent consumption of red meat, or cigarette smoking. For most physicians, asking a person to become involved in prevention places them in conflict with the goals of their profession and their own personal interests, and it removes them from their realm of expertise and experience. Many physicians may indeed recognize, agree with, and even promote the obvious benefits of prevention, but there are many who may not, at least not wholeheartedly. For this reason and others, health promotion administered through traditional medical practice is not likely to have a great impact.

Some of the emphasis of traditional medicine on the treatment of disease and lack of interest in prevention is weakening. In the mid-1980s, the number of health maintenance organizations (HMOs) in the United States has been increasing rapidly. HMOs typically provide all of an individual's medical care for a specified annual fee. This arrangement provides an incentive for prevention: Given a fixed amount of money per patient, it is in the HMO's interest to focus on reducing the risk of disease as a way of avoiding more costly medical procedures.

The reasons for conducting health promotion programs in the workplace derive from the nature of the workplace itself. More often than not, the majority of the workforce is quite stable and tends to remain with the same employer for long periods of time. For an organization with interests in reducing health care costs, this stability is critical. It means that the workplace population is perfect for health promotion interventions, which generally have their greatest impact on cost management over the long term. The stability of the workforce means that an organization's initial investment in health promotion is likely to be repaid with "interest" because the employees still will be with the organization when the benefits of the health promotion programs are reaped.

Of course, it should be recognized that long-term stability of the workforce is more characteristic of some industries and organizations than of others. Representatives of industries with a relatively transient workforce properly may question whether an investment in the health of their employees will be repaid to them or to some other future employer.

However, workplace health promotion programs can produce other benefits as well, and their time course is widely varied. Some benefits—for example, improved morale and absenteeism rates—occur almost immediately. Another associated short-term benefit may be improvement in employees' general sense of well-being, which may quickly translate into reduced usage of the costly health care system. This has been demonstrated emphatically in a study of approximately 85,000 federal employees and residents of Hawaii eligible for Medicaid. Access for this population to short-term psychotherapy to reduce transient anxieties produced a 37 percent decrease in total medical bills, a savings of nearly $16 million (Mervis, 1985). Other benefits such as reductions in risk behavior begin to appear as more people adapt healthier behavior patterns for longer periods of time. Long-term health benefits—for example, a reduction in the number of heart attacks in top executives—may take from months to years to materialize. The more stable the workforce, the more of the initial investment in health promotion will be repaid.

A final reason why the workplace is an excellent place for the delivery of health promotion services is that participation in such programs has been demonstrated to be much greater when sponsored by the organization than when offered by an outside group. Among the reasons for this increased participation are (1) the convenience of the location, (2) the reduced cost of the service, (3) the "esprit de corps" or continued support of the workplace, (4) organizational incentives, and (5) the generally positive reputation of the medical department (in organizations that have one) relative to that of other organizational departments.

Conclusion

Workplace health promotion programs are clearly associated with the evolution of the concepts of health and disease in our society. We believe that all people involved in this new and expanding field of workplace health promotion need some basic understanding of these concepts and their background to make sense of their activities in the field. Up to this point, we have not addressed the "nuts and bolts" of workplace health promotion; rather we have set out the context in which the principles of general health promotion and specific efforts at the workplace can be understood most clearly.

An understanding of both controllable and uncontrollable risk factors and the nature of their relationships to behavior and health is necessary to effective health promotion. The thoroughness with which you will need to educate yourself in this area depends on your professional background and the role you will play in the health promotion program. If you feel the need to undertake further reading, refer to Resource B, which contains a comprehensive list of publications for health promotion professionals.

Health promotion in society as a whole and in the work-

place in particular is an activity whose time clearly has arrived.
With increasing demand for health promotion services, there is
an increasing need for information, both technical and theoretical, on how programs actually work and why they work. This
book provides not only the hands-on information necessary for
the successful development, implementation, and evaluation of
workplace health promotion programs but also a general understanding of the major issues involved.

3

Health Promotion in Perspective: Relationship to Organizational Goals

Consider for a moment the goals of workplace health promotion. The more immediate objective may be to provide the means by which people can improve their health and prevent premature disease and death. The ultimate goal, however, is to manage the health care expenditures associated with absenteeism, disability claims, and overall insurance costs by developing a healthy and productive employee population. Health promotion historically has attempted to achieve these goals by encouraging the employee population to make behavioral changes that reduce the risk of disease. In a healthy workplace, the main risk factors for disease and disability leading to premature death are either controlled or mitigated, resulting in gains for both individuals and the company. This chapter addresses the question of whether the current structure of most health promotion programs is adequate to achieve the ultimate objective of management of health care costs.

Consistent with the emphasis on risk factor reduction, workplace health promotion programs have concentrated on helping individuals to recognize and act on the link between behavior and health (particularly in relation to the major risk factors). This concentration enables individuals to take responsibility for behaving in a way that reduces the risk of disease. The association between behavior and health is critical; educating people about this relationship and then motivating them to make changes is truly a challenge. Those who have tried to convince a cigarette smoker to quit or struggled with a smoking or weight problem of their own know that changing behaviors can be complicated and difficult.

To meet these general goals of health promotion, we propose that encouraging individual behavior change be only one of a number of strategies employed. Although many organizations may not be willing or able to make a complete commitment to the broader view of health promotion as described in this chapter, practitioners need to understand the full potential of the process. To appreciate this broader view, we will examine the assumptions underlying workplace health promotion as it is currently practiced.

Assumptions Underlying Workplace Health Promotion

Current practice in workplace health promotion rests on three general, perhaps implicit, assumptions:

1. Absenteeism, insurance claims, and disability are due primarily to disease.
2. These diseases, for which considerable corporate health care dollars are spent, have significant behavioral components.
3. These behaviors, which increase the risk of disease, have modifiable determinants whose loci are within the individual (for example, lack of knowledge, skills, and motivation).

By suggesting that these assumptions underlie the practice of workplace health promotion programs, we do not mean that everyone associated with a program necessarily would agree with our list. Anyone in the personnel or human resources field would disagree with the first assumption. And in fact, these assumptions might be irrelevant to programs developed not for purposes of cost management but instead for raising morale, enhancing recruitment, and so on.

Our point in stating them is to demonstrate that program structure is driven by these assumptions even if practitioners do not endorse them. We wish to demonstrate further that these assumptions, regardless of their validity or logic, may restrict the vision of practitioners and may limit the variety of interventions in the workplace health promotion repertoire. As we examine each of these assumptions in the context of the overall goals of health promotion, recognize again that our interest is in how programs reflect these ideas even if practitioners disagree with them.

Assumption #1:
Absenteeism, Disability, and Insurance Claims
Are Due Primarily to Disease

Since the field of health has long been a subspecialty of the field of medicine, it is not surprising that this first assumption is based on the medical model of disease: that the presence of a pathogen yields palpable physical changes that constitute symptoms that in turn lead to behaviors such as medical help–seeking, staying in bed, and self-medication (Figure 1). This model is familiar and powerful, yet it seems neither necessary nor sufficient to describe the patterns of absenteeism and organizational health care expenditures.

Figure 1.   Workplace Health Promotion.

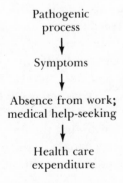

Studies have demonstrated that absenteeism reflects considerably more than health problems; for example, it has been shown to be associated with organizational, attitudinal, and personal factors (Cheloha and Farr, 1980; Hammer, Landau, and Stern, 1981; Mowday and Spencer, 1981; Watson, 1981). For example, the effect of a "sick day" policy on absenteeism is great. When Sherer Brothers Lumber Company allowed one or two weeks of sick leave, "it was amazing how many people were getting sick exactly five or ten days each year," said Gregory Scherer (in Boal, 1984, p. 7). These observations and others suggest that reductions in absenteeism, one of the endpoints of workplace health promotion programs, may be accomplished by means other than those designed directly to address the factors that contribute to disease. To the extent that workplace health promotion programs have been successful in reducing absenteeism (Chapter Four), studies suggest that this success may be attributable not only to improvements in health but also to more general factors associated with company-wide increased awareness of health issues, changes in policy, or even the delivery of a highly desirable program to grateful employees.

Policy changes aside, it should be recognized that this assumption, based on the traditional medical model of disease, oversimplifies the series of events culminating in health care expenditures. The most immediate determinant of health care expenses is the behavior of individual employees and their dependents. For example, seeing a physician is the event that leads to a claim against insurance. The oversimplified chain of events described by Figure 1 ignores the fact that between pathogenic process and health care expenses is a series of decisions made by the employee, and these decisions will have a major effect on the ultimate outcome. The sequence of events begins with the physiological changes in the body that lead to feelings associated with those changes. Decision 1: "What do these sensations mean? Am I sick?" Decision 2: "What, if any, health action should I take?" Figure 2 presents an expanded view of this series of events and suggests that the immediate determinant of sensations is physiological changes in the body.

The traditional medical model holds (1) that the physiological changes that produce the sensations are disease processes

Figure 2.   A Social-Psychological Model of Workplace Health
            Promotion.

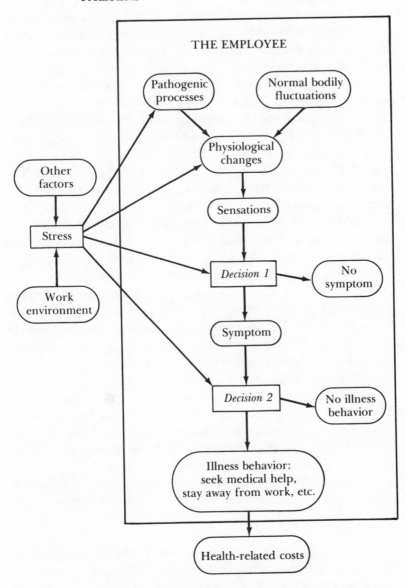

and (2) that the sensations are symptoms. In contrast, the model presented in Figure 2 indicates that there are several determinants of physiological changes: disease processes, normal

bodily fluctuations, and stress. For example, whether the result of objective work environment conditions or of subjective pressures to perform, stress has been associated with a wide assortment of uncomfortable and distracting physiological changes (such as headaches, stomach upset, nausea, back pain, and so forth) that resemble symptoms of pathogen-related disorders. Many studies identify the sources of stress at work: the lack of person-environment fit (Beehr and Bhagat, 1985), frequent and sudden changes in the work environment or work load (Holmes and Rahe, 1967), an understimulating, too demanding, unsupportive, and/or highly conflictual environment (French and Caplan, 1972), role ambiguity and conflict (Kahn, 1981), as well as a number of other variables (Adams, 1980) that have been shown to increase levels of stress significantly.

Not only has stress been implicated in the production of health conditions that resemble disease conditions but it also has been demonstrated to produce real pathogenic processes associated with heart disease and other conditions. For example, laboratory studies of animals exposed to social stresses develop significantly greater coronary artery atherosclerosis than nonstressed animals do, even when these animals are fed precisely the same diet (Kaplan and others, 1983). Other studies also indicate the pathogenic consequences of stress.

Finally, the body is not rigid but is constantly undergoing regular fluctuation of biological systems. These fluctuations also may lead to physiological changes that in turn lead to sensations. Under certain circumstances, these sensations may be interpreted as symptoms, thus starting the process that culminates in health care expenses.

Once a physiological change has been produced and a sensation results, a decision must be made regarding the nature of the sensation.

Decision 1: "What Do These Sensations Mean?" The onset of a sensation initiates a search for identification of a cause. Research in psychology has demonstrated that such a search occurs for conventional emotional experiences and for sensations arising from within the body (Michela and Wood, 1986). The traditional model of workplace health promotion, based on the medical model, assumes that the cause of these sensations is an underlying pathological (that is, disease) condition and that people behave in a way consistent with this understanding and identify the sensation as a symptom.

However, there is often real ambiguity regarding the origins of these sensations. Social psychologist James Pennebaker, recognizing that our bodies are constantly undergoing physiological changes and events that may be identified as symptoms, has examined the factors that influence symptom identification. One such factor appears to be the *fit* between the person and the environment, a concept that may be familiar to human resource professionals. In a series of laboratory studies, Pennebaker and his colleagues (Pennebaker, 1983) had subjects perform a task at a self-determined pace. After working at this pace for some time, subjects reported any physical symptoms they had experienced while performing the task. Following this report, subjects were assigned to work at one of three paces: 50 percent faster, 50 percent slower, or at the same pace. After working at this assigned pace, subjects again reported on symptoms. As predicted, both the slow and fast paces led to greater reports of symptoms than did the original pace; that is, when the *personal* characteristics and work *environment* were inconsistent with each other—when P–E fit was poor—subjects reported a greater number of symptoms than when P–E fit was good. These differences occurred even though physiological measurement of bodily changes indicated no difference between conditions.

Pennebaker's work suggests that the relationship of bodily sensations and physical symptoms is not direct but rather is influenced by other factors. One such factor is the relationship of the preferences of the person and the characteristics of the work itself. This person–environment relationship was developed to operationalize the somewhat vague concept of stress more precisely (French, Caplan, and Harrison, 1982). Therefore, it appears that stress influences the decision regarding the identification of bodily sensations as symptoms.

A significant body of evidence also demonstrates that

under stressful conditions, people are highly likely to misattribute stress-related physiological changes to disease processes and behave in a manner consistent with that misattribution: stay in bed, see a physician, and take medication. Similarly, individuals with boring and undemanding jobs (also a condition shown to be quite stressful) have higher rates of symptom-reporting and absenteeism (Taylor and Fiske, 1978). With lower levels of stress, physical experiences are less likely to be seen as symptoms, thus reducing the likelihood of costly illness behavior.

To summarize, it appears that people develop hypotheses regarding bodily sensations and their origins. These hypotheses guide our identification of the sensations as disease-relevant symptoms or disease-irrelevant sensations. They even determine whether or not we notice the sensations at all. The implication for workplace health promotion is obvious: Factors other than the mere presence of symptoms are involved in decisions about whether one has a disease. Some of these controlling factors arise within the workplace. Only when the decision is made that a symptom of a disease is present does Decision 2 ("What health action should I take?") become an issue.

Decision 2: "What Health Action Should I Take?"   Absence from work and/or obtaining medical treatment, the most proximate causes of health care expenses, are not perfectly associated with the presence of symptoms. There are certainly occasions when employees with symptoms, even serious ones, still come to work and avoid medical treatment. Conversely, there are occasions when medical attention is sought in the absence of symptoms. What determines whether an employee decides to be absent depends on a variety of factors. A report by Verbrugge (1985) explores this issue. Given the presence of symptoms, people were three times more likely to restrict their physical activity when they felt general malaise or if they experienced bad moods than if they did not experience such moods. Malaise and bad moods also serve as triggers to seeking medical care when symptoms are present. For example, given the presence of symptoms, medical care was sought on 8.9 percent of the days when subjects had bad moods but only 3.7 percent of the days when they did not.

These findings clearly suggest that the mere presence of physical symptoms is not sufficient to account for the behaviors that result in health care expenditures. Decisions made by individuals intervene between the presence of symptoms and actions such as medical help–seeking and absenteeism. The designers of workplace health promotion programs must consider, therefore, that reductions in health care costs will not be perfectly associated with the reductions in disease these programs are designed to produce. Program designers need to explore other avenues as well as the traditional ones in attempts to control the costs commonly associated with disease.

In sum, the series of events culminating in health care expenditures demonstrates that the traditional model of workplace health promotion is overly simplistic. Disease agents, stressful situations, and regularly occurring bodily fluctuations produce detectable physiological changes in our bodies that are often identical to one another. These sensations, regardless of etiology, may be identified as symptoms and attributed to disease or they may not be so identified. Given this identification of symptoms, a decision about how to behave in their presence is made. This decision triggers the set of behaviors traditionally associated with pathogen-related conditions—that is, visiting a physician, not going to work, staying in bed, taking medication, and so on. These *illness behaviors,* as distinguished from disease itself, constitute the basis of corporate health care costs (Figure 2). Just as the individual's ultimate health action will be based on an understanding of the cause, so must the health promotion specialist's actions reflect an understanding of the causes. Accordingly, an effective workplace health promotion program must take into account the psychology of the individual employee's health behavior.

What are the implications of this revised model for the first assumption (that absenteeism, disability, and insurance claims are due primarily to disease)? How people feel about their work, the level of conflict and comfort they feel at work and elsewhere, the level of engagement with that work, the stress they experience, and transient psychological and physiological states, whether work-related or not, all have a major effect on:

1. physiological changes in the individual employee
2. whether the person identifies these changes as symptoms of disease
3. whether medical help and/or medication is sought for the symptoms
4. whether one decides to be absent from work

In Chapter Two, we explored the current definition of health, which includes not only the absence of pathology but also the presence of a sense of well-being. It is clear that one's sense of well-being at work can have a powerful influence on one's perceived health and related behavior. It is equally clear that one's sense of well-being may be in part determined by aspects of the work environment (as well as factors away from work). Work climate, as a determinant of health and health behavior, is beyond the conceptual scope of most health promotion programs (Sloan, 1987). Nevertheless, these organizational determinants must be considered as potential areas of interest to achieve more thoroughly the goals of workplace health promotion. It may be the case that disease-related symptoms and work-malaise-related symptoms share equally in accounting for high rates of insurance claims and absenteeism. In its revised form, Assumption #1 should read: *Health care costs associated with absenteeism, disability, insurance expenses, and reduced productivity are the result of disease states, work climate, and other factors.*

Assumption #2:
The Major Diseases for Which Companies Accrue
Medical Care Expenses Are Considered to Be
Lifestyle Related—That Is, They Have Significant
Behavioral Components

This assumption is critical to the logical progression of ideas that underlie the current practice of workplace health promotion. It narrows the area of focus from disease in general to behavior-related disease, thus implicitly identifying the cause (behavior) as modifiable and therefore amenable to intervention.

The relationship between behavior and the major diseases of our time has been explored in Chapters One and Two. As long as the structure of workplace health promotion programs is guided by the first assumption, that disease is primarily responsible for the problems of absenteeism, reduced productivity, high insurance premiums, and so on, the second assumption remains relevant. However, if program structure reflects the fact that disease is not the only source of these problems, as we have demonstrated, the relevance of the second assumption requires review.

Up to this point, we have referred exclusively to the phenomenon of "disease" as opposed to "illness" or "sickness." The reason for this is that the term "disease" connotes the observable, verifiable presence of a pathogen or organic basis. "Illness" and "sickness," on the other hand, are terms used to describe a set of normative and socially sanctioned behaviors and experiences that frequently, but not always, appear in conjunction with disease. Staying in bed, monitoring one's temperature, taking medication, seeking a physician's advice, and "taking it easy" are all legitimate illness behaviors that can occur either in the presence or absence of a disease state. Moreover, there exist cases in which the confirmed and documented presence of pathogens or organic dysfunction is not associated with illness behavior. Given that the main source of health care expense is, in fact, illness behavior, whether that behavior is in response to a pathogenic process or misattribution of bodily sensations, it becomes critical to expand the search for activities that reduce health care expenses to include those that address illness behavior both in the presence and absence of confirmed disease. Figure 3 illustrates the expansion of the focus of workplace health promotion to include not only the prevention of disease but also both disease-related and nondisease-related illness behavior.

Figure 3 suggests that the legitimate boundaries of workplace health promotion extend beyond those usually accepted. That is, because health care expenditures are the problem for which workplace health promotion is usually suggested as a solution and because these expenditures are dependent on a

Figure 3.   The Broader Focus of Workplace Health Promotion.

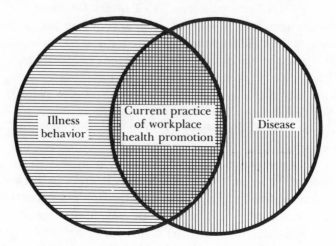

Legitimate boundaries of workplace health promotion

variety of factors in addition to pathogenic processes, the scope of programs must expand to encompass these additional factors. Such factors as organizational climate and stress in the workplace must be addressed. As previously mentioned, evidence suggests that workplace health promotion programs as they are currently constituted may have their effect through generalized changes in employee morale and satisfaction with the organization instead of through the reduction of risk factor behavior leading to changes in health.

Accordingly, let us revise Assumption #2: *The most immediate determinant of medical expenses in an organization is illness behavior, which is only imperfectly related to the presence of demonstrable physical disease.*

Assumption #3:
The Determinants of the Behaviors That Increase
the Risk of Disease Are Within the Individual's
Control and Are Modifiable

This assumption further limits the scope of health promotion in the workplace. The progression of assumptions has moved from disease as problem, to behaviors as risk factors for disease, and now to individual determinants as the cause of the health-related behaviors in question. Although we have shown that this focus has served an important function in organizing workplace health promotion efforts, too often it has served to shift attention away from a larger, more comprehensive view.

The social science disciplines long have agreed on the notion that behavior is "overdetermined," which means that all behavior is the result of a complex array of forces. A limited list of some of the factors that have been shown to account for differences in health behavior among individuals includes intelligence level, knowledge, ethnic and cultural background, peer pressure, level of education and income, family history, personal history and habits, various psychological traits such as self-esteem and locus of control, and numerous situational variables. No single factor provides necessary and sufficient cause for a given behavior. These factors interact with one another in individuals and groups, leaving behavioral theorists with restricted power to predict and influence specific behaviors (or lack of behaviors).

Clearly, some of these determinants are not modifiable and are therefore not amenable to intervention. Among those determinants that are modifiable, certain ones are more amenable to change than others. Among those more easily changed, some require a simple change strategy involving only a few time-limited interventions; others require more complex, continuous efforts. For example, lack of the particular skills needed to make a change can be overcome by providing knowledge, support, and the opportunity to practice; improving an individual's self-esteem, on the other hand, may require at least repeated opportunities to succeed in important events. People who specialize in changing the behavior of individuals must wade through a maze of alternative behavioral determinants related to the targeted behavior and arrive at a theoretical position that allows them to intervene most effectively and efficiently to produce behavior change.

A common assumption among professionals in workplace health promotion is that people fail to care for themselves properly because they are ill-informed, lack self-esteem, or may have no opportunity to acquire the necessary knowledge and skills. As a result, people become sick, seek medical care, and do not come to work, or they make the decision not to work hard while at work. Given these assumptions, it is reasonable to focus health promotion efforts on the individual.

However, among the modifiable determinants of health behavior are some factors that have been excluded from the scope of workplace health promotion: (1) the cultural norms of the work community, (2) the pressure of immediate peers, (3) constraints imposed by the work situation itself that prevent and/or discourage positive health behaviors, and (4) a work environment that in and of itself may be a contributor to disease, possibly through the stress it generates.

Certainly the typical approach to promoting health at work, which has consisted of informing individuals about their health risks to help them change their behavior to reduce those risks, is critical to improving individual health, as well as improving the overall health of a given community. However, unless the new behaviors themselves are recognized, facilitated, supported, and reinforced by the organization and by the powerful individuals within that organization, these attempts will be less than completely successful.

Even those executives and managers who enthusiastically support efforts of people to stop smoking and lose weight have difficulty understanding their own role in creating a healthy workplace beyond encouraging individuals to change. It may help to think of an example: Consider a manager who strongly encourages her subordinates to participate in a stress management class. Although she is aware that people in her group seem to be under a great deal of stress, she does not see a need to participate herself, let alone how she might find the time to do so. She does not consider her erratic management style, her methods of assigning and closely supervising work, or her stormy relationships with subordinates to be connected to either the elevated level of stress or the high rates of absenteeism and turnover in her group. In a situation like this, a stress management program designed to help this manager's subordinates learn to cope becomes a mere palliative. Although it is possible to intervene to reduce the source of stress, typically the focus of the effort is instead on the recipients of stress.

We spend about one-half of our waking lives at work. Some of the most powerful role models and authority figures in our lives are those to whom the hierarchical organization of work exposes us. There is no doubt that the workplace imposes distinct norms for behavior, not the least of which is how we take care of ourselves. If a workplace accepts, allows, or even encourages drug or alcohol use on the job, if our upper-level management smokes and/or disagrees with the individual's right to a smoke-free environment, if value is placed on the number of hours worked overtime rather than actual production, attempts to improve employee health and reduce the associated costs will be sabotaged effectively. The message is clear: The company wants employees to be healthy simply because a healthy workforce costs less money; it aims to achieve that end by providing some means for helping employees to change their behavior; and it is unwilling to address the sources of the problem—the need to change the organization's own behavior.

Several important issues arise. The lack of cultural support for positive health behavior substantially weakens the effect of even the most compelling individually oriented behavior change program. Second, the individual focus of such an intervention leads to a situation in which people who are unsuccessful at making changes may be held personally responsible for their lack of success (Allegrante and Green, 1981; Allegrante and Sloan, 1986). We discuss this issue in greater detail in Chapters Eight and Thirteen. Although this is a strong statement of the possible negative outcomes of a completely individually oriented health promotion program, without broader organizational understanding and commitment to health promotion, efforts will tend to range from the mildly effective to the unsuccessful and even destructive and divisive.

These considerations suggest that Assumption #3 be revised to read: *The modifiable factors that contribute to positive health behavior and reduce illness behavior include the norms, values, and practices of the workplace and of manage-*

ment, as well as individual factors such as lack of knowledge, skills, and motivation.

Implications of a Broader View of Health Promotion

Let us consider why it is important to understand this broader view and what it implies about the planning and implementation of programs.

Each workplace is a system, a highly interactive environment in which changes in one area lead to changes elsewhere. The overall goal of workplace health promotion essentially is to change the system from one in which illness behavior is prevalent to one in which illness behavior is reduced. Reductions in illness behavior may produce health care and other cost savings. As we have seen, workplace health promotion has traditionally attempted to intervene with individuals on the assumption that if enough individuals make changes, the diseases resulting from risk behaviors will slowly and surely decline, eventually producing a significant reduction in health care costs. This assumption is undoubtedly true, although the time frame needed to accomplish the goal may exhaust the patience of those who demand a reasonably swift return on their investment in health promotion. The larger view of health promotion embraces both individual elements of the system and the system itself as appropriate, if not necessary, places to intervene to create a truly healthy organization and reduce incidence of disease, risks for disease, and illness behavior.

The implications of this idea for planning and implementation are many, and the specifics will be dealt with more extensively in later chapters. However, one important idea should be considered as you organize yourselves conceptually to approach the task. In an optimally designed workplace, the organizational goal is to produce as much and as effectively as possible. People are not maximally productive when poorly managed and when they work in poorly designed jobs that promote inefficiency or stress, which in turn may contribute to disease and/or illness behavior. Many organizations have elaborate management training programs, organizational effectiveness specialists, and "quality of work life" committees already working to change the work climate and management practices that underlie productivity problems. The addition of a health promotion program that is integrated with these internal groups can be a powerful, effective, and efficient way to complement these existing programs. The activities and expertise of each are different, but the efforts of each reinforce those of the others, and the goals are identical: an optimally productive workplace where a minimum of illness behavior results from disease or other factors. Workplace health promotion has a great deal to contribute to the success of organizational effectiveness and management training programs, just as these programs have a great deal to contribute to the overall success of workplace health promotion. A consortium of internal groups that recognizes their separate functions but common goals and that work cooperatively to achieve them is the ideal in such cases.

In smaller companies and organizations, the individual internal divisions devoted to these separate functions may not exist and all efforts to increase managerial effectiveness and quality of work life are undertaken by individual managers or perhaps by a single personnel officer. In such organizations, these may be the people who will be initially supportive of the idea of health promotion. Getting their ideas and suggestions and commitment of support for a health promotion effort is critical. These managers will also be able to see the need for a broad and comprehensive health promotion effort, since they believe the system itself is an appropriate place to intervene for positive change.

Conclusion

The field of workplace health promotion has progressed tremendously over the past ten years. Part of that progress has entailed the institutionalization of ideas and expectations about the legitimate domain of health promotion in the workplace, the kinds of concerns it should address, and the kinds of activities that should address those concerns. A reexamination of the assumptions underlying current practice of workplace health promotion suggests that the field has addressed only a part of the total picture. By supporting risk-related behavior change, incidence of disease will be reduced over time; but disease-related absenteeism and insurance claims account for only part of the overall corporate health costs. Organizational factors influencing illness behavior clearly are responsible for another large portion of the total cost of health care. It is critical that practitioners understand the reciprocal relationship between the organization and the individuals who compose it. For workplace health promotion to have its fullest impact, programs will have to address both the organization and the individuals.

4

Making the Case
to Top Management

It is often the case that those within an organization who recognize the need for a workplace health promotion program—even those who will be ultimately responsible for its implementation —do not have the authority to make the basic decision to develop the program. That decision usually rests with an official at the vice-president, if not at the chief executive level. As a result, one of the fundamental problems in establishing a program is to persuade the decision makers not only that the program is needed but also that the organization potentially will benefit from it. More than being personally persuaded is needed to "sell" the company on the idea. As we will see in later chapters, once a program is established, its success requires that it be "marketed" to employees. This chapter is devoted to another sort of marketing: making the case for workplace health promotion to the key decision makers in the organization.

The chapter is divided into two sections: (1) presentation of the most current evidence regarding the benefits and costs of workplace health promotion to organizations and (2) recommendations regarding how to begin the process of health promotion in your organization by securing permission to begin a preliminary investigation.

Health Promotion and the "Bottom Line"

It was once said that "the way to a man's heart is through his stomach." It might also be said that "the way to a CEO's heart is through the wallet." Most human resources professionals have come to realize that the programs they promote, whatever their other merits, must be shown to have an impact on the organization's "bottom line." Although there are exceptions to this rule, it is generally the case that a workplace health promotion program must justify its existence by demonstrating that it will benefit the organization.

"The bottom line," however, does not always mean the same thing to all people. Even if the bottom line is understood to be financial success, the ways in which organizations attempt to achieve it may differ widely. For some, the bottom line consideration is that a program lead to improvements in morale or job satisfaction of the workforce. For a CEO who holds this view, there is an implicit assumption that improvements in morale translate to greater productivity and through it, improvements in the organization's financial picture.

A specialist in orthopedic injuries in the workplace recounts the following anecdote: She had been hired first to conduct an ergonomic evaluation of the facilities of a large aircraft manufacturer and then develop a program designed to reduce the high incidence of musculoskeletal injuries. After her presentation of a proposal to initiate an extensive series of "back schools" to prevent back injuries and reduce back pain, a corporate vice-president, feeling that the recommendations were too costly, remarked that "here at _____ , we don't make back schools. We make airplanes." The specialist's response was immediate. "No, here at _____ , you make *money* by selling the airplanes you make, and if you want to make airplanes more efficiently so that you can make more money, you will act to reduce the incidence of back injuries," she said. The moral: even if the bottom line is agreed on, multiple ways exist to achieve it.

Benefits of Workplace Health Promotion

Making the case for workplace health promotion requires examination of (1) the justification for these programs, that is, that the program goals are desirable and (2) the evidence that the programs can work to achieve their goals. Such an examination is complicated because the goals may vary widely. In a following section, we present some case examples of successful workplace health promotion programs. To appreciate what constitutes a success, however, we first must discuss the possible benefits of such programs.

What are the potential benefits of a workplace health promotion program? The list includes at least the following:

1. employee satisfaction with the program
2. improvements in employee morale and job satisfaction
3. improvements in productivity
4. reductions in employee turnover
5. greater ease in hiring new employees
6. direct cost savings, including
    a. reductions in the cost of health care insurance
    b. reductions in disability and workman's compensation
    c. reductions in costs associated with absenteeism and tardiness
    d. reduction in overtime pay
    e. in the case of smoking, savings on cleaning costs and fire insurance and reduced wear-and-tear on air conditioning and ventilation equipment

Each of these benefits merits some discussion.

Satisfaction with the Program

Participant satisfaction is an obvious benefit, one that should accrue to any program. Related, but distinct, is overall employee satisfaction that the program is offered. Both of these outcomes are essential to program success, and any subsequent benefits depend heavily on satisfaction with the program. Associated with satisfaction are possible improvements in employee morale and increases in job satisfaction. Because a workplace health promotion program is liked by employees, their perception of their work and of the workplace may change, presumably for the better. According to a survey of 300 Colorado organizations conducted by the Institute of Health and the Colorado Department of Health (Davis and others, 1984), improved morale is the most common benefit of workplace health promotion programs. As Herzberg (1966) informs us, morale and job satisfaction are dependent on a variety of factors not necessarily related to the work itself.

Improvements in Productivity

Improvements in productivity are highly touted goals of American industry. Productivity has become a buzz word, a goal toward which virtually all aspire. Whether improvements in productivity are expected to be produced by a health promotion program or by the purchase of new equipment, productivity remains extremely difficult to quantify and measure. This difficulty, however, should not prejudice the case for workplace health promotion; it has become just as legitimate to expect improved productivity of a health promotion program as it is to expect it of a new accounting system or new system of management. Unlike program satisfaction and improvements in morale, which may occur over a relatively short period of time, improvements in productivity are assumed to require greater time to emerge.

Reductions in Turnover and
Attractiveness to New Employees

Reductions in employee turnover and greater ease in hiring new employees are, in some sense, opposite sides of the same coin. To the extent that a health promotion program is seen as desirable, that is, employee satisfaction with it is high, the program may contribute to employee decisions to remain with the organization and not look for work elsewhere. Similarly, the existence of a well-received program may be an attractive feature of the organization to potential employees. Employee turnover and hiring are both costly to organizations in that they require the expenditure of considerable resources, human and otherwise. To the extent that a health promotion program reduces turnover and facilitates hiring, the organization's resources are conserved. The effect of the programs comes about both through the specific offerings and the delivery of the message that the organization is concerned for the welfare of its employees.

Potential to Manage Health Care Costs

Finally, for many, the most attractive aspect of workplace health promotion programs is their potential to cut into the rapidly increasing health care costs currently afflicting all organizations. Cost savings may be associated with reductions in the cost of health care insurance, disability payments, and workmen's compensation; these will be the result of reduced incidence of disease and accidents, among the other factors indicated in Chapter Three. In addition, a healthier workforce will miss work less frequently and will arrive promptly more frequently. Each of these may in turn result in reduced overtime pay to employees who take on the work of others in addition to their own. Another cost savings, one that often escapes notice, is the potential to reduce cleaning bills, fire insurance premiums, and maintenance of heating and ventilation systems by reducing and ultimately eliminating smoking in the workplace.

General Cost Savings

Of course, all of the previously mentioned benefits are also associated with cost savings, although less directly. For example, to the extent that an organization experiences reduced employee turnover, the costs of searching for, hiring, and training a new employee are reduced. Improvements in productivity are surely associated with cost savings: Increases in the organization's output of products with no increase in the amount of resources consumed is cost saving. Finally, most employers realize, although sometimes grudgingly, that employee morale and job satisfaction are important cost considerations: Whether employees work to their full potential or only half-heartedly depends in large measure on their willingness, which in turn depends on their feelings and perceptions regarding their work and the organizational climate.

The Time Course of Benefits and Its Effect on Evaluation

The time course of these potential benefits is widely varied. Some (participant satisfaction, for example) are relatively short term. The rest are thought generally to be longer term; there is little expectation that cost savings will emerge immediately after the program's implementation. It is obvious, therefore, that whether a program is determined to be effective or not depends not only on what the program goals are (that is, what benefits are expected) but also on whether one looks at short-term or long-term benefits.

Evidence on the effectiveness of workplace health promotion programs is still emerging. How good the evidence is depends, to a large degree, on whom and how you ask. The behavioral scientist may find the quality of the evidence suggestive but seldom conclusive. The vice-president for finance also may draw no firm conclusions. Program participants may find the programs effective and desirable. The health promotion manager may call the evidence mixed.

Why this diversity of opinion? First, the quality of the evidence depends on which evidence you examine. Workplace health promotion programs are expected to produce multiple benefits. When people ask about workplace health promotion effectiveness, we must ask which goal is being addressed. A program may be a rousing success in improving employee morale but may not be effective in reducing health care costs.

Some companies offer workplace health promotion programs simply because they believe that they will be liked by employees, which will contribute to an overall improvement in the organizational climate. A recently published survey of health promotion for small businesses (Yenney, 1984) indicates that this reason is surprisingly common. For these companies, the program is effective only if it is well received. If it also reduces the incidence of disease and accidents in the workplace, all the better.

For other companies, however, the objective of a health promotion program is to reduce health care costs. Anything short of this objective will be inadequate. For such companies, the fact that employees love the exercise or smoking cessation program is irrelevant. Determination of program effectiveness in these companies is considerably more elaborate. It is widely held that if this is the goal of a workplace health promotion program, then the company must be prepared to wait, perhaps five or ten years, for the program to demonstrate its value. Reductions in health care cost are expected to evolve relatively slowly, over a period of time that corresponds to the gradual reduction in use of the health care system, which is presumed to result from the gradual decrease in disease in the workforce. Recall, as discussed in Chapters One and Two, that most workplace health promotion programs currently act to reduce risk factors for chronic diseases by facilitating changes in risk factor behavior of individuals. A smoking cessation program may not demonstrate its impact on health care costs for several years because the health consequences of smoking and/or quitting do not occur overnight. The same is true of hypertension control or cardiovascular fitness programs. Figure 1 displays the temporal relationship of health promotion benefits.

Figure 1.   The Relationship of Health Promotion Objectives over Time.

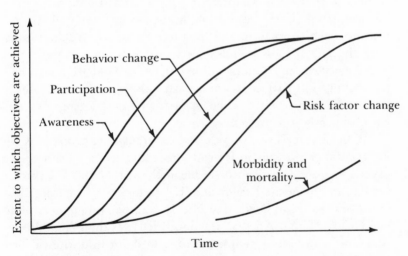

Source: The Minnesota Heart Health Program, Henry Blackburn, Principal Investigator.

It is for this reason that many long-term studies of health promotion programs designed to reduce risk factors are underway. These studies hypothesize that over a long period of time, programs that modify risk factor behavior will ultimately produce reductions in the incidence of chronic diseases such as cancer and heart disease. As these reductions occur, the need to use the costly health care system will also be reduced, thus saving the organization money.

Because of their emphasis on the control of chronic diseases, only a few workplace health promotion programs have yet been demonstrated to have the expected impact on health care costs. This is not because they are not effective; rather, it is because the programs will have their effect in the long run, and the data are simply not available yet. In light of these considerations, some companies, especially those with many employees, have resorted to statistical and epidemiological analyses to develop estimates of program effectiveness. (This approach can be seen in some of the case examples that follow.)

For understandable reasons, the evidence on the success of such behavior modification programs is still accumulating. Although the evidence is still incomplete, we have every reason to believe that once complete, it will be consistent with expectations. However, we question the generally accepted distinction between short-term and long-term benefits. We do not dispute the fact that in well-designed programs, some benefits will occur early on and others will occur later. What we question is the assumption that cost savings can only be seen much later in the sequence of events, when in fact such cost savings may occur quite early in a program.

In Chapter Two, we referred to an ongoing project involving federal employees in Hawaii. Providing access to short-term psychotherapy significantly reduced the use of the health care system and associated medical bills, producing a 37-percent savings (Mervis, 1985). Note that in this example, no medical treatment was offered. All that was modified was the availability of someone with whom people could talk about important issues, including the symptom. This opportunity had an immediate effect on the use of the health care system. The same kind of reasoning applies to absenteeism and even productivity, each of which has immediate cost implications for an organization.

In summary, savings due to reductions in the use of the health care system and in absenteeism may arise in both the short and long terms. In the short term, employees may see a doctor or be absent less frequently, not because their actual health has improved but rather because they feel better about themselves or about the organization. These changes may be consequences of a workplace health promotion program. Many fitness programs report that participants show positive changes in self-esteem. The moral: People see a doctor or are absent from work for a variety of reasons; poor health is only one of them. When employees are absent from work, organizations suffer greater expenses. Similarly, people visit physicians for a variety of reasons, and poor health may only be tangentially related. To the extent that employees use the health care system, for whatever reason, organizations will bear the costs. Short-term and long-term influences on productivity also are similar. Finally, it is not necessarily the case that evaluation of the cost-saving potential of workplace health promotion programs must await long-term findings. Only evaluations of potential savings that derive from reductions in incidence of chronic disease must wait.

Case Examples of Workplace Health Promotion Programs

The cases presented are not necessarily representative of the great majority of workplace health promotion programs; however, they are excellent examples of programs that have received some degree of systematic evaluation. Included are examples of simple as well as complex programs. Many aspects of the cases are generalizable to all kinds of organizations.

Blue Cross and Blue Shield of Indiana

In 1977, Blue Cross and Blue Shield of Indiana began a comprehensive health promotion program, "Stay Alive and Well," to its 2,400 employees and their spouses and to retirees. From the outset, a five-year controlled evaluation was planned. Among the Stay Alive and Well offerings were programs in nutrition, weight loss, smoking cessation, fitness, and stress management. All programs were offered on-site, and most were on company time. Other incentives included health passports (personalized health records), health risk appraisals, publicity in the company newsletter, posters, slide shows, and encouragement from management. The program was delivered in four phases: planning, screening, intervention, and follow-up.

Two groups of employees, 667 participants and 892 nonparticipants, were compared to determine the effect of the program on use of health insurance benefits. Participants generally submitted more claims than nonparticipants but the average cost/claim was lower for participants than for nonparticipants. Program costs and savings also were computed. Included in cost estimates were office rental, utilities, staff training, salary, fringe benefits, lost wages while employees participated in the program on company time, publicity expenses, and so on. The total program cost was $98.86 per employee. (Note that the cost of the program was computed per company employee not per participant.) That is, the cost was computed on a company-wide basis. Similarly, average savings were computed on a company-wide basis.

In addition, savings were discounted to take into account what the investment would have earned had it been invested elsewhere. Average savings per employee were $143.60. Therefore, the savings ratio was 1.45:1. This return on investment (ROI) figure is highly conservative in that the $98.86 per employee includes one-time start-up costs. If these start-up costs are amortized over the entire five-year period of the analysis, the average yearly cost per employee drops to $57.23, raising the savings ratio to 2.51:1 (Gibbs and others, 1985).

It might be argued that only those who were already quite healthy participated in the program, thus skewing the outcome figures in the predicted direction. (In fact, some outcome studies show dramatic program effectiveness without considering this important fact.) However, in this case, the calculation of the program costs and savings on a company-wide basis controls for this possibility (Mulvaney and others, 1985).

Johnson & Johnson

Johnson & Johnson has been a leader in the workplace health promotion movement, pioneering large and comprehensive programs. "Live for Life," the Johnson & Johnson program, provides programs in health risk appraisal, physical fitness, diet and nutrition, smoking cessation, hypertension control, stress management, weight control, and health education. Individual Johnson & Johnson companies decide whether or not to implement Live for Life. Special attention has been devoted to evaluation of the program and reports of the effect of the exercise and fitness program have just been published.

The exercise and fitness program consisted of a three-hour seminar on lifestyle, emphasizing among other things, the importance of regular exercise. The seminar also introduced a wide range of health promotion activities and facilities available at the workplace. Employees had the opportunity to participate, on their own time, in the regularly scheduled programs. In addition, there were highly visible health education campaigns.

Researchers compared employees at four Johnson & Johnson companies that offered "Live for Life" with employees at three companies that did not during the same two-year period. "Almost 20 percent of the women and 30 percent of the men in the health promotion program companies began regular vigorous exercise over the two-year period compared with 7 percent and 19 percent of the health screen [nonparticipating] companies" (Blair, Piserchia, Wilbur, and Crowder, 1986). Not only did the number of employees exercising at participating companies increase, but, as you might expect, the overall physical condition of the participating companies' employees improved relative to employees at the nonparticipating companies. Finally, those employees who showed the greatest improvements in physical fitness also showed increased feelings of general well-being, reduced depression, and reductions in coronary heart disease risk factors.

These changes represent reductions in risk factor behavior that are believed to produce actual reductions in health care costs in the longer term. A recent report has demonstrated that some of these latter changes have taken place. Two groups of Johnson & Johnson employees were followed for a five-year period. For one group of 8,451 employees exposed to the Live for Life program, the mean annual in-patient cost increases were approximately $43. For the group of 2,955 employees who were not exposed to Live for Life, the mean annual in-patient cost increase was $76. Groups exposed to Live for Life also had lower increases in number of hospital days per year and in total hospital admissions (Bly, Jones, and Richardson, 1986).

AT&T Communications

AT&T Communications conducts one of the most extensive and thoroughly evaluated workplace health promotion programs. Interest in the development of a program arose from the anticipated increase of stress associated with the breakup of the AT&T system. The program, "Total Life Concept (TLC)," was initially proposed not so much as a cost-cutting measure but as a way of helping employees cope with the disruption caused by massive reorganization of their work environment. TLC offers a comprehensive approach to the development of a healthy lifestyle. It begins with an orientation session to which potential participants are invited. During the orientation, employees are introduced to the ideas of wellness, behavioral health, and health risk, a short film is shown, printed materials describing program offerings are distributed, and a health risk appraisal (HRA) is conducted. Associated with the risk appraisal process is the measurement of such variables as blood pressure, serum cholesterol and high-density lipoprotein levels, and height and weight.

In a subsequent meeting, participants are helped to interpret their health risk appraisal and are encouraged to make a long-term plan for changing behavior in relation to health. They are offered the opportunity to enroll in the wide variety of intervention programs. These programs include stress management, smoking cessation, exercise, blood pressure control, back pain control, cholesterol reduction and nutrition, weight management, and interpersonal skills training.

Because of the relative novelty of TLC, it was subjected

to a pilot study and rigorous evaluation. Three groups were followed. Group 1 participated in the orientation and HRA in May 1983. It was invited to enroll in the health promotion programs listed and completed a second HRA in May 1984. Group 2 completed HRAs in May 1983 and May 1984 and received feedback and interpretation of the HRA but was not invited to participate in the programs. Group 3 completed an HRA in May 1984. By designing the evaluation in this way, AT&T-C was able to determine not only if TLC had an impact (by comparing data from Groups 1 and 2 in May 1984) but also if the act of completing an HRA alone might have a positive impact (by comparing Groups 2 and 3).

Both the health and financial results from the pilot study were impressive, sufficiently so that AT&T-C decided to implement TLC at all of its locations. Relative to Group 2, Group 1 showed significant decreases in the amount of smoking, serum cholesterol, weight, and, importantly, in the risk of heart attack and cancer. In May 1983 (Time 1), risk of a heart attack at AT&T-C was 3,620/100,000. In May 1984 (Time 2), heart attack risk for Group 1 had been reduced to 3,280/100,000. Extrapolated to the entire 110,000 AT&T-C population, over a ten-year period, TLC would reduce the number of heart attacks by 374. At an estimated cost to the organization of $250,000 to $1 million per heart attack, the savings accruing to TLC for this disease alone are $93.5 million. But the pilot results showed that TLC also produced a significantly reduced risk of cancer, which would reduce further the expenses associated with medical care, organizational disruption, overtime, searching, hiring, and training replacements (Bellingham, Johnson, and McCauley, 1985).

Extrapolated over all of the AT&T-C system, the TLC annual budget will be $4 million. Again using organization-wide figures, the $40 million spent on TLC over ten years will yield a savings of $93.5 million, a savings to cost ratio of 2.3:1. This ratio, of course, is for death due to heart attack only. For the same costs, TLC will also reduce the number of cases of cancer, thus saving even more money. Finally, although the analysis did not examine incidence of more minor illnesses, it seems certain that TLC will reduce expenses associated with these conditions, too. For example, it is well known that stopping smoking reduces the incidence of respiratory infections. In summary, AT&T's TLC program appears to be successful in the eyes of management, behavioral science, epidemiology, and the participants.

Canada Life Assurance Company and
North American Life Assurance Company

The Canada Fitness and Lifestyle Project (Shephard and others, 1982) compared the head offices of these two large Canadian life insurance companies in regard to a workplace health promotion program. Data on hospital admissions, medical claims, and physical fitness were collected for the year prior to and following the institution of an employee fitness program at one of the companies. Comparisons of the two companies were made of all employees who came to fitness evaluations, not simply of those who actually participated in the fitness programs. Initially, hospital use for the test company (the one at which the fitness program was offered) was higher than that for the control company. Following the implementation of the fitness program, this relationship was reversed: The employees at the control company had a higher rate of hospital use. At the outset, both companies were similar in total medical care costs. After implementation of the fitness program, no overall change in medical care costs was found in the test company but a significant increase was seen in the control company; this suggests that had it not been for the fitness program, the test company also would have shown an increase.

Finally, and most surprisingly, it was demonstrated that the reduced health care costs at the test company were shown not only by the participants in the fitness program but also by the nonparticipants as well. This finding suggests that the implementation of an employee fitness program may have effects on a company's health care costs even for those employees who do not participate. The mechanism of this effect remains to be investigated.

On the basis of these findings, it was estimated that the

program produced a savings of greater than 0.5 hospital days per employee per year plus $28.50 per year in medical costs other than hospitalization. The potential overall savings for the test company as a result of the fitness program were $84.50 per employee per year. (Note that these figures are based on Canadian medical care costs, which are considerably lower than American ones. Especially striking is the fact that these estimates are based on $100 per day for hospitalization. In the United States, daily rates for most hospitals are at least three times this figure, thus the savings for American companies would be considerably greater.)

Data on absenteeism and employee turnover also were collected in this evaluation. In the test company, turnover among program participants was reduced from 15 percent to 1.5 percent, and among high adherents to the program, absenteeism was reduced by 22 percent (Cox, Shephard, and Corey, 1981). These two changes also have considerable economic impact.

Speedcall Corporation

The case of Speedcall Corporation in Hayward, California, provides an excellent example of what a small company—about 35 employees—can do to promote health and have an effect on health care costs. The Speedcall program is as elegant as it is simple: The company issues weekly bonuses ($7) for not smoking on the job. According to Rose Glover, administration manager, the company philosophy is not to penalize people for smoking but to reward them for not smoking. The program is long term, continuing as long as participants are employed by Speedcall. Employees are entirely on the honor system to monitor their smoking.

Within one month after program initiation, the percentage of employees smoking at work declined from 67 percent to 43 percent. After four years, the number of smokers had fallen by 65 percent when compared to pre-program levels. Further evidence of the program's effectiveness is found from examination of former Speedcall employees. Former employees showed only a 22 percent reduction in smoking when compared to the pre-program baseline, whereas current employees showed a 60 percent reduction. This suggests that the continued availability of the $7 per week incentive for continuing employees has a significant impact in maintaining smoking cessation.

Net resource savings amounted to $38 per employee per year. These savings do not include the health insurance savings. The overall cost of the program was $246 per year per employee. The benefits in employee morale improvements are difficult to quantify.

During the 1976-1979 period, under the $7 per week incentive, the average health insurance claims at Speedcall rose at a slower rate than the national average. Moreover, the loss ratio on health insurance (the amount the insurance company has to pay on medical expenses relative to the cost of insurance premiums) declined considerably, which permitted Speedcall to find health insurance at a lower cost. In addition, the experience of a small sample (N = 5) of Speedcall employees is especially instructive. The health insurance claims of these five employees after quitting smoking (as a result of the program) were 50 percent of that prior to quitting. Because Speedcall is such a small company, it is difficult to assess accurately the overall financial impact of the program, but the findings are clearly suggestive (Glover, 1982).

New York Telephone

The New York Telephone Company is one of many organizations to offer hypertension screening and control programs. Unlike other similar programs, New York Telephone conducted an extensive evaluation of the program. The program was evaluated over a five-year (1978-1982) period during which 5,211 employees were identified as hypertensive. The program consisted of standard pharmacological treatment offered at the workplace. Program costs included payment for physicians, nurses, and drugs and amounted to $99.59 per hypertensive employee per year.

Using a sophisticated computer analysis to estimate the

effects of leaving untreated a population this size, the hypertension control program saved 53,363 disability days in the five-year test period. The value of these saved disability days was estimated to be $2,495,154. In addition, savings in medical expenses were estimated to be over $390,000. The total cost of the program was $2,005,141. Over a five-year period, the New York Telephone hypertension control program saved over $800,000 (Collings, 1982).

What Do These Cases Demonstrate?

We have presented several case studies of workplace health promotion programs, not because they are representative of workplace health promotion in general, but rather because they represent the *potential* of systematically developed, well-conducted programs. They illustrate a wide variety of approaches to health promotion in the workplace and equally broad methods of determining program effectiveness and benefits. As might be expected, large organizations tend to implement large, complex programs, and smaller organizations understandably are attracted to smaller-scale ones. Similarly, the sophistication of program evaluation is generally greater with large organizations than with smaller ones because of the availability of greater resources for conducting such evaluations.

Differences notwithstanding, each of the programs is successful by its own definition and standards of performance. Speedcall's $7 per week incentive, for example, has little in common with the sophisticated epidemiological evaluation that characterizes AT&T Communication's TLC program. For Speedcall, it is sufficient that smoking in the workplace is greatly reduced. In light of the overwhelming evidence relating smoking to health risks and to associated organizational costs, this approach is entirely understandable, especially when considering the limited nature of Speedcall's program. For Blue Cross and Blue Shield of Indiana and for New York Telephone, however, each with a much more extensive and costly program, firmer evidence of success was deemed necessary and was available.

Making the Case for Workplace Health Promotion:
The Pre-Planning Phase

These examples demonstrate that workplace health promotion programs can be successful and can benefit the organization. Armed with this information, what does one who is interested in encouraging program development do next? At this stage, planning for the development, implementation, and evaluation of a health promotion program is premature. First, it is essential to determine whether a health promotion program of any sort is not only desirable but needed and feasible. Second, one must secure the permission of the responsible decision makers in the organization to proceed, which generally requires determination of the need and feasibility for such a program.

Designing a health promotion program is covered in detail in Part Two. The remainder of this chapter discusses what is needed to reach the design phase. First, you must conduct an examination of the organization to determine whether or not pursuit of workplace health promotion is justified; that is, the organization's health must be analyzed. Although the details of such an analysis are discussed thoroughly in the next chapter, conducting such an examination requires a mandate of sorts from the CEO or other responsible administrator.

Securing Management Support
for an Organizational Health Analysis

The ease of securing management support at this stage depends heavily on the characteristics of the individual organization. Small organizations typically are characterized by relatively flexible hierarchies. If this is the case, then securing support for the analysis may be relatively simple; it may require only that you ask permission. Of course, if your position in the organization is such that the authorization of another person is not necessary, then this is not an issue.

In larger organizations, however, it is often the case that permission must be granted for you to undertake a task that temporarily may reduce the amount of time you devote to your other responsibilities. In some ways, this is a "chicken and egg" problem because the information you need to make your case to management for release time to conduct the analysis is precisely the information you will want to acquire through this investigation. You can use much of the information presented earlier in this and the other preceding chapters to justify to management the need for an organizational health analysis. This information, of course, may not be directly relevant to your organization, but it can help you to justify an investigation to uncover this more relevant information.

Should you need to secure permission to conduct this research, more than likely you will need to make a written and possibly an oral presentation documenting the need. Note again that the need in this pre-planning phase is to secure permission to conduct the analysis, not the need for a health promotion program. Until you conduct the research, you have no basis to determine whether a program is needed and, if so, how it may benefit the organization. Top managers are not inclined to look favorably on requests to devote precious organizational resources to a program whose need is not adequately demonstrated.

The next section presents some guidelines regarding how one might structure the approach for permission to conduct the analysis. In what follows, we present a discussion of the preliminary investigation and following that, a brief discussion of how to structure the approach for permission to conduct it. This apparently inverted order of discussion is intentional; to secure permission for the analysis, you must first know what information you will need to collect.

A Preliminary Investigation

Since the focus of your interest is the benefits associated with workplace health programs, that is, health care cost management, reductions in absenteeism, and improvements in morale and job satisfaction, the most relevant information is the organization's recent history of expenses associated with disease: reports from the medical department (if one exists), insurance claims, and attendance records. The medical department may have detailed records of visits organized by ailment. Aggregated data will help to address whether there is, for example, a steady stream of employees visiting the health service for stress-related or smoking-related problems. Does it appear that a large fraction of the workforce is overweight? Do medical records indicate an unusually high frequency of certain kinds of injuries? At this stage, you are looking for general information to justify the need for further inquiry.

Similarly, the benefits department or personnel department may have relevant information on the extent to which employees use the health care system and the overall costs to the organization associated with this usage. Either the personnel department or the insurance company will have information on the number of claims filed by employees over a given period of time. In addition, the dollar value of the claims should also be available. All of this information probably will be available only on a confidential basis and should be in aggregated form to be useful. Sometimes insurance companies will appear reluctant to provide this information. For this reason, it is imperative that you secure the authorization to collect it.

It may be necessary to collect other information, either because medical and insurance information is not available or sufficiently well organized or because it alone is not sufficient. Health statistics, available through the federal and local government and from insurance companies, may indicate the frequency of certain diseases and conditions, and these statistics may be further organized by geographic and demographic categories. For example, it may be the case that the incidence of certain kinds of cancer is especially high for certain populations or in certain geographic regions. If in your workforce this population is heavily represented or if most of your employees are from this geographic region, it will be worth investigating a health promotion program designed to reduce the risk of these kinds of cancers. To take a specific and different example, it is clear that compared to whites, blacks suffer a much greater incidence of hypertension. If your workforce has a high percentage of black workers, it is likely that hypertension and related conditions such as heart disease and stroke are a concern for the organization.

Finally, other similar companies, either in your area or elsewhere, may have investigated workplace health promotion programs and collected some information you might find helpful in illustrating the scope of the problem and potential solutions. Their experiences may be instructive to you during this pre-planning phase. Trade organizations may have relevant information on health care expenses for the industry as a whole as well as recommendations for cost management strategies.

Proposal to Conduct the Analysis

The proposal should be structured along the appropriate lines for internal communications within your company and should conform to norms of language and length. Information from previous chapters in this book as well as other current facts will be useful. Resource C contains a list of likely sources of such current information.

The following is a sample outline for the proposal:

I. Describe the problem.
   A. Present the rising costs of medical care in the country and for your industry in general.
      1. insurance costs rising at ____% annually
      2. cost of medical care rising at ____% annually
   B. A relatively large fraction of these costs are avoidable.
      1. costs associated with lifestyle factors
         a. for example, the cost of cigarette smoking to a corporation
         b. for example, the cost of one heart attack to a corporation
      2. costs associated with organizational factors and illness
         a. for instance, sources of absenteeism
   C. Disease produces direct and indirect costs to the organization.
      1. insurance usage
      2. absenteeism

           3.   losses in productivity
           4.   disability
           5.   turnover, replacement, and so on

II.   Show how organizations have saved substantially on health care costs by investing in various forms of health promotion.

    A.   Present one example of a large, comprehensive, well-evaluated wellness program.

       1.   briefly describe the program
       2.   describe the findings
       3.   detail the cost and projected savings

    B.   Give examples of one or two corporate health promotion programs in companies that approximate yours in size. Include the same information as in the preceding subsection A.

    C.   Extrapolate these findings and benefits to your organization.

III. Secure permission to investigate these matters in your own company.

    A.   Request time from your assigned duties to conduct the analysis. Determine to whom you will report the findings of the analysis.

    B.   Request access to information (in aggregate form only). Departments should be mentioned by name, and examples of types of data to be requested should be included.

    C.   Request permission to poll employees. Surveys should be anonymous.

    D.   Secure agreement regarding what form the results of this analysis will take and to whom they should be submitted.

Conclusion

Making the case for workplace health promotion is a multiple stage affair. Although we have seen organizations that suddenly implement a cardiovascular fitness program immediately after the CEO has a heart attack and with no organizational health analysis whatsoever, many organizations behave more systematically and less reactively. The first stage of development is to demonstrate, using the kind of information discussed in this chapter and in previous ones, that health promotion programs are worthy of consideration. Because the planning and implementation of a workplace health promotion program is likely to require the dedication of significant resources, it is necessary to demonstrate need, whether revealed by an examination of internal organizational experience or extrapolated from the experience of other similar organizations. This stage of organizational analysis will help to shape the health promotion program to meet the organization's unique requirements. Always remember that the analysis may indicate that no program at all is necessary or desirable.

5

Analyzing the Organization's Health Needs and Resources

An important first step in planning for a workplace health promotion program is to analyze the organization's needs and readiness. The purpose of such an organizational analysis is to provide management with a comprehensive picture not only of the organization's state of health and of the probable determinants of this state but also of the organization's resources. A comprehensive analysis is conducted (1) to determine if a program is practical and (2) to guide program development to address only those health problems for which a program is likely to be effective. Always remember that an organizational analysis may reveal that the development of a workplace health promotion program is not justified: the company's health indicators are about as good as reasonably can be expected, the problems that are revealed are beyond the scope of health promotion, or there is insufficient employee interest.

We should indicate that we have used the word "analysis" rather than "diagnosis" in this chapter. "Diagnosis" connotes medicalization of a problem (that is, detection of a disease). We prefer to call this process "analysis" because the primary focus of workplace health promotion is the prevention of future disease and its correlates rather than the treatment of existing disease. Moreover, as this chapter will indicate, in analyzing rather than diagnosing the organization, information is collected on the resources of the organization to conduct a workplace health promotion and on the interests, needs, and health habits of the employee population as well as on frequency of disease, disability, and medical care costs.

Analyzing the organization requires information from many sources. The organization itself must provide considerable data. A related source of data is the insurance carrier or administrator. The employees represent a third source of information. Finally, other sources such as government (local, state, and federal), health organizations, both local and national (for example, American Lung Association, American Heart Association, YMCA), and the insurance industry can help in the analysis.

How extensive the analysis should be will vary from company to company. Some organizations will rely only on simple estimates of program needs. For example, the mere perception that a sizable fraction of the workforce smokes may be all that is necessary to justify the development of a smoking cessation program. Such a perception may be based on no data collection at all; it simply may be the product of a judgment about the prevalence of smoking in the workplace. Alternatively, an organization may undertake a detailed investigation of the prevalence of health conditions, stratified by organizational division, employee sex, or management level. Such an investigation may be quite complex. The complexity of the analysis will be a function of a variety of factors including the organization's size, resources, and, especially, the preferences of top management.

How Organizations Conduct Health Analyses:
Case Examples

AT&T Communications

AT&T Communications conducted an extensive epidemiological study of its health promotion program, Total Life Concept (TLC). In so doing, baseline data on absenteeism, turnover, health care claims, and incidence of disability were collected. The stated objective of collecting these data was (1) to deter-

mine the need for a health promotion program and (2) to have a
basis of comparison for the program outcomes. In reality, these
data were collected more for the second reason than for the
first, which further underscores the importance of recognizing
that analysis is often a less-than-scientific procedure. Published
reports suggest that the real inspiration for TLC was not the
data-based discovery that significant health problems existed at
AT&T-C but rather the expectation of serious adverse health
effects of the divestiture of the AT&T system in the early
1980s. The need for TLC and the form it took could have been
established with far less sophisticated (and less costly) efforts.
Of course, the epidemiological study also was used for program
evaluation.

Plaskolite, Inc.

Case examples from smaller companies further underscore this
point. At Plaskolite, Inc., a light manufacturing company in
Pennsylvania, the health promotion program began with little formal analysis. It was known, for example, that the workforce was
relatively young and presumably in good health. The only serious problem in the use of the health care system was that use of
the emergency room appeared to be higher than expected. This
information led to an analysis of the medical conditions that
brought employees and their families to the emergency room.
The analysis disclosed that in many cases, nonemergency problems were being treated. It was discovered that many employees
did not have family physicians to whom they could turn for
routine treatment.

     Plaskolite also examined absenteeism rates across company
divisions and discovered an unusually high rate in one area. Further examination disclosed that this high rate was due not to disease but rather to problems with the area supervisor. Other analytic strategies employed included surveying employees to collect
information on smoking and other health habits, providing annual physical examinations, and collecting information on employee preferences in regard to health promotion activities.

Scherer Brothers Lumber Company

At the Scherer Brothers Lumber Company, organizational analysis took the form of a needs assessment. Employees were surveyed about their preferences for programs. Note that no health care utilization data were collected to determine if a workplace health promotion program were necessary. It was assumed that such a program was desirable, irrespective of the state of the organization's health care situation.

Skeptics may scoff at the apparent capriciousness of this assumption, believing that health promotion programs in the workplace must justify their existence by amassing evidence that a need exists. In this regard, however, Scherer Brothers behaved no differently than AT&T Communications: Both acted not on the basis of evidence collected but rather out of the widespread recognition that (1) the organization's health care costs are enormous and that (2) workplace health promotion programs have the potential to reduce those costs and significantly improve employee morale. In fact, at Scherer Brothers, the primary justification for the program is that employees like it, not that it may contribute to health care cost management.

These cases present excellent examples of the variety of information used to justify the development of a workplace health promotion program. To be sure, AT&T-C collected information on relevant health variables, for example, absenteeism and health care claims, but the basis for proposing TLC was the very reasonable expectation that the enormous convulsions produced by divestiture of an American institution would increase the risks of costly diseases and disabilities.

Further support for this minimalist approach to analysis comes from a brief and nonrandom survey of workplace health promotion programs in the Mid-Hudson Valley of New York. The survey revealed that although many companies had health promotion programs or were developing them, none had conducted organizational health analyses. All companies indicated that their interests in these programs had arisen from the expectation that such programs might reduce medical care costs as well as improve morale and reduce absenteeism among employees. This survey underscores the nonquantitative nature of the judgments made by many organizational executives in development of workplace programs.

These case examples and the survey, as well as reports on other workplace health promotion programs, reveal that as currently practiced, organizational health analysis is a less scientific and more "seat-of-the-pants" process. Even in the case of AT&T Communications, an enormous company with equally enormous resources, the justification for the development of a health promotion program was based more on expectations of adverse health outcomes of divestiture than on rigorous analysis of data on health practices, absenteeism, and medical care use. Of course, the expectation of adverse health outcomes was based on decades of scientific study of the impact of preventive actions on the incidence of disease.

Almost all organizational health analyses depend heavily, although not necessarily exclusively, on such judgments. The zeal to quantify virtually every aspect of an organization has made many managers and program developers reluctant to admit their dependence on rational information unavailable in quantitative form. In this regard, it is essential to recognize that the decision to embark on a program of workplace health promotion is a business decision and that many business decisions are made without quantitative information, regardless of what graduate schools of business currently teach. We believe that the decision to develop a workplace health promotion program is for most, but not for all, companies a prudent one.

These considerations clearly suggest that the analysis an organization undertakes should be guided by a realistic view of (1) what data can be collected, (2) the expense of collecting them, and more importantly, (3) the meaning of the data. For these reasons, we recommend collection of the following information for an organizational analysis:

1. data on basic employee (and dependents, retirees, and spouses) health practices
2. survey information on the preferences of employees (and

dependents, retirees, and spouses) regarding various health promotion activities

3. relatively simple data on insurance use and absenteeism
4. a complete survey of community and intra-company health resources

Below we present an outline of information that can be used in analyzing the organization. The outline contains much more information than is necessary for any one company. It is presented in such great detail because individual organizations may find that some of the information listed is either more important or more accessible to them. In reading the outline, keep in mind that you probably will not need to collect all of these data. Data collection should be guided by the needs and characteristics of each individual organization.

Because organizations differ so widely in their structure, the outline is organized according to categories of information that may be used in the analysis rather than by organizational divisions from which this information may be collected. For example, information on medical care costs may be collected in the personnel department in some organizations and in the benefits department in others. Small organizations may not have such discrete departments and have instead a single person who serves these functions. What is important for purposes of analysis is the information itself, not where it is located.

Workplace Health Promotion Organizational Analysis: An Outline

I. Data from the Organization

A. Medical Care Costs and Utilization. Among the most relevant information to be collected from the organization is the annual utilization of the medical care system. For most organizations, this information is available through the medical, personnel, or benefits departments. Typically, the relevant data are the insurance premiums. Analysis of costs and utilization should also include accident and disability information. One may examine this information in at least two ways: (1) the cost of medical care and (2) the frequency of utilization. Although the two are related, the relationship is not always perfect, as we will discuss soon.

As we indicated earlier in the book, the Chrysler Corporation paid more than $6,000 per employee in health care costs in 1983. Health insurance premiums in that year totaled $373 million. But, one might ask, "How can we know whether or not this amount is excessive?" To answer this entirely reasonable question, one might compare the cost of health care to other organizational costs. Chrysler did this and discovered that it paid more in 1983 for health care than for any other single supplier. Another way to assess the magnitude of the annual costs of health care is to compare them to past years. Chrysler did this in an unusual way: It discovered that the cost of health care in 1983 amounted to more than $600 per car sold, whereas in 1970, the figure was $75 per car sold.

However you analyze it, an essential part of the organizational analysis is to determine the annual medical care costs and to make meaningful comparisons of these figures. Such data not only permit you to determine the necessity of a health promotion program but will also provide the opportunity, after a program is underway, to evaluate its impact on medical care costs.

Once this information is secured, the challenging part of the analysis begins: how to meaningfully interpret it. Perhaps the most basic question one can ask of data on medical care costs is about the absolute magnitude of these costs over the past several years. How much is spent on insurance premiums? Are these costs stable, or are they increasing? If increasing, at what rate? How does this rate of increase compare to the national rate of inflation of medical care costs? At the national level, for example, health care costs rose at a rate of 7.7 percent when compared to a 1.1 percent increase in the consumer price index (Pear, 1987). How do these trends compare to the costs of other services?

Beyond analysis of global medical care costs, subsidiary analyses can be conducted. Adequate interpretation requires at least two additional considerations: (1) Which groups use the medical care system and (2) which medical care benefits are used?

B. Which Groups Use the Medical Care System? Questions can be asked about the distribution of medical care costs across the organization. For example, are the overall costs distributed equally across the organization or are they greater in some categories, for example, employees, dependents, retirees, upper-level executives, entry-level positions, or manufacturing division versus finance division? In other words, which groups are making the most use of the medical care system?

An important distinction to be made is between employees on the one hand and spouses and dependents on the other. On a national level, 70 percent of organizational medical care expenses go to claims from spouses and dependents. This percentage obviously varies from company to company and according to the characteristics of benefit packages, but determining the fraction of medical care expenses associated with employees relative to spouses and dependents will be important in shaping the health promotion program.

Information can be categorized not only according to organizational units but also by demographic categories, for instance, sex, age, race, ethnicity. Disability at a major New York metropolitan company, for instance, is most frequent among women from age twenty to thirty-five. The cause of this disability is pregnancy. This example reveals several important aspects of an organizational analysis. First, it demonstrates the utility of examining medical care and other related costs according to their distribution across organizational categories and employee groups. Second, the conclusion to be drawn from an analysis revealing that pregnancy is the leading cause of disability is that it is unrealistic to expect a workplace health promotion program to have an effect on this particular medical care expense.

C. Which Medical Care Benefits Are Used and How Much? The pattern of medical care utilization within the entire organization and within individual groups should be examined for trends.

How much is each benefit being used? Working with your insurance company or administrator will be helpful here. Utilization data can be classified according to "major diagnostic categories (MDCs)," the twenty-three general groups of "diagnosis-related groups (DRGs)." The latter are over 400 specific medical diagnoses that are often used in analysis of claim utilization. Table 1 presents a list of the major diagnostic categories. Using MDCs as the basis of the analysis, you can determine which medical con-

Table 1.   The Major Diagnostic Categories for Medicare, 1983.

MDC 1:	Diseases and Disorders of the Nervous System
MDC 2:	Diseases and Disorders of the Eye
MDC 3:	Diseases and Disorders of the Ear, Nose, and Throat
MDC 4:	Diseases and Disorders of the Respiratory System
MDC 5:	Diseases and Disorders of the Circulatory System
MDC 6:	Diseases and Disorders of the Digestive System
MDC 7:	Diseases and Disorders of the Hepatobiliary System and Pancreas
MDC 8:	Diseases of the Musculoskeletal System and Connective Tissue
MDC 9:	Diseases of the Skin, Subcutaneous Tissue, and Breast
MDC 10:	Endocrine, Nutritional, and Metabolic Diseases
MDC 11:	Diseases and Disorders of the Kidney and Urinary Tract
MDC 12:	Diseases and Disorders of the Male Reproductive System
MDC 13:	Diseases and Disorders of the Female Reproductive System
MDC 14:	Pregnancy, Childbirth, and the Puerperium
MDC 15:	Normal Newborns and Other Neonates with Certain Conditions Originating in the Perinatal Period
MDC 16:	Diseases and Disorders of the Blood and Blood-Forming Organs and Immunity
MDC 17:	Myeloproliferative Disorders and Poorly Differentiated Malignancy and Other Neoplasms NEC (not elsewhere classified)
MDC 18:	Infectious and Parasitic Diseases (Systemic)
MDC 19:	Mental Disorders
MDC 20:	Substance Use Disorders and Substance Induced Organic Disorders
MDC 21:	Injury, Poisoning, and Toxic Effects of Drugs
MDC 22:	Burns
MDC 23:	Selected Factors Influencing Health Status and Contact with Health Services

ditions are the most prevalent. This information may provide you with the best estimate of the health conditions that afflict the workplace population (and the other insureds), and in turn who are the most likely candidates for a health promotion program.

Once you have determined how most effectively to break down the overall population making use of the medical care system, for example, emloyees, dependents, retirees, intra-company divisions, and so on, and have further determined the organization-wide pattern of health conditions leading to medical care utilization, you may wish to go further and ask about the pattern of medical care utilization between groups. For example, a national computer consulting company recently wanted to address an unexpectedly high rate of psychiatric utilization among a specific group of employees in contrast to other diagnostic categories and to other employee groups. The realization of the high utilization of a specific benefit by this specific group of employees suggested a detailed examination of the work conditions and health habits of this group, which in turn led to specific recommendations for changes in each. Without such a detailed analysis, the organization might know only that general medical expenses had increased at a rather unexpectedly high rate. It would not have understood the source of this increase.

For many organizations, this information on medical care costs and utilization is available only through the insurance carrier. Even organizations that self-insure contract with insurance companies or other organizations to administer their insurance programs. The extent to which detailed analyses of insurance data can be conducted will vary from carrier to carrier. According to Dr. Charles Arnold of Metropolitan Life Insurance Company, even the most sophisticated of software is not capable of doing more than determining the distribution of insurance claims among the MDCs. Even if this were completely possible, a thorough analysis would require, in addition, the collection of data on behavioral health practices of employees (which we will discuss shortly). Then, one might be able to say to top management, "Can you see that your rather high incidence of bypass surgery and care for other heart diseases as well as care for pulmonary diseases is related to this high rate of smoking?" The best information for guiding the direction of health promotion programs, in Arnold's view, is the combination of information from medical care utilization and the health habits of the employee population.

Some other qualifications are in order. When examining the frequency of medical care claims organized by groups of insureds, keep in mind that age plays a major role: The incidence of chronic disease is directly related to age. Consider, for example, that a group of upper-level managers may suffer from a higher rate of cardiovascular disease than entry-level employees. It is possible that the upper-level managers experience greater stress on the job. They may also smoke more, exercise less, or eat more poorly. It is also highly likely, however, that they are considerably older than the entry-level employees, and this difference in age may be enough to account for the higher incidence of cardiovascular disease. As far as organizational analysis and program planning are concerned, the most important information may be the health habit data: that this group of managers smokes, gets little exercise, and eats poorly. Even if these managers' risk for CHD is due primarily to age, if they smoke and get little exercise, their risks may be reduced through implementation of a health promotion program.

Another qualification relates to changes in medical care costs as a function of new medical technologies. Even if the incidence of a given disease is constant, the cost of insurance claims may increase due to the use of new (and more costly) medical procedures for that disease. If such technological advances are apparent, the more relevant information may be the frequency of claims for a given condition, not the total costs of claims for that condition.

The moral: Although insurance claim information may be useful, it may be extremely difficult to obtain and may not help all that much. A more sensible approach to analyzing the health of the organization may be to survey employees regarding health habits. On the basis of this survey information (and a corresponding survey of employee preferences regarding programming), you may be able to do quite well in planning a program that simultaneously meets organizational needs and employee preferences.

D. Absenteeism, Tardiness, and Turnover. Another important aspect of a workplace health promotion organizational analysis is the rate of absenteeism, tardiness, and turnover. Like data on medical care utilization, data on these indicators also can be examined on a global level or broken out by groups within the organization. It is highly useful to determine if absenteeism rates differ across divisions of the organization. For example, are they higher for blue-collar than for white-collar employees? Are rates in manufacturing different from rates in finance? Are men absent or late more frequently than women? What are the absenteeism figures for the company as a whole and by organizational division for the past several years? Are there seasonal or other temporal variations in absenteeism? If so, what are they and do they vary from unit to unit? The same questions also may be asked about tardiness and turnover.

Just as medical care information may be analyzed by frequency or cost, so can data on absenteeism, tardiness, and turnover. The preceding questions address the issue of frequency. We also want to know about costs. Is information available, for example, to determine the cost of absenteeism, again for the overall organization and by division? It will probably be useful to break down this information further by units within larger divisions.

As was the case with medical care expenses and utilization, you must be careful in interpreting data on absenteeism. Different companies and different divisions within organizations will have absenteeism policies that vary markedly. If, for example, your organization provides employees with a specified number of sick days per year, whether they are used or not will depend heavily on factors other than disease. A policy of sick-day accrual with no time limit will probably differ in its impact on absenteeism from a policy in which sick days must be used within a limited period of time. The meaning of absenteeism will differ still further if the company has no sick-day policy. And for executives above a certain level, attendance records often are not kept.

As discussed in previous chapters, absenteeism is not perfectly related to disease and disability. People stay away from work for a variety of other reasons. Therefore, data on absenteeism must be viewed with caution in relation to the value of a workplace health promotion program. Since some absenteeism and tardiness are due to factors other than disease, workplace health promotion programs that address risk factors for disease may not be expected to have an impact on these other factors. However, the impact of workplace health promotion programs also should be expected to exceed the limits of health and disease in that they are perceived as organizational benefits that will have an effect on employee morale and organizational climate.

E. Organizational Resources. No workplace health promotion analysis is complete without collection of information on the resources, both internal and external, available to the company and on organizational policies that may augment or constrain the proposed programs.

1. Existing departments. The most fundamental resource of any organization in this regard is the already existing departments that naturally relate to health promotion, for example, the medical or health and safety departments. Most organizations have some in-house medical service, ranging from a full-scale medical department with physicians, nurses, and allied health professionals to a single, part-time nurse. Similarly, most organizations have safety programs that vary in their scope, usually as a function of the size of the organization. The existence and nature of such departments provides a natural resource for workplace health promotion program developers and as such, their mandates and capacities should be understood. As an example, a large international advertising agency recently became interested in the development of a limited health promotion program for its executives. The program, although inspired by the human resource staff, was assigned to the occupational nurse for implementation. At Kimberly-Clark Corporation and Phillips Petroleum Company, the programs operate out of the human resources departments. Pillsbury's "Be Your Best" program is located in the employee health service department. At Du Pont, however, Health Horizons operates out of the health and safety department.

These examples suggest that in addition to health, safety, and medical departments, the human resources or training and development departments also may be relevant to the development of a health promotion program. Since these functions are involved in training in the workplace, they provide a natural resource and experience base for health education. Of course, an employee assistance program is a natural ally to health promotion programs. In Chapter Ten, we will discuss in greater detail the interrelationships of these various departments within an organization as they relate to program development and implementation.

We should note that most small companies do not have separate human resources, medical, and health and safety departments. For many of these companies, these functions are performed by a single individual as part of a still larger job. As already indicated, many small companies have inventive and effective health promotion programs, and these programs depend heavily on local community resources. Analysis of these resources will be discussed later in this chapter.

2. *On-going programs.* In examining the nature of the already existing departments in the organization, determine what programs these departments already have that may be relevant to workplace health promotion. Health and safety departments typically will have programs designed to improve safety aspects of the physical workplace, for example, reduction in noise or air pollution. A medical department may already conduct periodic physical examinations or cholesterol screening. The employee assistance program may have on-going programs in substance abuse awareness. Human resources departments may offer training in a variety of interpersonal skills/communications areas.

3. *Support of top management.* Resources other than relevant departments must be analyzed. An effective health promotion program requires support of top management. Knowledge of the company's physical facilities is essential. The nature of an organization's health promotion program depends heavily on the availability of space. The more ambitious the program, the more space will be required. Although relatively little room is

needed to conduct small group programs in smoking cessation or weight control, the establishment of a complete physical fitness center, such as those at Sentry Life Insurance or Pepsico, requires a great deal of space.

4. *Staff.* Another aspect of organizational resources concerns staff for a program. Will there be provisions for assignment or even hiring of staff to run the program, or will program coordination be an additional responsibility of an already busy employee?

5. *Finance.* Concerns about physical space and staff suggest that an essential aspect of a workplace health promotion organizational analysis is finance: How much money or other organizational resources will be available for development and implementation of the program? It may not be necessary for the organization to spend enormous amounts of money to develop the program; it may decide instead to reassign one or more employees. Reassigning employees represents as important a commitment as money. There is no denying that workplace health promotion programs consume precious organizational resources, and the degree to which these resources will be available must be determined by an organizational analysis.

6. *Communication channels.* Finally, it is important to assess the organization's communication media. What forms of communication are available? Public address announcements? Newsletters or magazines? In-house mail? Video and audio facilities? Electronic mail? Union publications? No workplace health promotion program, however cleverly conceived, can survive without proper communications. An important aspect of planning for the program is the development of a public relations campaign; to develop this campaign, you must know what your communication resources are.

F. Organizational Policies and Other Characteristics. Are there already existing company policies and regulations relevant to health practices, for example, a smoking policy or an automobile safety-belt policy, that may encourage or interfere with development of a health promotion program? As already indicated, a policy regarding sick days must be considered in analyzing organizational data. The policy regarding work schedules is also important to consider. The organization, or some part of it, may be on shift-work. Shift schedules will influence a health promotion program in two ways: Programs will have to be made available for all shifts, unless, of course, only a certain shift seems to have unacceptably high medical care use or poor health habits. In addition, shift-work has been demonstrated to be associated with numerous health problems, a factor in itself to consider.

Other aspects of the work schedule must be considered. For example, some or all employees may be on a flex-time schedule, which may make it considerably easier for employees to participate in the health promotion program.

II. Information from Employees

The collection of information from employees is as critical a component of an organizational analysis as any other. Even the most sophisticated analysis of medical care costs, insurance use, and absenteeism cannot provide enough direction for a developing health promotion program. Since employee health behavior is an immediate determinant of each of these, it is essential to collect information from employees. In addition, because a large fraction of medical care costs are associated with spouses and dependents, it may be important to collect information from them, too. In fact, one of the most important aspects of an organizational analysis is the determination of what fraction of medical care expenses is spent on spouses and dependents. However, keep in mind that medical care expenses are only one part of the total disease-related costs of an organization. Spouses and dependents are not absent or late to work in your organization. Similarly, they are not on the job in your organization so their behavior does not have implications for productivity. In the remainder of this section, we will refer to data collection from employees, but whenever it is feasible and consistent with your overall program design, you may want to collect similar information from spouses and dependents. You also may want to collect different information from spouses and dependents.

A. Employee Interests in Health Promotion Programs. An important issue is what program employees are most (and least) interested in. If offered the opportunity to take part in a series of courses or programs or to hear a talk, which would they attend? Every workplace is different in regard to employee interests. Do not assume that because a substantial fraction of the employee population smokes, for example, that there will be interest in smoking programs. Such interest may not exist. Even if it does, it may be secondary to areas of greater interest, for example, weight and nutrition or stress management.

Consider, also, that your employee survey might ask about interest in nontraditional programs less directly related to health. Such programs might be devoted to parenting, the problems of two-career families, healthy cooking and shopping, accident prevention in the home, especially for children, how to make the most use of the organization's health insurance program, and so forth.

In addition to information on programs in which employees are interested, it is important to collect information on employee willingness to attend such programs and when they would like them to be offered. Even if a program appears to be of considerable interest, scheduling it at the wrong time or in the wrong location will reduce participation.

B. Employee Health Practices. In addition to surveying the employee population on interest in health promotion programs, it is important to collect information on their current health practices. How many of the employees, for example, smoke? How much do they smoke? What fraction of the population is overweight? Sedentary? How many people experience excessive stress? What about blood pressure? Do employees wear safety belts when they drive? What are their diets like?

This information on basic health habits and interests in health programs may be broken out by demographic information: sex, age, educational level, or level within company. This may permit a more fine-grained analysis of employee health habits and interests and may suggest targeting different programs for different groups. Information on employee health habits collected during the initial analysis also can be used as a baseline against which change can be measured. In Resource D, we provide a sample employee survey.

Always remember, when collecting information on employee health habits, that this information must remain strictly confidential. Failure to provide this protection will compromise program success.

III. External Resources

Resources for health promotion programs are available outside as well as inside the organization. Most small companies, owing to their size, have limited internal resources for health and safety, medical, and human resources departments. Outside organizations can provide information relevant to program development and actual services for the program.

A. Information Resources. Valuable health statistics, for instance, frequency of disease and disability in the local area, may be available from government organizations at the local, state, and federal levels. Similar information is available through the insurance industry, either at the national level or through your local carrier. Resource C provides some sources of information. Trade organizations are another source of information. Many companies are members of specific organizations that represent the industry as a whole. These organizations may have valuable information on the health care situation of the industry.

Care must be taken when using information from these sources. Sometimes their relevance is questionable. For example, federal health statistics may report the frequency of diseases, even broken down by geographical region. At first, this may seem ideal as the basis for comparison with your own organizational data. Federal health statistics, however, include all people living in that geographical area, including people who do not work. Among these unemployed are people who cannot work because their health does not permit it.

B. Service Resources. Providing information is, of course, a service. But other services may be available from sources outside the organization. In virtually every community, various organizations can be useful in providing health promotion services. Such organizations include local chapters of the American Heart Association, American Cancer Society, American Lung Association, the Red Cross, the YMCA, the Auto Club, local hospitals, medical societies, universities, and school systems. Many of these community resources already have programs relevant to health promotion that either can be brought to the company or delivered for the company at another location. Resource C lists organizations that may be helpful to your program.

Other community resources include local vendors who specialize in health promotion services. Physicians, psychologists, social workers, and health educators may offer relevant programs.

Trade unions are highly important in many workplaces, and their cooperation and assistance can be invaluable. Because health promotion programs are relevant to negotiated benefits packages, many unions already have considered them and have established relevant policies. Some unions, for example, the United Storeworkers Union, have been highly innovative in the development of health promotion programs for implementation. In a unionized workplace, it is essential to include the union in the analysis and planning phases.

The availability of community resources is an essential aspect of the organizational analysis. However, not all community resources are of equal quality. Even high-quality ones may not be appropriate for the specific kind of program you plan to develop. Evaluating local resources is important. It does not necessarily follow that a program offered by the local affiliate of a prestigious not-for-profit national organization is of high quality. Similarly, local, independent for-profit vendors may offer high-quality programs at reasonable prices. In Chapter Ten, we discuss the issue of selection of outside vendors and consultants.

Some Qualifications

This chapter provides a general introduction to the issues involved in the analysis of an organization in regard to a workplace health promotion program. Given the need to collect information of this sort, many organizations, driven partly by the lure of high technology and opinions of consultants in the area, have attempted to implement enormously complex and apparently sophisticated assessment procedures. One example is the now widespread use of computer-based "health risk appraisals" that purport to analyze scientifically the lifestyles and medical histories of employees first to assess the risk of various diseases and then to provide recommendations for lifestyle changes that in turn are expected to result in reducing those risks. Resource E examines health risk appraisals (HRAs) in greater detail; however, we believe that HRAs have relatively little value in the context of organizational analysis. Although they may collect an enormous amount of information, the value of that information for development of a health promotion program appears limited. HRAs may be useful in other capacities, for example, the motivation of employees already enrolled in a health promotion program, but as analytic tools for assessment, they are unnecessarily detailed and costly. Their popularity derives primarily, we believe, from their scientific appearance and their use of computer technology.

The same may be said of sophisticated computer-based evaluations of insurance utilization data. Such evaluations may provide accurate information regarding frequency of insurance claims (for example, psychiatric versus respiratory), broken out by employee category (blue or white collar) or characteristics (men versus women, black versus white) and disease category. In our view, this information, although interesting, is not always useful in the planning of a workplace health promotion program. Why do we believe that both HRAs and sophisticated analyses of insurance utilization data are of limited value? At least three reasons exist: (1) the information they provide is generally superfluous, adding little if anything to the development of a health promotion program beyond that provided by much simpler means; (2) the traditionally limited view of the scope of health promotion programs restricts data collection to certain health areas; and (3) the meaning of the data collected is questionable. In some cases, these three reasons overlap considerably.

Providing Superfluous Information

Health risk appraisals collect information in great detail about a person's medical history, health behaviors, and, in some cases, emotional state. Recommendations then are made to address certain health areas, for example, lose weight, stop smoking, and so on. To be sure, these recommendations are worthy ones. However, the highly detailed information generated by sophisticated analyses of personal lifestyle and medical history provide us with considerable unnecessary information. For program development, all we really need to know about the employee population, for example, is how many people smoke, how many people have uncontrolled high blood pressure, or how many people are overweight. Simple information of this sort enables us to recommend the development of a smoking or weight control program with as much confidence as we would if we had a much more sophisticated HRA analysis.

Limited Scope of Workplace Health Promotion Programs

In Chapter Three, we presented an expanded view of workplace health promotion. That view suggests that objectives of health promotion programs are determined by many factors other than those with which the programs typically deal. To reiterate briefly, absenteeism and medical care costs typically are understood by the standard model of workplace health promotion largely to be the products of employee lifestyles such as leading sedentary lives, smoking, or eating poorly. Accordingly, health promotion programs attempt to induce lifestyle changes that produce risk factor reduction leading in turn to reductions in the incidence of disease and injury. This chain of events is thought to culminate in reductions in disease-produced absenteeism and medical care costs.

But as Chapter Three indicated, absenteeism and medical care costs also are determined by factors other than lifestyle-related disease and injury. The narrowness of vision characterizing most workplace health promotion programs is reminiscent of the "little boy and the hammer" problem. To this little boy, everything looks like a nail (and requires pounding); that is, since the arsenals of traditional workplace health promotion interventions typically are filled with individual behavior change approaches to risk reduction, health promotion programs are constructed as if all causes of absenteeism and high medical care costs were functions of behavioral risk factors such as smoking and not exercising. Even though most health promotion managers recognize that health care costs are multiply determined, the programs they manage are not designed in a way consistent with this recognition.

Thus, one fundamental shortcoming of traditional organizational health analyses is that they only collect information relevant to these common areas and fail to collect data on other factors influencing health promotion endpoints. Since these other factors are important, a realistic analysis should collect information on them as well.

The Meaning of the Data

Another way of approaching the same issue is to ask about the meaning of the data collected by HRAs and analyses of insurance utilization. Consider, for example, a finding that the absenteeism rate for one company is twice that for a comparable company. What do these data mean? What do they tell us about the requirements of a health promotion program designed to deal with absenteeism?

The model presented in Chapter Three indicates that both individual psychological factors as well as organizational factors play a part in absenteeism and health care use. To discover, as Plaskolite did, that one of its divisions suffered from high absenteeism requires us to ask about its cause, which in this case was the supervisory style of the manager. Another factor influencing absenteeism, as previously indicated, is the policy an organization has regarding sick days. Many companies allow employees a specified number of days of absenteeism due to disease each year. Some of these organizations permit sick-day accrual over the employee's tenure with the company. Others permit no accrual from year to year. It is no surprise, then, that in the latter organizations, annual absenteeism associated with "disease" is considerably higher than in the former organizations, which in turn will be higher than in organizations with no sick-day policy. One can expect that if sick days are not accrued, they will be exhausted each year. Such absenteeism figures reflect relatively little about the incidence of disease in the organization.

Recognizing the ambiguity of this information on absenteeism raises questions about its value for the planning of health promotion programs. Of course, as implied in Chapter Three, to the extent that the existence of a workplace health promotion program makes the company a better place to work, there may be a greater tendency to come to work, thus reducing absenteeism. *But such a change has nothing to do with reducing risk factors for disease.*

Similarly, although data on medical care costs and utilization may be important in an organizational analysis, they must be viewed with caution. Their value in connection with a workplace health promotion program assumes the clear causal chain culminating in insurance claims. These claims are assumed to be produced by medical care utilization for disease, which in turn is related substantially to lifestyle or, as we shall see later, to aspects of the organization. At every step in this chain, one may raise questions. Differences in benefits packages rather than variations in frequency of disease may account for substantial variation in the frequency of certain types of insurance claims. For example, one division of an organization may appear to have an extraordinarily high rate of psychiatric utilization compared to another division. You may be tempted to interpret this information as evidence that the first division experiences considerably greater stress than the second, suggesting the need for stress-management programs. However, the greater incidence of psychiatric disorders may be an artifact of the former division's superior mental health benefits; that is, rather than increased frequency of claims reflecting the causal influence of stress, it may well be the case that the cause is the benefit structure, and the consequence is the greater frequency of claims.

The point of this discussion has been to nurture a healthy

skepticism regarding the use of "high-tech" diagnostic instruments in preference to simpler data collection approaches that rely on common sense. Instances occur in which extremely sophisticated analyses may be of value for program development, but such instances are uncommon. In most cases, organizational analysis can be relatively simple and, as a consequence of this simplicity, inexpensive. Health promotion programs in the workplace are constantly asked to justify their existence to receive precious resources. One way to conserve limited resources is to take as "low tech" an approach to analysis as possible. Only rarely will the quality of the information you collect be compromised by this strategy. However, adopting such a strategy will permit you to demonstrate to top management your concern for bottom line considerations.

Conclusion

Clearly, we have presented much more information than is necessary for a conventional organizational health analysis. The scope of the analysis you conduct will depend on your resources, organization size, and interest. Use these factors to select among the categories presented above. And do not forget to use common business sense. Just because you have the opportunity to collect extremely detailed information using sophisticated technology does not mean that you have to do it.

Finally, recognize that collecting information on employee preferences and organizational resources in regard to workplace health promotion is essential. Sacrifice the collection of other information if you must (we do not recommend this, though), but do not fail to poll employees. Not only will you collect important information but you also will begin your public relations efforts.

6

Planning: Developing the Mission, Business Plan, and Budget

Proper, thoughtful planning is essential to the success of any program, whether it be in health, finance, marketing, or manufacturing. Planning requires hard work, thought, commitment, and most importantly, time. There is no reason why the planning of a health promotion program must be conducted overnight. Failure to provide sufficient time for planning almost always guarantees that mistakes will be made, some of which may be costly and avoidable.

As is probably obvious by now, the implementation of a workplace health promotion program is more than a mere graft on to the organization of a program fundamentally unrelated to the rest of the organization. Workplace health promotion programs, to be successful, must address issues central to the organization's operations and values. Efforts must be made to ensure that health promotion is more than an irrelevant frill to be attached arbitrarily to ongoing operations.

The simplest way to move from the analysis phase through the planning phase is to think of the data (both formal and informal) you have collected when answering the following questions in relation to health promotion in your organization:

Who?
What?
Where?
When?
How?
How much?

The process we describe is fairly straightforward. It begins with the data and results in a complete business plan or proposal of the health promotion program. Figure 1 summarizes this process.

As the figure illustrates, the first activity in the sequence of events is the establishment of a mission statement. The goal(s) of the mission statement will help to direct the next two parallel stages in the planning process: the content and process of the health promotion program. The information gathered during the analysis phase should guide the planning of the activities, procedures, and policies of the program.

The final step of the planning phase is the creation of a business plan incorporating both activities and procedures into an overall package that answers the questions listed previously and includes a detailed budget. This business plan will serve not only as your proposal for funding the program but also as your guide for the first two years of the program's existence.

The Mission Statement

The initial impetus for development of a workplace health promotion program may be widely varied. It may be the inspiration of a single individual convinced of the need for such a program on the basis of its cost savings potential or its appeal to employees. It may be the result of a generalized awareness on the part of many individuals about the increasing costs of health care and rising absenteeism. It may be the product of personal experience of a CEO who is committed to a healthy diet or running. It may arise during contract negotiations with a union.

The function of a mission statement is the guidance of all subsequent activities in program planning and development. As such, the logical first step in planning a health promotion program

Figure 1.   The Business Plan.

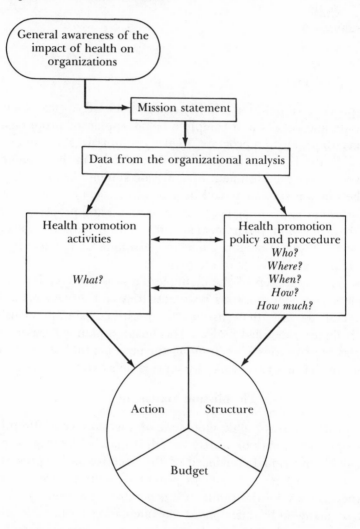

at the workplace is the establishment of a mission. The mission will vary from company to company, and, typically, it will be established (or at least approved) by a top-level executive. Ultimately, the responsibility for executing the mission falls to the health promotion staff and committee.

As an example of a health promotion mission statement,

the vice-president for personnel of a major Connecticut-based company drafted the following: ". . . an integrated Human Resources approach to health and wellness, which will help the employees and the Company to realize an increase in productivity, morale, and general well-being, while reducing health-related costs." Following this statement were five specific goals:

- improve organizational performance and individual productivity through reduced absenteeism and turnover, improving alertness on the job
- reduce expenditures for worker's compensation, health insurance, and disability insurance
- help employees cope with individual and organizational stress resulting from change
- provide positive programs to help attract and retain highly motivated employees
- promote the concept that employees have primary responsibility for their own health and wellness

As you can see, this set of statements is very general. By their nature, mission statements lack specificity. Their function is not to identify specific tasks but to set direction for others to follow. Mission statements from upper-level management are important because, in organizations characterized by competing demands for scarce resources, the mantle of institutional authority is often necessary to gather those resources. In addition, the statement provides a unifying set of standards by which progress toward program development can be measured.

Other examples of less lengthy mission statement include:

To create a corporate culture that is supportive of a healthy lifestyle (AT&T Communications, TLC Program).

Our objectives include measurable, sustained lifestyle improvements among the greatest number of employees possible in regular exercise, smoking cessation, weight control, stress management, health

knowledge, and awareness of medical intervention
programs (Johnson & Johnson, Live for Life Program).

To create and support a healthy lifestyle and attitude both in the workplace and at home (Scherer
Brothers Lumber Company).

The issues discussed in Chapter Four, the case for workplace health promotion, and Chapter Five, organizational analysis, give mission statement authors a basis from which to begin.
The establishment of a mission statement, the planning of the
program, and organizational analysis are interdependent: The
relationship between organizational analysis and the establishment of a mission statement is a "chicken and egg" problem.
The mission statement may establish the need to conduct the
analysis but at the same time, the analysis determines which objectives are appropriate for the program.

However, even in the absence of a detailed analysis, some
basic information about the company's medical care costs, expenses associated with disability and workmen's compensation,
productivity, morale, absenteeism and turnover, and so on, can
be used to develop general objectives. Recognize, however, that
this information is not the only source of data for development
of the program mission. In addition, you must consider political
and economic realities of the organization, the workforce, and
the environment. For instance, even if it appears that, on the
whole, the workforce gets adequate exercise, it may be desirable
to offer a fitness program. The justification for such a decision
may be based on its expected impact on morale, not on even-
tual reduction in cardiovascular morbidity and mortality.

Because the goals of a mission statement are highly general, the development of the specific tasks required to achieve
these objectives is delegated to the employee(s) assigned the responsibility for planning the program. The health promotion
manager must translate these general objectives into a tangible
program with measurable outcomes.

Developing a Business Plan

Once the mission statement has been drafted, you are ready to use it for direction in planning the specifics of the program. As mentioned, the next two stages should take place in a parallel fashion, each informing the other. The fact that the "Activities" section appears prior to the "Policies" section is arbitrary. To advance further your business plan, you may wish to contact some organizations with special expertise in workplace health promotion. In Resource C, a selected list of such organizations is provided.

Activities

Stage 1: Organizing the Data. It is likely that you have not been able to collect all of the information described in the analysis chapter. Even though this may be the case, it is critical that your plans be based on some objective facts about your organization. At a minimum, you will need information on: (1) employee interests, (2) employee health practices, (3) internal resources, and (4) community resources.

Using any and all information about the health status and interests of employees, organize the information into general categories of health concerns. For example, consider the following hypothetical case:

1. Company medical records indicate that there is a year-round high number of visits to the nurse for respiratory infections in contrast to other causes.
2. The employee health questionnaire indicates that about 45 percent of the employees smoke.
3. The employee interest questionnaire reveals that a substantial concern of nonsmokers is that the smoking policy is not enforced.
4. The union representation has expressed concern that the smoking issue will be brought up in the next contract negotiations.

In this case, one of the general health topics important to this organization is smoking. The important point here is to find areas or topics for which there is broad-based concern and/or evidence of need, expressed in different forms of data. You can anticipate that smoking stress, fitness, and food, generally appearing in that order, will be the product of your data organization. Your organizational analysis may reveal different concerns of equal validity; but generally speaking, the traditional limitations of health promotion make it difficult to ask questions that address issues beyond these health concerns.

Two case examples present data from actual organizational analyses. Later in the chapter, the programs designed to deal with the problems revealed by these analyses are discussed.

The Alpha Corporation is a Northeastern-based company that specializes in providing consulting services for computer operations for business. Organizational analysis revealed, first of all, that the increases in medical care costs they had been experiencing were not spread uniformly across all divisions of the company. The increases were restricted largely to a single group of employees, the sales staff. Moreover, dramatic increases in insurance claims were seen for only one category of disease: psychiatric. In spite of changes in the benefit structure designed to control increasing psychiatric treatment, claims had still increased 21 percent from the previous year.

Demographic data on the sales staff indicated that most people were male, relatively young, and white. Analysis of their health habits indicated that they were under considerable stress. Further analysis pointed to certain aspects of their lives and the nature of their work: a heavy travel schedule (suggesting irregular eating and sleeping patterns), extreme competitive pressure characteristic of the computer industry, and a management approach to compensation that placed the sales staff at a disadvantage compared to other company employees. These data suggest that stress is a central problem in this division.

The Beta Hospital, in the Southwest, had a different sort of problem. The hospital is a large institution with approximately 6,000 employees. The director of employee health had decided that a health promotion program was both necessary and desirable but that to persuade management of the need for a full-scale program, the first step was to identify a single health area to address. Organizational analysis revealed several problems: (1) 42 percent of the total employee population smoked and although smoking was more common among the service staff (transporters, cleaners, mechanics, and food service), it was also common among nurses, technicians, and administrators; (2) stress-related disorders were high among nurses in certain areas (the emergency room, cardiac care, and pediatric oncology); and (3) obesity was a significant problem, especially among members of the service staff.

Stage 2: Defining the Possible Universe of Activities. Once you have identified three or four general topics, take a week or so, ask for help from anyone you contacted during the analysis phase, and brainstorm any and all of the points of view, issues, and possible activities you can in relation to each of the topics. If you have been working with an employee health promotion committee during the analysis phase, involve it heavily in this process. Be creative! Go wild! Refer constantly to the analysis data to orient your thinking toward the company-specific issues. Chapter Nine should stimulate your thinking.

The following are examples of a range of ideas generated in response to data that reveal that smoking in the workplace is a serious problem. We have selected smoking as an example because it is likely to be a problem area you will encounter. Remember, brainstorming by definition is not constrained by reality.

Educational Activities

- Institute a smoking education program during work group meetings/safety meetings/monthly assemblies.
- Form an employee committee to problem solve about smoking in the break room and rest rooms.
- Develop a literature display for the cafeteria, documenting the dangers of passive smoking.
- Consult with the American Heart Association, the American

Cancer Society, and the American Lung Association about the range of activities and support materials they have to offer. Also get their advice about model workplace programs.

- Obtain an ecolyzer (a device that measures carbon monoxide in exhaled breath) and offer to test smokers outside the cafeteria every day for a week.

Financial Impact

- Reward nonsmokers with $1.00 per day.
- Obtain an engineering estimate of the extra burden imposed by smoking on the air-conditioning and ventilation system.
- Obtain similar estimates from the fire insurance carrier on extra costs of premiums for smoking workplaces and from cleaning services for additional cleaning costs.
- Arrange for nonsmokers to get a break on life insurance.

Interpersonal Support

- Set up an "adopt a smoker" program.
- Ask opinion leaders to take a leadership role in their constituency in encouraging co-workers to quit.
- Set up a nonsmoking support hotline.
- Convene a weekly support group for ex-smokers.
- Collect a list of names of ex-smokers who would be willing to act as support buddies for new quitters.

Quitting

- Offer to pay smokers to quit.
- Participate in the Great American Smokeout in a big way.
- Offer an incentive to pregnant women to stop smoking.
- Offer smoking cessation clinics at work on work time, at no cost to employees.
- Subsidize smokers' attendance at smoking cessation clinics or classes elsewhere.
- Organize "quit-teams" and hold a competition between departments.
- Train ex-smokers to deliver smoking cessation programs.

Policy

- Change the smoking policy to prohibit smoking in the building.
- Change the personnel policy to not hire smokers.
- Declare every Tuesday a nonsmoking day.
- Clearly mark areas where smoking is permitted.
- Recognizing that smoking is a form of stress reduction, set up a committee to investigate stress at the workplace and to make recommendations about future actions of the health promotion program based on the findings.
- Ask for a clear policy statement about smoking from the CEO and publicize it widely.
- Take cigarettes out of the vending machines and canteens—they no longer will be sold on company property.
- Create a nonsmoking policy for all vendors who provide services to the company.

Public Relations

- Publish nonsmoking messages in all editions of all internal newsletters.
- Publish the names of all new nonsmokers (three months of abstinence) in a company paper or newsletter with congratulations.

Stage 3: Refining the Universe of Activities.   Once you have completed the brainstorming process (and it may take considerably longer than a week, depending on how many other people are involved), classify each suggestion as to the expense, the effort (how much labor is involved), and the lead time necessary. For example, convening an employee committee to investigate the development of the smoking policy requires few expenses, moderate organizational time (obtaining organizational mandate, appointing an effective committee, sending invitations, scheduling meeting space, briefing the chairperson, providing background material), and only moderate lead time (one to two months). On the other hand, company payment or copayment for smoking cessation programs may involve great expense (from $40 to $500 per participant), great organizational effort (to develop guidelines, mechanisms for legitimate reimbursable methods, and referral lists; to recruit the smokers to participate; and to follow up on their participation), and enormous lead time (the politics of getting such a program in place often takes the involvement of many different organizational systems). Knowing how things are accomplished in your organization is critical to the success of this exercise.

Once you have thought through what it would take to implement each of the ideas you have gathered under each general topic, make three lists for each topic. The first list is for quick projects, that is, ongoing or time-limited activities that require little money, effort, and lead time. The second list is for medium-sized projects and should include long-term and short-term activities that require more lead time and organizational time but modest monetary expense. The third list is a kind of wish list that contains the activities that would be wonderful to undertake if you were not constrained by organizational and financial resources. Include on this list ideas that your cocontributors develop and for which they would be willing to take primary responsibility. A number of ideas will be eliminated as decisions about policy begin to impose reality on the proposed activities.

Stage 4: Determining What Is Feasible. The next step in designing the business plan is to contact the appropriate internal and external resources, already identified by your organizational analysis, that would need to be involved in the delivery of each activity on each list. Talk about the activity and ask for information on its feasibility, the kind of support the resource can offer, and for any other general words of wisdom. The development of policies and procedures will help to reduce the number of items on your list. It you organize your lists properly, you will find that there are a few central resources to which many of the items can be referred. For example, on the previous sample list, many of the ideas about smoking activities are reasonable topics for comment by the personnel director or someone in a similar position.

Establishing these contacts is important for several reasons. First, it will allow the constraints of reality to reduce your lists to a manageable size. Second, it begins to make the health promotion program a part of the future planning process in relation both to internal and external resources. For example, the personnel manager in charge of the company smoking policy may ask you to wait until the policy is released in six months before convening a committee to address the same issues. As another example, the American Heart Association has designated a month during which it heavily promotes high blood pressure control activities, and it can offer a complete package of activities for you to implement if you wait until then.

In short, at this point in the process, it is appropriate to develop a more precise idea of what contributions your internal and external resources can make available and to determine accurately what each activity will entail. Be aware, however, that until the business plan is approved and funded by your organization, it is inappropriate to commit to any particular activities, programs, or committees. You should now have an annotated list of different activities, organized by subject and complexity, which is the basis for your final business plan.

Alpha Corporation and Beta Hospital Revisited

Analysis of Alpha Corporation revealed that stress was a significant problem within the organization, specifically for the sales staff. During program planning, the health promotion manager, with assistance from an interested and helpful insurance representative, considered numerous possible activities to deal with the problem. The constraints of reality, that the sales staff was frequently on the road, imposed severe limitations on the viability of many activities. Nevertheless, the manager was able to develop a reasonable program proposal, one which was consistent with the staff needs and organizational limits.

The program was devoted, of course, to stress management. A special training program was developed and tailored to the specific needs revealed by the analysis. Among the traditional elements of the program were training in relaxation methods and the use of physical exercise to reduce stress. What made the program unique was that it was designed also to help the staff cope with the health-related problems that could arise as a result of frequent travel (for example, how to eat on the road, how to unwind after the day is over and you are in a strange place, how to deal with being away from your family on a frequent basis, and so on). Finally, recommendations were made to modify the compensation structure so as not to penalize these employees. This suggestion is related to the concerns presented in Chapter Thirteen on health promotion through organizational change.

The case of Beta Hospital was different. In that organization, analysis indicated that numerous health problems existed. Moreover, these problems were not confined to any single group. Armed with this information and recognizing that at the outset, resources would be limited, the director of employee health decided that the most sensible approach would be to select a single problem and to develop the health promotion program around it. She reasoned that once it proved to be successful, the program would expand to address other areas. Smoking was selected, because research data on workplace smoking programs indicate that they are the most cost effective of the traditional health promotion programs.

Two different approaches were established. First, steps were taken to develop a smoking policy in the hospital. Members of different employee constituencies were appointed to form a committee with this mission. Representatives of the various unions were part of the committee. The committee decided that its objective would be the establishment of a nonsmoking workplace within two years. Second, the local Lung Association was contacted to deliver smoking cessation programs to all hospital employees. As an incentive for employees to participate, part of the program cost was underwritten by the hospital. Other incentive programs to encourage employees to quit smoking were rejected on the basis of budgetary constraints.

In addition to the partial subsidy of the program fee, the hospital used the Great American Smokeout as a focal point of its efforts.

Policy and Procedural Issues

The information you will use to develop policies and procedures for the health promotion program is generally less formal than that used to plan activities. For this development, you will rely more heavily on anecdotal information and ongoing and frequent consultation with appropriate individuals in various decision-making positions throughout the company. We highly recommend that these decisions be made by an interdepartmental committee appointed by the sponsoring manager. In Chapter Ten, we discuss the importance of a health promotion committee in greater detail.

Regardless of who makes these decisions, the goal of this stage of planning is to answer five questions:

"*Who* participates in the program?"
"*Where* does the program take place?"
"*When* is the program offered?"
"*How* is the program delivered?"
"*How much* will it cost?"

To guide you through this process, we have formulated more specific questions and have noted some of the relevant challenging issues.

Will all employees be able to participate? Many companies offer their health promotion programs only to top executives. This policy may be the result of limited resources or a decision that they have a greater investment in top executives than in any other group of employees. Although the latter may be true, it may also be the case that the greatest fraction of the company's medical care expenses comes from other employees. Decisions regarding to whom the program is offered must be made after consideration of all the factors.

Will family members of employees be included in all or

any of the health promotion activities? As stated previously, the majority of insurance claims nationwide originate with family members. Data from the organizational analysis will address this issue. Clearly, the messages of health promotion are equally applicable to family members. Should this concern be a priority for the program? How can the company be certain those messages spread to all of those who are involved in the company either directly or indirectly?

Will the program be offered on company or employee time? The obvious disadvantage to offering programs on company time is that employees will spend less time at work, which raises both financial and logistical problems. However, if programs are offered at lunch time or before or after work, other problems may arise. Because of family commitments, for example, employees may be unable or unwilling to participate at these times. The result can be decreased participation. Also, offering the programs on company time indicates to employees a serious commitment on the part of management.

Will the program be delivered on- or off-site? Some companies, most notably International Business Machines (IBM), make extensive use of local off-site facilities for such programs as exercise and fitness training. This may be an especially attractive opportunity for small companies whose limited resources do not permit them to develop extensive in-house facilities. It also may be an effective way to involve both employees and their families with the health promotion experts in their communities. On the other hand, most research has shown that in-house facilities and programming enhance participation; obstacles such as transportation, parking, and the extra time associated with travel to another location are reduced.

Will the program be conducted by the organization's staff or will outside resources be used? Again, depending on the organization's resources, a company may call on local consultants, university-based professionals, or voluntary health organizations such as the American Lung Association or American Heart Association to staff the program. An evaluation of the company's resources will determine whether full- or part-time staff is possible.

What kind of support is needed from top management?
How can it be obtained? It is safe to say that if top management
is not thoroughly supportive of a health promotion program, it
cannot succeed. In addition to supporting programs designed to
help employees, management must be prepared to balance such
efforts with efforts to implement complementary organizational
changes designed to ensure healthy and safe working conditions.
Failure to do so may render suspect any health promotion efforts directed at employees.

What procedures will be developed to ensure confidential-
ity of information and protect the rights of employees? Information collected during analysis and afterward is highly confidential and must be treated as such. To ensure confidentiality,
many companies store these data in medical departments along
with other sensitive information.

How will the program be funded? Programs may be funded
in at least three different ways. First, the company may support
it entirely. Second, the company may require a copayment
from employees. Third, the company may provide facilities but
expect employees to pay all of the costs associated with their
participation. Of these three, the latter is least desirable because
it poses a barrier to participation. Copayment is effective because employees, through their copayment, have a sense of
ownership in and commitment to the program. Full company
support is also effective because it demonstrates to employees
that the company is serious about the program. The organizational analysis can address this issue.

Will the program be offered all at once or will its delivery
be staggered over time? It is highly advisable that a program be
gradually implemented to permit correction of flaws and elimination of obstacles. Even the best conceived and best funded of
programs have undergone extensive pilot testing and gradual implementation.

What kind of organizational arrangements and incentives
will be developed to enhance participation? This question addresses one of the most critical aspects of any health promotion
program. The most advanced program is likely to be a failure
unless organizational mechanisms are developed to encourage

participation. Such arrangements as "flex time," a strategy used by Tenneco, provide employees with the opportunity to alter their work schedules to permit visits to the fitness center. Speed-call Corporation, as indicated, provides financial incentives for quitting smoking. Other companies provide such incentives as competitions, lotteries, T-shirts, availability of the program to families, and public recognition for participation. Companies with on-site facilities might provide for showers and lockers. As a means of encouraging participation, some companies provide gym clothing.

The Business Plan

At this point, you should have two important documents. The first is an annotated list of possible health promotion activities. The second is a list of policy and procedure recommendations that provide the underlying structure on which the activities are based. Using the mission statement and your knowledge about how the company actually operates, the next phase is to lay out a proposed schedule of implementation. Remember that workplace health promotion is not a short-term activity. Accordingly, consider laying out a two-year schedule that fits the anticipated resource and time constraints, while addressing as completely as possible the desires, interests, and needs of the organization. This time line will be a compromise.

Here are some planning hints:

- Whether you are starting off with a pilot program or with a complete one, it cannot emerge gradually from the shadows. You should organize some kind of ceremony or grand kick-off event to legitimize the program and to mark its inception.
- Plan a maximum of three major events per year and use them as pivotal, expectable events to be promoted annually.
- Careful pacing of long- and short-term events and activities is important (1) for you, so that you are not overextended; (2) so that participants can plan ahead and not be forced to choose between simultaneously scheduled and desirable activities; and (3) so that the image of the program always will be present and visible.

Budget

Two-thirds of the business plan is complete: the activities and the policy and procedures of the program. What remains is the estimation of the cost of implementing these activities. Developing a budget is as important as any aspect of the program design process. Since health promotion programs are implemented largely because they are seen to produce quantifiable benefits to the organization (although these benefits may be long term), it is entirely reasonable for management to expect the health promotion manager to budget properly for the program. We cannot provide you with specific information on costs of program components. What follows, however, will provide the general budgetary categories for you to consider. Throughout the program design process, you will be able to collect information on costs.

Salaries and Benefits

Whether you hire a full-time program manager or allocate a limited number of hours per week from a current employee, you must budget for the time spent on the program. Include in this part of the budget salary information for all program personnel. You can obtain the fringe benefit rates from your personnel department. If you hire outside consultants, budget for their time. Distinguish operating costs from development costs in this and all other budget items. You will confront development costs only once; operating costs are ongoing.

Supplies, Marketing Expenses, Communications,
and Travel

To run an effective program, you will need standard office supplies such as stationery, typewriters or word processors, and pens and pencils. As part of your marketing campaign, you will have postage and telephone expenses as well as printing costs for posters, graphics, and reproduction. There may be other media expenses, for example, video and radio, too. Courses that you offer will require teaching materials such as workbooks, handouts, blood pressure cuffs, and calorie counter books. It may be necessary or important for you to visit other health promotion programs or to attend relevant conferences. As in the case of salaries and benefits, distinguish between operating and development costs for these expenses.

Space and Overhead

Unless you are constructing a new facility for the program, you will use rooms that already exist. When you budget for use of this space, take into account how frequently it is used by activities other than the health promotion program. The best estimate of the cost, often referred to as the "opportunity" cost, is the value of other activities displaced by your program. If the space is never used, then the cost to the organization of the space is zero. On the other hand, if your program displaces another activity, then the "opportunity" cost is an estimate of the expense to provide similar space for the displaced activity. Depreciation expense (on a square-foot basis) may be a good estimate of this cost. Estimate the costs of utilities, too.

Equipment and Facilities

Many health promotion programs, especially those in physical fitness, require (or desire) equipment and facilities. Since both equipment and facilities may last for a relatively long time, it is appropriate to budget for the cost over their projected lifetime. One estimate of this cost is the depreciation expense. Of course, you should also indicate the initial cash outlay.

Costs Associated with Employee Participation

If employees participate in the health promotion program during the workday, it is appropriate to consider the time away from work as a program expense. However, this pertains only to the case where employees do not make up the work on their own time. Whether this is the case may depend on the level of the employee within the organization. A receptionist, for example, may not be able to make up for time spent at a weight con-

trol program by working later in the evening. A manager, however, can make up for lost work time.

Financing the Program

One essential element of the budget is the source of development and operating funds. An obvious source is the organization's (or specific department's) operating fund. If the organization believes that a health promotion program will be cost
beneficial in the long term, then it may be willing to fund its
development and operation as an investment.

Other sources of funding for the program include fees
from participants. Many programs operate on a cost-sharing
basis, with individual participants and the employer contributing to program costs. Some organizations offer cafeteria-style
benefits programs from which employees can choose certain options, for example, life insurance, vacation days, sick days, different levels of medical coverage, and a health promotion program. Organized in this manner, the company provides the
health promotion program to employees for free and as a substitute for other benefits. If you consider a cafeteria-style program, make certain that you investigate the tax implications of
this arrangement. Another possibility for program funding includes making arrangements with insurance carriers who may be
interested because of the prospect of reduced claims. Also,
some organizations have developed health promotion programs
through contributions from unions.

Conclusion

The culmination of the planning phase of workplace health promotion is the creation of a document that explains and details
the elements of the business plan; that is, it must begin with the
mission statement, present the program objectives, and specify
how these objectives will be accomplished. To do this, the proposal must present organized summaries and interpretations of
the data, collected during the organizational analysis, that justify
the plan for implementation. The implementation plan should

include the activities to be conducted (an annotated schedule of proposed activities) and the policies and procedures by which the program will be administered (where and when the activities will be conducted, who will participate, and so on). Included in the implementation plan should be an outline of evaluation activities (Chapter Seven) that will be undertaken to determine the degree to which the objectives have been met. Finally, the details of the program's budget must be presented.

This business plan may serve as a proposal for the funding of the health promotion program if this has not yet been accomplished, or it may serve as the program manual, a working document that will serve both reference and guidance functions. In either case, development of the document will enable both you and management to have a clear and complete picture of the program and a valuable reference point as the program grows and the workplace changes.

7

Evaluation: Assessing Program Effectiveness from the Outset

The third major task of designing a successful workplace health promotion program is developing an evaluation plan to assess the extent to which a program is effective in achieving measurable objectives toward a demonstrable goal. The importance of determining how program effectiveness will be assessed is often overlooked in the design stages of program development. Specifying the goals, expectations, and design of an evaluation plan at the outset of program development is essential if the program and its evaluation are to be successful. According to Dr. Andrew Brennan, former director of the Center for Health Help and currently director of Group Insurance Marketing at the Metropolitan Life Insurance Company, "Although designing an evaluation plan at the outset is critical, many practitioners fail to grasp its significance in their enthusiasm to get things started."

Formulating the evaluation plan early in the program development process permits data that have been collected during the organizational analysis to be used as a baseline in gauging the immediate impact and long-term outcomes of the program on both individual participants and the organization itself. Thus, evaluation to assess program effectiveness attempts to answer several questions at several levels; some of these questions address the process and appropriateness of the program itself, others deal with documenting the effects the program has on participants and the benefits these effects have for helping to achieve organizational goals.

This chapter provides a basic conceptual framework with which the health promotion manager can develop an understanding of the need, purposes, and role of evaluation in workplace health promotion. In addition, the chapter presents a hierarchy of specific options for a feasible evaluation design. Several of the designs are especially useful for assessing the value of health promotion programming within the range of practical and financial limits that are almost always imposed by "real-world" conditions. The chapter's emphasis will be on helping you to appreciate evaluation—whether simple or complex—as a systematic process that continues throughout the duration of programming and that is critical to establishing accountability in the eyes of participants and program decision makers.

Why Programs Can Fail

As we saw in Chapters Five and Six, designing a program involves skilled organizational analysis and planning. In addition, a successful program involves setting in motion a series of activities (the health promotion program) based on adequately conceptualized theory and then instituting a system of evaluation that is capable of detecting the effects these activities are intended to produce. Before designing any evaluation plan, it can be useful to examine the possible reasons why programs can fail to achieve their goals. Programs fail for many reasons. In analyzing and conceptualizing program failure, Weiss (1972) found that programs can be unsuccessful for at least one or some combination of three distinct categories of reasons.

Program Failure

A program may fail because a causal process (the program) intended to produce a goal is not activated or set in motion. This usually results when the organizational analysis has been inadequate or haphazard or when the data generated from the analysis has been misinterpreted.

The most common form of program failure occurs because of faulty implementation. No matter how good the design of a workplace health promotion program or the adequacy of the theory underlying the program, it will fail if it does not have managerial, financial, and other supports set in motion and sustained according to the original design. For example, ensuring that the number of sessions believed necessary for a given program is in fact conducted would minimize the possibility of program failure. In Weiss's framework, setting the program in motion is usually the immediate goal of a program. Program failure thus can be considered a failure to achieve the most immediate goals.

Thus, many well-conceived workplace health promotion efforts are said to have failed when in fact they may not have been adequately tested: An otherwise sound program may not have been implemented as intended. As a result, evaluations of programs under these conditions reveal that the program ostensibly has had no effect or less than the desired effect. It becomes essential for the evaluation to monitor the extent to which implementation of the program occurs as a way of guarding against program failure.

Theory Failure

The second category of reasons for unsuccessful programs can be described as a failure of theory. This type of failure occurs when the theory underlying the program (for example, how people make changes in health behaviors) is inadequate to achieve the goal. As Weiss stated, theory failure occurs when realization of immediate program goals fails to lead to the final desired outcomes. Even if the program may have been set in motion and implemented with adequate resources and fidelity to the original program design, a program based on inadequate theory is unlikely to achieve the desired effect. Again, careful assessment of needs, of the learning style and capabilities of adult participants, and of what works with whom under what circumstances, together with a conceptual framework that takes these considerations into account when formulating the design of the program, can help reduce the likelihood of theory failure.

To illustrate, many well-intentioned professionals have designed health promotion programs based on what we might call the "informal" theory that people behave in unhealthy ways because they do not know any better. The program resulting from this theory, an inadequate understanding of human motivation and health behavior, is usually one in which the targets of the effort, employees, simply are told how they should behave. Such programs often are unsuccessful because they fail to understand the specific underlying motivations for health-compromising behavior and how these motivations might be changed to encourage health-promoting behavior. Numerous examples can be found in workplace health promotion efforts to help people change their diets, exercise more, and stop smoking cigarettes—behaviors that can be difficult to change, and where an understanding of the complex motivations and specific techniques that work to help people change becomes critical.

Measurement Failure

The final category of reasons for unsuccessful programs is measurement failure. In this case, a program derived from adequate theory has been set in motion with adequate support, but the final outcome may go undetected because of an inadequate evaluation design or because of inability—due to lack of available instruments or tests that are valid, reliable, or sufficiently sensitive—to measure the effects of the program. In other words, the objectives of the program may have been achieved but not noticed because of an insensitive evaluation.

To summarize, and as Figure 1 illustrates, the likelihood of a successful workplace health promotion program and an evaluation that is capable of demonstrating its success depends on three ingredients: a causal process with adequate underlying theory to achieve stated goals; programmatic resources and administrative support that ensure a level of implementation consistent with the original design; and the use of feasible evaluation design and measurement procedures that enable the desired effects of the program to be assessed. With this framework of possible reasons why programs may fail, we can move to a dis-

Figure 1. Categories of Program Failure.

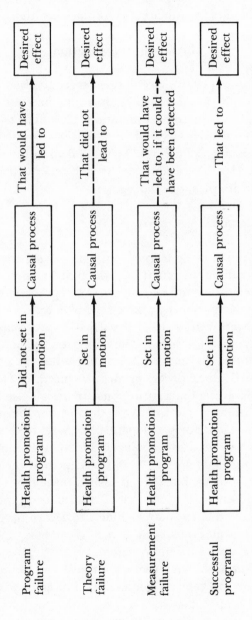

Source: Adapted by permission from Carol H. Weiss, *Evaluation Research: Methods of Assessing Program Effectiveness* (Englewood Cliffs, N.J.: Prentice-Hall, 1972), 38.

cussion of the three levels of evaluation and some case illustrations of their roles in evaluating workplace health promotion.

The Levels of Evaluation

Green and Lewis (1986) have defined three levels at which evaluation of health promotion programs may be conducted: process, impact, and outcome evaluation. The objects of interest for evaluation at each level differ as do the criteria for program success in achieving objectives. Figure 2 depicts the relationship of these three levels of evaluation to each other when applied to workplace health promotion programs.

Process Evaluation

Process evaluation is concerned with measuring the quality of the program and the extent to which it is implemented. In workplace health promotion, we can assess program quality and level of implementation by asking several questions: How many participants were attracted to a particular program? Were the specified number of sessions comprising the full program conducted according to design? Were the programs perceived as being helpful? Did the programs meet the needs of participants? How valuable were the instructional materials used? Was the program instructor effective? Were the location and time of the program convenient for participants? Answers to these kinds of questions are essential for refining and further developing a program. Thus, not only are such questions asked at the end of any programming activity, but they are asked throughout as well.

In addition to collecting data from participants in a program, process evaluation may include a review of program goals, procedures, and methods using panels of outside experts during the formative stages of the program, prior to implementation. This kind of process (sometimes referred to as formative) evaluation can serve to assure a minimal level of quality even before the program begins. Process evaluation designed to elicit data about the level of implementation and participant satisfaction, as well as to assure quality in the initial design of the program,

Figure 2. **Three Levels of Program Evaluation.**

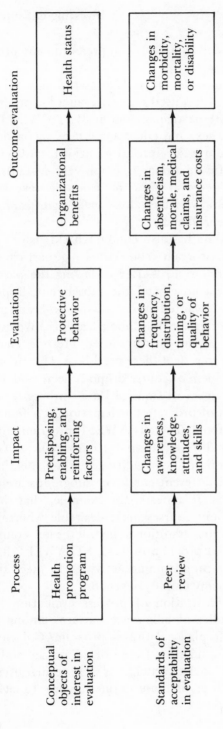

Source: Adapted from Lawrence W. Green and Nancy P. Gordon, "Productive Research Designs for Health Education Investigations," *Health Education* 13, no. 3 (May/June 1982): 6.

should be included as a basic component in any program's evaluation plan.

To illustrate, let us look at two organizations. Control Data Corporation has used process evaluation to determine the characteristics of participants in its "STAYWELL" program. Data about age, sex, and educational level of participants were collected and used to generate information useful in tailoring programs for specific subgroups of employees. Data from a process evaluation conducted in 1982, for example, revealed that these three demographic variables alone yield significant information about program enrollment.

Control Data has also conducted extensive evaluation of the STAYWELL program's courses to gauge participant response. Merrill (1984) reported, "After reviewing the participant's reactions to those courses and the subsequent dropout rates, it was clear workers wanted more 'how-to' skills and actual behavior change activities and less 'book learning.' We quickly found out that most of our instructor-led lifestyle change courses needed revision to reflect these needs" (p. 13). By making these changes, the problem of course dropout decreased markedly.

Another aspect of Control Data's process evaluation was to analyze rates of program participation as a function of program format offered. The STAYWELL program now offers different courses in different formats (for example, self-study, interactive computer-based, or traditional group meetings) and has determined that different employee subgroups are attracted to different formats. It appears, for example, that the sales staff finds the self-study courses most desirable whereas office and clerical staff prefer traditional instructor-led courses. By collecting data about program process, STAYWELL had modified continuously its programming activities to meet the needs of Control Data's many employee groups.

Another illustration of process evaluation can be seen in Pepsico's studies of adherence patterns among participants enrolled in their physical fitness program. Colacino and Gulbronson (1984) studied patterns of adherence and found that only 26 percent of the participants were regular users of the fitness center, with regular use defined as five to eight visits per month. Process data of this nature can be considerably more useful in guiding program refinement and future development than solely knowing, for example, that 82 percent of the workplace population participated during the test quarter. Such findings have led Pepsico to place more emphasis on attempting to increase individual adherence to an exercise program once participants begin.

Impact Evaluation

Impact evaluation is concerned with measuring the extent to which the program has produced changes in awareness, knowledge, attitudes, beliefs, skills, behavioral intentions, and actual behavior. Was knowledge gained or beliefs changed during a program? Were the proper skills developed for participants to change their behavior? Did these changes, in turn, result in changes of the actual behavior of participants? Evaluation designed to answer such questions serves both to verify the assessments undertaken during the analysis of both individual and organizational needs and to enable program developers to monitor progress toward achieving program objectives based on these needs. This level of evaluation is a commonly found component of most workplace health promotion program evaluation plans.

Typical measures of impact in a workplace health promotion program designed, for example, to reduce cardiovascular disease risk would include awareness and knowledge of physical inactivity as a risk factor, the extent to which participants can demonstrate the skill to monitor their pulses during exercise, and the frequency with which they exercise as a result of participating in the program. These measures provide indicators of the program's effect on those factors that predispose and enable behavior conducive to reducing cardiovascular disease risk, as well as of the distribution, frequency, timing, and quality of the desired behaviors.

The Johnson & Johnson "Live for Life" program conducted evaluations to assess impact. Live for Life, a comprehensive workplace health promotion program discussed in Chapter Four, was offered to four Johnson & Johnson companies. In three comparison companies, only the health risk appraisal was offered. One specific focus of the program evaluation was to measure the effect on physical exercise. According to Blair, Piserchia, Wilbur, and Crowder (1986) who evaluated the effect of the program, "Almost 20 percent of the women and 30 percent of the men in the health promotion companies began regular vigorous exercise over the two-year period compared with 7 percent and 19 percent in the health screen [health risk appraisal] only companies" (p. 923). These differences were significant, indicating that the presence of a comprehensive health promotion program produced a greater impact on exercise habits than did the health risk appraisal intervention alone. Another indicator of program impact was actual physical fitness, as measured by performance on a stationary bicycle. Compared to employees in the health screening companies, employees in the companies with the comprehensive health promotion program were significantly more fit after two years.

The impact evaluation of Live for Life also compared changes in risk factors as a function of physical fitness. Using data on employees from the health promotion program companies only, the analysis demonstrated that significant reductions in risk factors for coronary heart disease were associated with improvements in physical fitness.

Outcome Evaluation

Once a program has been implemented over a period of years, outcome evaluation can provide answers to questions about the long-term effects of program participation. Outcome evaluation is concerned with the extent to which it can be demonstrated that a program has had effects that translate into organizational benefits and improvements in the health status of participants. Organizational benefits include lowered absenteeism, increased morale, and reduction in medical insurance claims. Changes in health status of participants can be established through records of morbidity, mortality, or disability of employees.

Although it is often difficult to attribute cause and effect in outcome evaluations, effects such as those just noted can be determined by analyzing the changes in morbidity, mortality, disability, and the costs associated with these events, up to several years following program implementation. One example of the difficulty of establishing cause and effect in such evaluations would be erroneously attributing reduced absenteeism as an outcome of a workplace health promotion program when, in fact, the reduction may have been due to a company's addition of more discretionary holidays. Similarly, although an outcome evaluation might suggest that it was the workplace health promotion program that resulted in lower employee medical costs, the reduction actually may have been the outcome of increasing the deductible of the company's health insurance plan or making available to employees membership in a health maintenance organization. Careful records of the organization's benefit plan provisions must be maintained if outcomes of workplace health promotion are not to be confused with other interventions.

Conducting assessments of workplace health promotion programs at this level of evaluation usually requires a substantial commitment on the part of an organization to provide the technical and other costly resources necessary to track and collect data on large numbers of participants for long periods of time. It also requires an interest in developing a scientifically rigorous evaluation designed to demonstrate with an acceptable degree of confidence that the programming has resulted in such outcomes. Because of these requirements, only the largest of organizations have undertaken this level of evaluation of their programs.

One of the more notable evaluation efforts has been conducted at Blue Cross and Blue Shield of Indiana. In their evaluation, the health care costs of both program participants and nonparticipants were followed for five years following implementation of the health promotion program. Results on the initial outcomes (organizational benefits) indicated a general tendency for participants to have submitted more medical claims and to have made more payments than nonparticipants. As Gibbs and others (1985) have explained, these somewhat surprising results may have been due to the program's focus on risk detection, which may have led to an initial increase in use of the health care system. Over the entire five-year evaluation period, however, the health care expenses of participants was 76 percent of that for the nonparticipants, indicating that the program had in fact produced the desired outcomes.

This case illustrates the use of evaluation to determine the effect of a program on the important topic of health care costs. Of note, this evaluation was not concerned with impact evaluation: changes in health behavior. Only longer-term outcomes, changes in health care costs, were evaluated.

Choosing an Evaluation Design

Choosing a "grand design" to serve as the blueprint for the evaluation is important, but it does not have to be complicated or difficult. The following hierarchy of evaluation designs proposed by Green and Lewis (1986) is intended to help you choose a design right for your evaluation needs. The hierarchy includes six designs, presented in ascending order of complexity, ranging from the simple and more feasible historical recordkeeping approach (which can be used in virtually all evaluation plans and conducted as a matter of routine administrative function) to the sophisticated evaluative research project (which is limited in its application because of the technical requirements of the design itself and the financial resources necessary to undertake it). Each design has its own strengths and weaknesses, and the process of conducting each can be reduced to two or three major steps.

The Historical Recordkeeping Approach

This approach to evaluation is reasonably straightforward because most workplace health promotion programs in formal organizations will have developed administrative and monitoring functions that permit the routine collection, tabulation, and charting of data contained in various records. The first step in developing this approach is to establish a system that allows you regularly to capture data on the process, impact, or outcomes of interest over a period of time. The second step is to institute a regular collection and tabulation of the data of interest, form a data base, and chart these on a graph. In the third step, you then compare the charted data against the criteria for accept-ability that have been stated in the objectives of the program.

An example is shown in Figure 3. In this case, a graphical representation of participation as a process measure of interest

Figure 3.   Participation in a Stress Management Program.

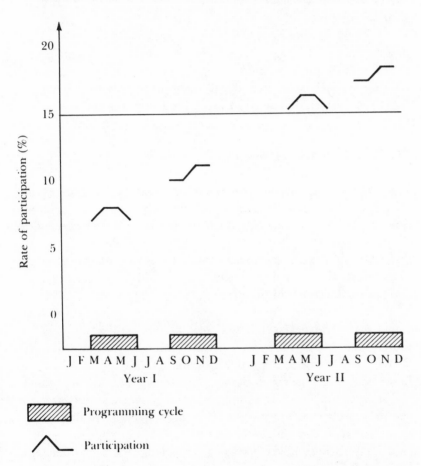

Source: Adapted from L. W. Green and F. M. Lewis, *Measurement and Evaluation in Health Education and Health Promotion* (Palo Alto, Calif.: Mayfield, 1986).

in a workplace stress management program is illustrated. The data have been inventoried and plotted by program cycle over a two-year period. From the graph, we can tell that during the first year the program did not achieve its objective of recruiting at least 15 percent of the workforce to participate in the programming. During the second year the objective was reached. Other discernible information is that relatively more employees participate during the winter cycle of both years than in other cycles, perhaps suggesting higher levels of need at these times to cope with stress.

These kinds of data and the information they yield about programming, although simple and straightforward, can prove valuable in helping to understand the effects of a program on a continuing basis. The recordkeeping approach therefore constitutes the essential element in all of the following evaluation designs.

The Periodic Survey Approach

This approach combines the historical recordkeeping approach with special periodic efforts to collect additional data that may not be part of the routine recordkeeping system. Together with the routinely collected data, these additional data may be required to refine the evaluator's understanding of program effects. Such data can be obtained by conducting periodic spot surveys of the program population.

The first step in this approach is to establish a series of target dates during which the special data collection will be undertaken. These dates may be determined by what you may know from previous experience or the experience of others to be critical stages in the program. The second step is to conduct the surveys and from the data collected generate an estimate of the program's progress toward achieving objectives at that stage.

In workplace health promotion, this approach to evaluation can be helpful in assessing knowledge gain or behavior change following programming. Again, the changes being assessed are "historical" in that they are defined in relation to some prior period in the same program or target audience.

The Normative Approach

This approach to evaluation uses the historical recordkeeping approach to make comparisons with other programs at sites where similar data have been or can be collected. The value of this approach is that it permits the evaluator not only to make historical comparisons of process, impact, or outcome within a program over time but also to make comparisons with other programs.

The first step is to identify sources of similar data on a comparable program offered at some other site. The second step involves gaining access at the other program site to a common data base similar to your own or cooperating with the other program in developing a standardized procedure for collecting the data and creating such a data base. The third step then is simply to make periodic comparisons between the two programs.

Figure 4 illustrates how this evaluation approach is an extension of the recordkeeping approach presented in Figure 3. Note how participation in a company's stress management program being offered in one building compares to participation in the same program being offered in another building. Similar comparisons could be developed between companies in different locations whose stress management programs might have the same objectives.

The Controlled Comparison or Quasi-Experiment

This approach is similar to the normative approach; however, the controlled comparison usually attempts to compare impact or outcomes in a setting receiving a program (the "experimental" site) with a setting not receiving the program (the "control" or comparison site). The evaluation is considered a quasi-experiment because the populations are not randomly assigned. The first step in this approach is to identify an organizational setting with a target population similar to that of the organization offering a health promotion program but that is not going to participate in the program. In large, multiple-site organizations, another building or company location might serve as the

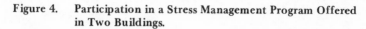

Figure 4.   Participation in a Stress Management Program Offered
in Two Buildings.

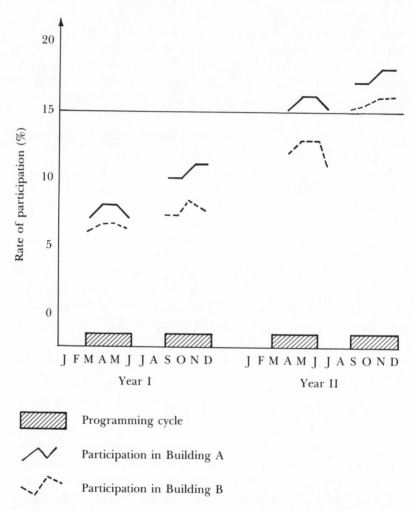

Source: Adapted from L. W. Green and F. M. Lewis, *Measurement and
Evaluation in Health Education and Health Promotion* (Palo Alto, Calif.:
Mayfield, 1986).

comparison site. Next, the evaluator implements either the recordkeeping or periodic survey approach, or a combination of the
two, to collect data in both the experimental and the control

sites. Comparisons on the data of interest are then made periodically to assess the effects of the program.

Ford Motor Company has used this approach in a project designed to evaluate the effects of three programs to control hypertension among its employees. The experimental programs included testing different approaches to detection and referral at two of the company's plants and one approach designed to provide on-site treatment of hypertension at another plant. A fourth plant, which received no program, served as the control site. This design features a reasonably feasible approach that can be implemented in most larger organizational settings, especially ones with multiple sites. Moreover, the design enables you to say with greater confidence at the end of an evaluation that your program made the difference.

In another evaluation study, Michela and Allegrante (1986) used a quasi-experimental design to assess the impact of a workplace health promotion program for inner-city school teachers. In one district, ten schools offered the program, and five schools served as comparisons. Pre- and post-program data were collected using a health risk appraisal and a questionnaire designed to measure common stress symptoms, organizational climate, and job satisfaction. Comparisons between the two groups of schools showed significant changes in the weight and physical activity of teachers in schools receiving the program. In addition, teachers' perceptions of their work environment were significantly improved, particularly in terms of perceived control over work activities and participation in decision making.

The Controlled Experiment

This approach is similar to that of the quasi-experimental approach, but differs in that the controlled experiment relies on the evaluator to make random assignment of participants to at least two, and sometimes more, different programs. In this sense, the approach is comparable to the randomized clinical trials that medical researchers often use in evaluating new drugs or disease treatments. Once the evaluator has randomly assigned participants to one of the approaches being assessed, the procedures for conducting this evaluation are the same as those outlined for the controlled-comparison evaluation.

New York Telephone is one of few organizations to have conducted and reported a controlled experiment in the evaluation of one of its own health promotion programs, a cholesterol reduction program (Bruno and others, 1983). In this evaluation study, 145 employees at New York Telephone were enrolled in the program and were randomly assigned to treatment groups or to a control group. The treatment group programs consisted of a multifaceted, fourteen-session program designed to modify eating behavior. Employee participants assigned to the control group met periodically only for the purpose of collecting data that would be compared to data collected on those in the treatment groups. Evaluation of the immediate impact of participation in the treatment groups revealed that these participants improved significantly on a nutrition quiz following the course, whereas the control group showed no such change in knowledge. More important, the program led to a significant reduction in average cholesterol levels for the treatment group. For the control group, no significant reduction was noted. These findings suggest that the immediate impact of the program not only increased knowledge of nutritional practices and their relationship to blood cholesterol but also resulted in important changes in eating behavior that, in turn, resulted in more long-term changes in cholesterol levels, representing a reduction of risk for cardiovascular disease.

The Evaluative Research Project

The last approach to evaluation, which we only briefly mention here, is that which Green and Lewis have called the full-scale evaluative research project. This design is the most ambitious because it is the most scientifically complex, costly, and least feasible. The steps for implementing this design are the same as those for the controlled experiment, but participants in such evaluations are randomly assigned to multiple program groupings where sophisticated combinations of the educational and other program strategies are varied to test the cost effectiveness of the different approaches. This design permits evaluators to analyze both group and intragroup effects of programming.

Conclusion

Evaluation should be an integral part of the program design in workplace health promotion. Specifying the level of evaluation and the objects of interest for evaluation (for example, knowledge, behavioral changes, organizational benefits, or actual health status changes) at the outset of a program design enables the evaluator to establish measurable objectives toward which program activities and resources can be directed. In other words, it provides you and the program with a sense of direction, while at the same time fostering accountability to participants and decision makers. Anticipating the reasons for possible program success or failure also can help you to think more productively about what goals you wish to achieve, the means by which these goals can be reached, and the design and methods by which you can detect both the short-term and long-term effects of the program. Depending on the goals and those resources available, you should be able to identify at least one evaluation approach that will prove both practical and feasible for your organization in evaluating your health promotion program.

8

Dealing with
Ethical Issues and
Other Problems

Designing workplace health promotion programs not only requires organizational analysis, planning, and evaluation but also
sensitivity to potentially important ethical issues and other
problems that can arise in the course of developing such programs. Consideration of such issues and problem identification
during the early stages of designing the program can prove critical to gaining employee confidence. A high degree of employee
confidence is necessary to ensure program acceptance and participation throughout the organization.

As discussed in previous chapters, workplace health promotion can be an important strategy in an organization's effort
to reduce absenteeism, improve morale and productivity, and
reduce the high cost of health care. However, workplace health
promotion efforts are not without the potential for misuse. Nor
are the goals and intervention methods of such efforts entirely
without ethical implications for the organization and the health
promotion manager whose responsibility it is to develop and implement such programs.

This chapter will discuss how workplace health promotion may pose specific ethical and other difficult problems that
are not always apparent at the outset of program design. These
problems relate to ensuring fairness in the approach to solving

health problems in the context of the workplace, minimizing the likelihood that such programs will have unintended consequences that can prove damaging to either employees or the organization, protecting employees from coercion, and guaranteeing employee privacy and the confidentiality of records. Several ethical issues and other problems typically arise during the design stage when an organization attempts to encourage employee lifestyle changes believed conducive to promoting health. We discuss some of the attendant moral dilemmas these issues and problems present for the health promotion manager and suggest possible strategies for dealing with them.

Conflicting Loyalties: For Whom Do I Work?

In designing workplace health promotion, probably the first issue the health promotion manager will face is that of conflicting loyalties. This dilemma is expressed by the question: For whom do I work? Often, because of the nature and range of strategies that can be undertaken in the development and implementation of programs, the professional responsible for workplace health promotion programming may question whether allegiance and loyalty are to the employer, the employee, or both. Whose advocate does the professional become when workplace health promotion is involved, and under what conditions does the dilemma of conflicting loyalties present itself as an ethical problem with consequences for the way a program is designed?

   The question poses a potentially perplexing moral dilemma if the organizational goals and management agenda of the employer turn out to be in conflict with the perceived health needs and desires of the organization's employees. Consequently, the health promotion manager may be caught between these two legitimate but conflicting interests. For example, as a representative of management and member of the middle-level executive structure of the organization (as many health promotion managers are), you might be expected to design a stress management program at the workplace. One or perhaps both of two distinct approaches to reducing known stressors or their effects in the work environment can be taken (House, 1981). One approach would focus on reducing exposure to the harmful effects of the stressors by altering the immediate work environment, thus effectively removing the stressors. The other approach would seek to "buffer" the effects of the stressors by providing opportunities that enable employees to develop personal coping skills necessary to compensate for stress. The focus of the former intervention approach is organizational in nature, the latter is individual behavior change.

The dilemma of conflicting loyalties arises when the professional responsible for program design recognizes that in reality the compensatory approach alone—what one recent study (McLeroy and others, 1984) found to be the dominant conceptual approach in the design of most workplace stress management programs—may not solve or mitigate the problem. This approach does not attempt to remove or reduce the harmful stressors from the work environment but rather focuses on developing health promotion solely through individual change. Such an approach is common because attempting to deal with the stressors themselves—like those of assembly-line production, sitting at a workstation in front of a computer terminal, or an overly authoritarian manager—may be perceived as unacceptably altering the fundamental organizational priorities and economic goals of management. The organization-change approach may threaten the values of authority and productivity held by the employing organization. However, focusing on the individual as the locus for change usually does not address fully the root causes of health problems and may result in alienating those employees for whom such limited strategies are intended.

What do you do in this situation? How can you balance or reconcile the goals and needs of both the employer and the employee in the design of the program? Can you be responsive to the interests of both? And, perhaps most important, how can you maintain your sense of professional integrity, your sense of fairness, and your own moral hygiene under such circumstances? Although it is possible to be responsive to both sets of interests simply by being sensitive to and conversant with the issues involved, how you answer each of these questions depends, in part, on your personal, professional, and even your political values. To a great extent, it also depends on how you may have learned to perceive the victims of illness—a perception that can present a distinct ethical problem, which we now discuss.

Blaming the Victim

Certain factors have to be taken into consideration when designing a health promotion program for the workplace. These same factors can influence the selection of the targets of our intervention strategies. How we ensure fairness in the approach to solving health problems of employees and in selecting the targets of intervention thus becomes a central question for the health promotion manager during the design stage of program development. The tendency of too many efforts in workplace health promotion has been to focus solely on the individual rather than on the individual along with the nature of the work and the organization itself. How does this create problems? To answer these questions, you must first understand what it means to "blame the victim" (Ryan, 1976).

According to a prominent theory in social psychology (Lerner and Miller, 1978), we tend to perceive the world as a just place in which people get what they deserve and deserve what they get. This notion applies not only to those people who are the beneficiaries of positive events but also to those who are victimized by misfortune. The theory holds that we are threatened when confronted by an apparently innocent victim suffering from a misfortune. As a way of protecting ourselves from the possibility that such a thing could happen to us, we seek to reduce this perceived threat either by discovering something that the person did to bring on the misfortune or, failing that, by disparaging the person. The latter serves to restore a sense of justice by convincing us that the victim is the kind of person who deserves this fate. In either case, the victim is blamed for the problem.

Some of our own research (Gruman and Sloan, 1983; Sloan and Gruman, 1983) has demonstrated that this theory can be extended and applied to health and illness. If people become ill, we tend to attribute the causes of their illness to them and their behavior (Crawford, 1978; Sontag, 1979). A contemporary example is the tendency for some people to think of those who have become infected with AIDS (acquired immune deficiency syndrome) as suffering divine punishment for engaging in socially unacceptable or morally undesirable homosexual behavior or drug abuse. In this way, at least psychologically, we protect ourselves against the possibility that we will suffer from the same illness by focusing on our "socially desirable" behaviors and characteristics. Following this logic, it is culturally appropriate to believe that we have ultimate control over health and disease. It thus becomes both consistent and convenient to target health promotion programs at individuals rather than at organizations or larger social problems, because the behavior of individuals, as victims of disease, is seen as the cause of illness and under their control.

Evidence in previous chapters justifies to some extent both the current conceptual and programmatic focus on the individual that is found in workplace health promotion. As indicated, we know from over two decades of epidemiological research that certain cardiovascular diseases and forms of cancer are influenced considerably by behavioral risk factors. It is thus appropriate that efforts to prevent disease and promote health at the workplace be designed to intervene on and modify those risk factor behaviors that we now know are often, but not always, related to health status and the quality of life. However, it is clearly a mistake to believe that factors under the direct control of the individual (which, in reality, may not always be the case) are solely responsible for the development of disease. Regrettably, this is what many ill-conceived workplace health promotion programs seem to assume, thus implicitly blaming the victims.

Historically, too many early efforts in workplace health promotion have placed the burden of organizing for change on employees and not on the more powerful elements of management (Galanter, 1977; Minkler, 1978). This orientation in workplace health promotion has thus had the effect of blaming the victim for poor health rather than focusing on the circumstances responsible for the problem. Carcinogenic substances in the workplace, overly stressful work conditions, and the inefficient or inhumane operations of an organization all constitute examples of circumstances not conducive to maintaining health at work. The potential for victim-blaming in workplace health promotion is vast, if you allow yourself to think about health as a solely individual responsibility (Allegrante and Sloan, 1986).

We do not mean to suggest that individuals have no responsibility whatsoever in the causal nexus of health. However, blame for many of the deaths due to lung cancer, for example, cannot be assigned exclusively to individuals who may have been assaulted with persuasive messages from advertisers at cigarette vending machines in every foyer of the organization's building or who may have worked daily for years with known carcinogens. We believe that the professional manager designing health promotion programs has to realize that the assignment of responsibility and culpability for illness is a complex matter requiring an understanding of the multiple factors—operating both in and out of the workplace—that can cause disease. In light of such complexity, we believe that rather than dividing professionals and simplistically distorting the issue of whether an individual or systems approach should be taken, a combination of approaches should be encouraged (Green, 1986). Thus, the design of any good health promotion program has to balance the use of behavioral-change approaches with enlightened management practices intended to address organizational-level factors that contribute to health risk of employees. Moreover, even approaches that foster the empowerment of workers to participate in identifying what can be done to reduce risk at work also become important strategies in any comprehensive program design.

Can Coercion Be Justified?

Another problem with some workplace health promotion efforts is the potential for employees in an organization to perceive that they are being coerced into participating, exercising, losing weight, or otherwise doing things they do not wish to do voluntarily. This is especially a problem when programs have not been developed with the needs or expectations of employees in mind and when management appears to dictate a policy of collective good over individual rights. Potential program participants who have not been involved in the planning phase or whose interests have not at least been represented through consensus may sense that if they do not participate in a program, or if they participate but do not meet behavior-change objectives, they may risk their job, fail to be promoted, or lose social status among fellow workers.

In recent years, this problem has arisen in many forms. For example, in 1987 a large corporation tried unsuccessfully to dictate that employees must stop smoking both on the job and away from work or lose their jobs as a result (Phillips, 1987). The company, which manufactured products containing mineral fibers thought to be hazardous to workers who were also cigarette smokers, planned initially to conduct lung tests to monitor the smoking behavior of employees. Experts indicated that the plan raised several legal issues. It was thought that such a plan involved invasion of privacy, violation of contract rights, and discrimination. Following negative publicity, the company announced that although employees who violated the ban on smoking would not necessarily lose their jobs, smoking violations would be reviewed on an individual employee basis. The company also indicated that testing would be used ostensibly to monitor the health of its employees, not their smoking behavior.

It is important to remember that when encouraging individual behavior change in essentially healthy individuals, coercion to participate has no legal place and can never be morally justified in health promotion programming. In most cases, employees should have the right to decide for themselves whether they shall participate, and they should not be made to feel embarrassed, ostracized, or penalized for failing to do so. Voluntariness of participation thus becomes the *sine qua non* for health promotion programming.

Minimizing Unintended Consequences

The final ethical dilemma is that of unintended consequences. As in any effort to bring about change through planned intervention, there can be unintended consequences of workplace health promotion. Some of these consequences can prove damaging in varying degrees to employees, the organization, or the programming effort itself. Although it is probably not possible to anticipate all of the possible unintended consequences that can result, it is possible to minimize their likelihood through analysis during the design stage. The following are some examples of the possible unintended consequences of developing workplace health promotion programs.

Reducing Benefits

The first example illustrates how changes in one aspect of an organization's policy may influence changes in other policy aspects. In 1983, the *New York Times* (Berg, 1983) published a front page story titled, "Major Corporations Ask Workers to Pay More of Health Cost." The article reported that for the first time, during the previous summer, five of the nation's largest corporations—three of which have been among the vanguard in developing workplace health promotion programs—had entered into negotiations with groups of employees during which management had asked employees to pay an increased share of their health costs. The article also reported that several of the corporations had, in effect, dictated this new policy to their white-collar, nonunion employees. At two of the companies, both of which were bargaining with unions, the request that workers bear more of the burden for their health costs was bitterly resented. Union representatives flatly rejected the idea.

Although management at these companies eventually dropped the plan, the story is indicative of what appears to have become a trend in American corporate thinking. Data from a recent study of group benefits in a national sample of over one thousand business organizations showed that companies have been reducing benefits in response to escalating employee health care costs (The Wyatt Company, 1984). Conducted by an independent employee benefits, compensation, and actuarial consulting company, the study showed that employee medical benefits have eroded since 1980. Although 52 percent of the companies provided free coverage to their employees under major medical plans in 1980, only 39 percent did so in 1984. Similarly, in 1980 only 5 percent of the companies surveyed had plans with deductibles of over $100, over 40 percent had introduced such deductibles by 1984.

In this context, it must be recognized that increases in deductibles have been lagging well behind inflation and the consumer price index. Therefore, you may be tempted to regard such increases as long overdue. As indicated in Resource A, workplace health promotion is only one of many ways in which organizations are attempting to manage rapidly escalating health care costs.

Another approach is, for example, to shift some of the burden to employees. Both health promotion and benefit managers must realize that this is a highly complex issue and that evidence suggests that the shifting of costs to employees as a cost-management strategy may not be as effective as you might expect. As Herzlinger and Schwartz (1985) have said, "Health care costs are like a lump of rubber: punching down one part will only cause a rise in another. Piecemeal tactics for dealing with the problem have only made it worse" (p. 69). In an era of increasing emphasis on personal responsibility for health, attempting to shift costs to employees may provide reactions of puzzlement or, worse, resentment.

Although we do not wish to imply that workplace health promotion is causally linked to the reduction of benefits, the significance of these developments is that health care costs have produced enormous pressures within organizations to reduce benefits. Moreover, it is plausible to assume that when such pressures exist within an organization, the presence of health promotion programs may serve to strengthen the hand of management to undertake such reductions. This can mean that rather than providing health insurance benefits, employers are willing to leave the disconcerting impression in the view of many employees and organized labor groups that insurance benefits can be easily replaced with worker health promotion programs.

It would be unfair to view the recent reductions in employee medical benefits as an unintended consequence of the development of workplace health promotion in business and industry. But you can understand how this possibility or similar developments could threaten a programming effort and compromise the role of the health promotion manager. The early stages of program design is therefore the appropriate time to help both labor and management become clear about the motivation and expectations for health promotion at the workplace. Such programs were never intended to supplant medical or other benefits and are likely to be assiduously resisted by many employees if they are perceived as such. Keep in mind that such programs were originally conceptualized as being used in combination with other cost-management strategies; beyond that, any other motivation or expectation for their use can only ensure the failure of a program to achieve its goals.

Violating Confidentiality, Privacy, and Other Rights

Another potential unintended consequence of workplace health promotion activities is violating individual rights. For example, screening workers and drug testing have the potential to produce serious unintended consequences, including legal problems involving violations of confidentiality, invasion of privacy, and discrimination. Although corporate policies that have attempted to require employees to submit to urinalysis and other obtrusive tests for drug use are relatively recent developments, business and industry's interest in screening at the workplace has a long history. In the early 1900s, Frederick Taylor's (1911) "scientific management" position, at least in its application to the Ford Motor company, was one of the first efforts to conduct systematic screening of employees.

Whereas the interest at Ford was to maximize productivity by ensuring proper job placement, as guided "scientifically" by physical characteristics of employees, contemporary efforts to screen for drug use and such conditions as hypertension, colorectal cancer, risk for cardiovascular diseases, and the potential for job-related injury due to certain genetic predispositions and biological traits are motivated by management's interest in prevention of costly disease and injury. Although many of the current screening and drug testing activities conducted as part of workplace health promotion programs often are presented by management as benefiting and protecting both employee and employer, little, if any, serious consideration of issues related to privacy, informed consent, confidentiality, test validity or reliability, constitutionality, or discrimination is contained in the public statements of policy by organizations. For example, how are we to deal with risk assessments used widely in workplace health promotion whose validity and reliability have been questioned (Chaves and others, 1984)? Underestimating a risk for a disease can lead to inattention to potentially life-threatening behaviors, and overestimation can lead to needless preoccupation with one's health. Whether it is ethical to use such estimates that give the appearance of objective accuracy when their validity has not been firmly established is among the many critical issues facing the health promotion manager.

Our concern is that screening and testing of any kind can be misused or misdirected in the context of workplace health promotion programming. Moreover, the potential for using screening and testing to discriminate on the job and violate individual privacy under the guise of health promotion can jeopardize an otherwise well-intentioned and conceptually sound program design. Although several recent court cases have determined that broad mandatory drug testing of government employees without cause is unconstitutional, it is difficult to know the extent to which this practice occurs among privately owned organizations and whether it is constitutional.

A related issue is whether employers will be entitled, in effect, to discriminate against employees based on the results of screening technologies that enable us to focus on the identification of workers who have the genetic potential for health problems (Murray, 1983). Should, for example, organizations be

able to exclude potential employees with high levels of cholesterol on the grounds that these individuals are more likely to
suffer heart disease and will therefore increase the organization's medical care expenses?

Rapid advances in genetic screening and genetic engineering will make such testing a possibility in the future. Bylinsky
(1986) reported that California Biotechnology, a bioengineering
company, has under development a test capable of identifying
people "with a congenital *propensity* to form fatty deposits,
called atherosclerotic plaques, in their arteries" (p. 81, emphasis
added). Assuming such a test becomes available, prediction of
heart disease will become more accurate, and with this increasing accuracy may come more interest in screening at the workplace for potential heart disease. Mandatory testing of employees
for the presence of AIDS antibodies is yet another area of testing in which questions regarding the ability of both private organizations and public authorities to maintain confidentiality
and prevent discriminatory uses of data have been raised (Gostin and Curran, 1987).

The design stage of a health promotion program is a good
time to bring management and employee groups together and
work with both to establish an equitable company policy on
these issues. Any policy should be based on current research
findings regarding the validity and reliability of specific screening or testing procedures, as well as on existing court decisions
and precedent regarding the legality or limited uses of any such
procedures. Finally, it is important to establish as part of a
company's policy a set of procedures designed to ensure the
confidentiality of health-related data and protection of individual employee rights regarding release of such data or information derived from them. Such assurances of confidentiality regarding potentially sensitive information are critical to fostering
employee confidence and participation in programming activities.

Other Consequences

Many other possible unintended consequences of health promotion exist. Employees in exercise programs may spend more
time exercising than the program and management may have in-

tended for them. Accidental injuries or even disease problems might result or be exacerbated from some people participating in certain kinds of programs. Stress management programs could result in some employees feeling they should not "push" themselves at the job. The costs associated with cafeteria changes and healthful meal choices could become more expensive than anticipated for some organizations, thus presenting the dilemma of whether the health benefits justify the additional expenditure. Although it may not be possible to predict many of these and other potential unintended consequences, it is important to be prepared to avoid or minimize their effects.

Conclusion

This chapter has reviewed several ethical and other problems that arise in developing workplace health promotion. The attendant moral dilemmas that these and other issues raise, moreover, may leave the health promotion manager feeling a little like the proverbial monk in Gomorrah. Although we have shown that health promotion can be an important strategy in an organization's efforts to achieve economies and objectives for improving health and preventing disease, the perceived motives and expectations for such efforts can render them vulnerable to misuse and criticism and can ultimately jeopardize programming.

Expecting workers and others in an organization to assume greater responsibility for their health is undoubtedly necessary if business and industry are ever to achieve containment of costs associated with premature disease, death, and disability. However, if initiatives to promote worker health are not balanced with sensitivity to issues of fairness, protecting employees from coercion, and minimizing unintended consequences, together with spirited attempts to design organizational changes to ensure healthy and safe working conditions, health promotion programming can be undermined and fail.

Keep in mind during the design stage of program planning and development that the best efforts in workplace health promotion are those that go beyond simply encouraging the use of individual change strategies, which may merely result in helping those employees already predisposed toward making changes in their own behavior. Health promotion managers who are reflective about the potential ethical and social consequences of their work will see that the larger conceptual agenda of promoting health and preventing disease at work also can be considerably more advocatory than solely teaching employees how to assume greater responsibility for their own personal health. Finally, and equally important, your efforts also should be concerned with the practical possibilities and benefits of empowering workers and encouraging management to cooperate more fully in the formulation of negotiated policies that might prove effective in fostering health by focusing on the nature of the organization and the work itself—issues to which we will return again in Chapter Thirteen.

9

Tools of the
Health Promotion Manager

Through assessment of your organization, you should have a
fairly good idea about the issues on which to focus your program. This chapter discusses how you can reach individuals in
the workplace and influence the organization. Keep in mind a
number of assumptions as you read through the following cata-
logue of tools. First, people respond to different media and
activities, and a flexible, multidimensional approach to any issue
will increase the effect of the message. Second, the "critical
mass" of information, ability (skills), and cultural support necessary to motivate change in individuals or organizations differs
widely, and although it is impossible to predict an optimal level,
it is certain that change is most likely when all three of these
critical components are present.

The purpose of a health promotion program is not to get
people to sign up for an aerobics dance class, to get a mammo-
gram, or to go on a diet: These are mere vehicles. The purpose is
(1) to educate employees about the extent of their personal responsibility for their own physical and mental health, (2) to enable both the individual employees and the organization as a
whole to become critical consumers of health and lifestyle
choices, and (3) to facilitate individual and organizational
changes that can be sustained for the lifespan of both individ-

uals and the company. Neither these purposes nor the goals of workplace health promotion (reduction in insurance costs, absenteeism, and so forth) realistically can be reached through the inconsistent or brief infusion of information. These objectives only can be achieved by creating a workplace in which individuals are valued and are treated as whole people, not merely brains and hands—where there is a climate in which good health is seen as a vital part of doing a good job.

To orient you to the wide array of possible interventions used to accomplish the goals of health promotion, we have written this chapter on "tools." We call them tools because, for the most part, each is a neutral medium. However, each medium is appropriate for conveying many different kinds of health-related information and skills and increasing the level of awareness and support of these concerns in the work environment. Each of the "tools" we discuss is described in detail, with special attention paid to their use as part of a workplace health promotion program. Also included are suggestions for how they might be used most effectively.

Print Materials

Two general categories of print materials exist for use in health promotion: externally produced posters, pamphlets, payroll stuffers, calendars, newsletters, magazines, and booklets on specific or general health issues and internally produced publicity that can include announcements or program summaries appearing in the form of flyers, posters, newsletter announcements, or newspaper articles.

Externally Produced Print Materials

With the growth in popularity of health as a topic, relevant print materials, especially, have proliferated. Universities, extension services, newspapers, magazines, and hospitals have greatly increased their publication of materials for the lay reader, and a whole private industry has sprung up that is devoted solely to various forms and qualities of health information. Thus, a wealth of print health information is available, ranging from free to extremely expensive. (Keep in mind that, unlike watches or suitcases, more expensive health information does not make it necessarily more accurate or guarantee a more attractive package.) Because of this wide variety, it is often difficult to choose which information is both the most appropriate for your organization and the most accurate. This is especially the case with nutrition information, where there are a number of different schools of thought, new research developments daily, a broad divergence of professional opinion, and what seems to be a high level of emotional involvement among those with even minimal expertise. A similar, though lesser confusion can be found in relation to the other main health topics including, thanks to the efforts of the tobacco industry, smoking.

When evaluating information, consider using the federal government, universities, and the major voluntary health agencies as sources for basic content information; they employ appropriately trained experts, are generally conservative medically, and do not make health/behavior recommendations without a close examination of all available evidence. Additionally, they tend to frame the information in a very simple, easy to understand way to which you will be able to compare other print materials.

There are two other considerations in choosing print materials: (1) Threat is not a great motivator: Research has demonstrated that frightening pictures and "end-of-the-world" pronouncements are far less effective than a more positive, affirming message. This latter approach is more consistent with the overall health promotion position. (2) Be sensitive to the reading level and propensities of your main employee population. An effective choice of print materials will depend greatly on the orientation of employees to the printed word both in the workplace and at home. Remember that *Time* magazine is written at the ninth-grade reading level.

The following are some suggestions for using externally produced print materials in the health promotion program:

1. Set up a literature display at the entrance to the cafeteria or building or in the break room(s) or rest rooms. A litera-

ture display should center on one general topic (taking care of your heart, eating right, and so on), should offer a variety of information (different pamphlets), and should either be set up on a short-term, time-limited basis or should change topics frequently. It seems to take about a week before a literature display becomes as noticeable as an exit sign. Literature displays should include large signs identifying the current topic and should be publicized in the various internal publicity vehicles. Displays should be given interesting, attention-getting titles ("What Every Husband (and Wife) Should Know" for a display on breast cancer in women, or "Good News About Vegetables" for a nutrition literature display that includes a vegetable bowl, dietary recommendations from the American Cancer Society and the American Heart Association, recipes, menu suggestions, and comparative nutrition information about different vegetables (calories, vitamin C, and so on). Finally, literature displays must be serviced regularly and frequently to maintain a neat, well-stocked, credible appearance. Resource C contains a list of organizations that provide health promotion literature.

2. Send a health or safety newsletter, magazine, or calendar to each employee's home. This involves family members, if only peripherally, in the work community's concerns about health. A number of such magazines published by insurance companies and universities exist in addition to privately produced ones. This option can be fairly costly, since the price of both the materials and the mailing must be considered.

3. Target information to specific subgroups that you identify over time. The more specifically the information is tailored to the individual's concerns, the greater the benefit of the effort. A variety of ways exist to target information, and to some degree your ability to do so will depend on your access to sociodemographic information and the information about individual employee interests and health status. One way of targeting information is to do so by known risk factors. For example, all women, relative to men, are at increased risk for osteoporosis, breast cancer, and cervical cancer; anyone with elevated blood pressure readings is at risk for high blood pressure; smokers are at risk for many health problems; and so on. Another way to

target information is to identify areas of the company frequented by the targeted group. Identifying these groups can sometimes be tricky and attention should be paid to issues of confidentiality. Targeting information by employee interest may ensure good reception of materials, but those truly at risk still may not be reached. Targeting groups for distribution of printed material, although not requiring an internal mail operation, certainly is enhanced by one.

4. Information can be distributed as support for other health promotion activities. A summary flyer on community resources for the aging can support the information presented during a talk on "Helping Your Parents Age Comfortably." A sticker for the shower or mirror, distributed after a talk on the early detection of breast cancer, can remind women to practice breast self-examination. A packet of low-fat recipes can encourage attendees to follow the suggestions made during a talk about diet and heart disease. The careful choice of one or two supporting materials for an activity can ensure that (a) the information supplied in the activity is summarized and reinforced and (b) the item itself will trigger the memory of the activity.

Posters are another form of print media available to the health promotion program. Because posters communicate motivational messages as opposed to specific information, they are useful for increasing general awareness of issues but are not adequate in and of themselves to convey a complex message. The same can be said for most of the "bullet" types of health messages, such as payroll stuffers, bumper stickers, calendars, and so on.

Internally Produced Print Materials

The second type of print material useful in any health promotion program is that produced internally to publicize the activities, events, and services sponsored by the program. An enthusiastic and thorough marketing campaign not only boosts participation in program activities, but it also serves as a persistent reminder that health is a legitimate and widespread concern at work. It is definitely worth taking the time and energy to make certain that all communications issued by the program are of high quality. Some guidelines for writing such materials are:

1. present information in a simple and straightforward manner
2. reflect the positive, welcoming spirit of the program
3. use humor whenever appropriate
4. attach program logo or symbol whenever appropriate

Because such a wide range of flyers, leaflets, booklets, articles, and fact sheets is available on most health topics, it is unnecessary for the health promotion staff to spend time researching and writing its own materials. In fact, unless you are a highly skilled researcher or have access to one, it is not appropriate that you do so. For the most part, in-house materials will focus on the marketing of the program within the company and the community.

The following are some suggestions for using such internally produced materials.

1. Assuming you have an internal mail system, send announcements of events to each employee or to each targeted individual (for example, smokers, women, or middle-level executives). Do not forget to send all publicity material to each of the upper-level managers and executives.

2. Put together a quarterly or monthly newsletter with a preview of upcoming events, reports on past events, and solicitations for suggestions about activities and participation in planning committees.

3. Produce and distribute materials to draw attention to media events (particularly television and radio) that are health related and that the health promotion program can support through activities in the workplace. Exercise caution: There are some wacky ideas out there, and these often can be found on local access cable channels. If you have a chance to preview such programs, try to do so. If not, recommend programs offered over the major networks or the Public Broadcasting System.

4. Make contact with all internal publicity mechanisms: newsletters, union newssheets, weekly events flyers. Find out

who is the editor, what are the deadlines, who you must consult
before placing an announcement. Use these channels as much as
you can to promote the presence of your program.

5. Because the program will benefit from as much public
exposure as possible, make contacts with local newspapers and
other media. For this purpose, you will need to develop a press
kit. The kit should include a complete description of the program, calendar of events, and samples of announcements, articles
from company newspapers, and so on. After clarifying company
guidelines and practices regarding publicity, develop contacts at
each newspaper, find out about the kinds of things they are looking for, and ask about their deadlines. If you must work through
a company public relations staff, cultivate their interest as well.

6. Develop a catchy program name and colorful logo and
never organize any activity without the name and logo being
visibly present. This is one of the least expensive ways to identify your program events. Have posters made with the name and
logo on the top half and a plastic sleeve on the bottom. Use the
sleeve to insert current program information.

Audio-Visual Materials

In much the same way that relevant print materials have proliferated with the rise in popularity of "Wellness," so the production of audio-visual materials on various health themes has expanded. A number of catalogues and publications review new
materials (see Resource B), all of which are valuable but few of
which are adequate alone as a reference source for this material.
Films and videos may go out of date quickly, are expensive to
produce, and often are available only through distribution
houses. Slide/tape presentations often appear to be no more
than a lecture with a fancy blackboard. Nevertheless, the range
of audio-visual materials is fairly wide, and they should not be
excluded from your health promotion working plan: (1) film,
video, and to some extent slide/tape presentations allow for
learning "stories"—that is, the presentation of role models who
struggle with the same issues involving behavior change as does
the audience; (2) for groups who are visually oriented (or more

specifically, television oriented), a good film can be as effective as, if not more so than, a dynamic speaker, (3) an audio-visual presentation can greatly enhance a written or spoken communication by presenting the same information in a different form; (4) audio-visual presentations are less labor intensive, although they are equipment intensive.

When using audio-visual material of any sort, consider these guidelines:

1. Always preview material before scheduling its use: catalogues and reviews generally do not give you as much information as you need to make an adequate judgment about any items' appropriateness to your specific population.

2. As you preview, keep in mind the long-term goals of your health promotion program: Does this presentation give accurate information, discuss behavior in specific terms, recognize the importance of continuing positive health behavior over time, avoid threatening or frightening messages, and generally have a positive tone about change?

3. Do you have reliable working equipment (video player, projectors, and so on) to which you have dependable access? Do you know how to use this equipment? Be warned! Poorly functioning equipment seriously undermines the program's credibility and effectiveness.

Management and Authority

It may seem unusual to include management and authority as a tool for health promotion in the same general category as print materials. Nevertheless, the authority figures in the workplace convey a tremendous amount of information to the employee population, both directly in what they say and indirectly in what they do not say and how they behave. Although a health promotion program may be sanctioned at the highest level of your organization, it easily can be sabotaged, knowingly or unwittingly, by middle- and upper-level managers who do not understand it. Similarly, the program can be given a tremendous boost by those managers who make a personal commitment to the program's goals. It is important, as you consider what tools are available to you, that management commitment be seen as equal in importance to any other.

Use all of your resources to identify key figures in the work environment. Do not limit yourselves to upper-level management. Include in your list middle management, union leaders, informal leaders, anyone who seems central to the psychosocial functioning of your organization. It is important to pick role models here—not necessarily people who are fit and skinny but rather people who are concerned about their organization and their fellow employees and who are willing to struggle with the challenge of creating a healthy workplace, whether that means individually or as an organization.

The reason you will want to identify and market the program to the formal and informal leaders of your organization is that the health promotion program's message, although important in and of itself, requires the power and authority of the strongest voices in the organization to give it credibility and to carve out a respectable place in the everyday workings of the company. One of your goals should be that the program become part of "business as usual." To this end, set out to sell the program to each of the key executives in your organization. Take the time to seek each one out, explain the rationale for the program, and ask for active support. The following is a list of tasks for which leaders' help can be enlisted:

1. as an employee health promotion committee member
2. for informal endorsements to peers and formal endorsements for promotional literature
3. to allocate agenda time in meetings to the discussion and promotion of the program
4. to smooth the way by donating resources, secretarial time, an extra personal computer, the guaranteed cooperation of the maintenance staff, the permission for a weekend function, and so on
5. as a spokesperson
6. as participants like anybody else, not because they are the managers but because they are role models who can demonstrate that health is important personally and to the workplace community

Committees

The use of employee committees in overall workplace intervention can be a powerful way to expand the legitimacy of employee health concern in areas beyond the traditional individual behavior change strategies. By committees, we mean carefully appointed representative employee groups that are given a serious mandate to investigate, problem solve, monitor, and/or plan in areas that may affect employee health. Sometimes such a committee's mandate will need to be endorsed or even originate from upper management for it to carry the kind of clout needed to make committee membership meaningful, but this is not always the case.

When considering using committees as part of the health promotion effort, consider the following:

- Do not convene a committee unless there is a legitimate concern that can be clearly related, either directly or indirectly, to the goals of health promotion (for example, absenteeism, insurance use, and so forth), and there is a legitimate task to be done.
- Representation from appropriate groups can make a tremendous difference in the credibility of the committee, both with upper management and employee subgroups. Invest time and energy and enlist the advice of opinion leaders in this activity.
- Committees should be task oriented and time limited. If there is a need for an ongoing committee, limit the tenure of committee members.
- Clearly define for the committee where it fits into the overall program scheme, what is the purpose of the committee, and in what way is the committee accountable to the health promotion program (what kinds of reports, recommendations, and so forth, are expected).
- Work closely with the appointed/elected chairperson of the committee to make certain that the technical and informational support necessary to make the committee's activities useful and focused are included.
- Take responsibility, along with the committee, for making

certain that the product of the committee's efforts receives attention from the appropriate audience.
• Thank the committee publicly for its contributions.

The following are some examples of committees and their tasks that have contributed to health promotion efforts across the country:

1. The Employee Health Promotion Committee: Supports and advises the program in regard to policy, direction, and so forth (see Chapter Ten).
2. Employee Smoking Policy Monitoring Committee: Gauges employee satisfaction, compliance, and attitudes and makes suggestions for support activities to be sponsored by the program. This committee should be part of a larger smoking initiative (see Chapter Twelve).
3. Working Parents Committee on Child Care: Investigates employee needs in this area, assesses how family demographics affect absenteeism, and makes recommendations about possible corporate responses.
4. Food and Nutrition Committee: Monitors food available to employees through cafeteria and vending services, makes recommendations to internal agents responsible for vendors, and works with vendors (when appropriate) to make certain that healthy alternatives are offered.
5. Spring Fun Run Committee: Plans and takes primary responsibility for a major weekend family event.
6. Committee on Work and Stress: Identifies perceived sources of stress in the work environment, notifies and makes recommendations to appropriate bodies, and advises change as appropriate.
7. Fitness Committee: Identifies barriers to employee fitness at work, assesses and monitors interest, makes recommendations, and sponsors projects, for example, installation of showers or a corporate discount at the local YMCA.

Use of committees as a resource for the health promotion program is highly recommended. In addition to the obvious benefits, by involving many people in the program, employees feel a greater personal investment in health promotion activities. They feel a sense of "ownership" in the program, which is important. Use of committees, however, should not be unqualified. Remember that since the health promotion program is likely to be confronted by organizational "turf" issues, make certain that the committees you organize do not usurp the functions of already existing divisions within the organization. If territorial concerns arise, committees should work closely with those other divisions.

Microcomputer Software

New software products are being developed continually for the health promotion market as personal computers (PCs) are increasingly used as learning tools and as access to PCs increases. Interactive programs are available for almost any behavior change strategy from psychotherapy to weight loss to smoking cessation. Some programs, such as computerized health risk appraisals, orient users to the specific behaviors they need to change. Others use video games that incorporate health goals and messages. Many of these items are well conceived, well researched, and attractively designed. Before you start investigating what is available in this medium, consider these issues:

1. This medium involves one person at a time in a highly specialized, personalized way. You will need to define carefully the function it is to serve. Who uses the software? When? Under what circumstances? What place does the intervention play in the overall program?

2. This medium requires access to personal computers. Are personal computers available at your worksite? By "available," we mean not merely present but also available for use in the health promotion program. Because a computer program can be used by only one person at a time, health promotion software is not a particularly efficient way of reaching many people at once, although it can be very effective for individuals when used properly. Access to the hardware can be more of a determining factor in your decision to use this medium than the considerations of point 1.

3. What kind of role do computers play in the lives of

the employees at each worksite? There is a trade-off here: Those who are the least familiar with computers are those who attribute the most credibility to them and are also the most resistant to working with them, perhaps because of fears of incompetence. Regardless of how user friendly the program (and there is a tremendous effort to make these programs that, if nothing else), this resistance often may be great. This resistance must be factored into any plans to use personal computers as an intervention if your employee population is not comfortable with this medium.

In general, interactive software can be a creative, effective, and important means of identifying and changing health risk behavior and of supporting new behaviors. However, it will have an impact only if it is used in a way that is sensitive to the needs and cultural norms of a worksite.

Health Promotion Events

An excellent way to increase the visibility of the health promotion program in your organization is through the sponsorship of large, widely publicized magnet events. These events should be considered primarily as cultural interventions; they are not a particularly effective means of communicating information or motivating individual behavior change, but they are a great way to increase the salience of health as a legitimate concern in the workplace. Their objective is cultural change not health behavior change. As such, they are ideal for launching a new program. Here are some hints for successful use of this technique:

- Large events take a great deal of organizational effort. For this reason, try to plan only two or three main events per year and enlist a committee of volunteers who are willing to take over much of the planning and publicity for each event.
- Make an attempt to have each major event use as many "tools" as possible. The more multidimensional the messages, the greater the impact.
- Rather than spend a tremendous amount of money for such projects, invite your community resources to join your company in the effort.

- Focus the event. It is easier to organize diverse information when it has more in common than merely "health." For example, rather than a huge and diverse health fair, consider a heart health fair, where all information, films, and activities focus on the cardiovascular risk factors of lack of exercise, diet, high blood pressure, serum cholesterol, Type A behavior, and family history.
- Make your main events explicitly time limited and highly visible: The more unusual the event in the working day, the more attention it will receive.
- Consider the possibility of including one or two smaller events as well during the year. For example, use such an event to kick off a new cafeteria nutrition program or to attract participants to another health promotion offering, such as an after-work aerobics program or smoking cessation course. Again, the purpose of such events is to draw attention.
- Plan to make at least one of the events an annual occasion. It is important to consider how to become not only a normal part of work but also how to become a part of the tradition of your workplace, much like the annual Christmas party or spring picnic. If your workplace has no such traditions, then you have an opportunity to start some. One event can be The Great American Smokeout. It has the advantage of receiving widespread coverage by the national media. Free planning and publicity materials are available from the American Cancer Society.
- Have fun! And make sure that the participants do, too.

Lectures/Talks

There are two types of talks or lectures that are important in a workplace health promotion program. The first is a promotional talk in which you or another staff member speak to internal groups about the health promotion program itself. We discuss this topic in the section on program marketing in Chapter Ten. The second is a lecture by an expert on some health or program-related topic. These two types serve different functions, but both can be important to the overall working of the program.

Health-Related Talks

Scheduled talks by experts on different health-related topics and publicizing them well can contribute greatly to the goal of creating a work climate in which health is a legitimate concern. The following are some points to consider as you plan such activities:

• Plan to schedule talks during the lunch period and keep them to about thirty to thirty-five minutes (this assumes that the company allocates a full hour for lunch) so that attendees also can have a break from sitting. Advertise these talks as brown bag meetings.

• The voluntary health agencies are good sources of inexpensive or free public speakers. Hospitals, community health and mental health services, community colleges, professional organizations, universities, and their extensions are also good sources of speakers.

• Make an attempt to get good, effective public speakers who will be able to tailor their remarks to your employee population.

• Use only speakers who have nationally recognized credentials such as registered dieticians, exercise physiologists, social workers, dentists, registered nurses, and so forth, or who represent respectable organizations. Avoid quacks.

• Carefully define the topic of the talk: No one wants to hear about exercise in general; but specific aspects of exercise, for instance, how exercise contributes to weight loss, might be more attractive. Be creative and work with your speaker to develop topics that "sell" well.

• Be sensitive to the needs of your particular employee population(s). Use your analysis data, particularly demographics (age, dependents, sex, marital status) and employee interest.

• Consider putting together a series of talks all related to the same theme (see "Suggested Series and Topics").

• Publicize each talk as much as possible. Whenever a talk is being delivered by a hospital or voluntary health agency, publicize it as being cosponsored by your program and that institution.

- Elicit from your speaker an outline of the talk or some suggestions of relevant articles or books to read; prepare a handout with this information for attendees to take with them.
- Make certain that the speaker recognizes the time constraints and leaves time for questions from the audience.
- Solicit new topics of interest from the audience at the end of each presentation, through a questionnaire, by voice, or even on 3 X 5 cards deposited in a box at the back of the room.
- Send a formal thank-you letter to both the individual and the sponsoring agency if appropriate. If your program has some product such as a coffee mug or T-shirt with the program logo, you may want to send one along, too.

Suggested Series and Topics

Fitness in the 80s

No Pain, No Gain: Avoidance and Care of Sports Injuries
Fitness for the Whole Family
Actively Expectant: Fitness During Pregnancy
Fitness on the Road: Tips for Travelers

Food for Thought

Grocery Shopping for the Health of Your Body and Pocketbook
Healthy Heart Cooking
Cooking for ONE'S Health: A Guide for Singles
Low-Cost, High-Health Meal Planning
Myths and Legends About Weight Loss
What YOU Need to Know About Cholesterol
The Bottom Line on Vitamins
Making Vegetables Exciting
Eat to Win: What and How to Eat to Perform at Your Best
Healthful Holiday Eating
To Meat or Not to Meat: What Vegetarians Need to Know
For Women Only: Your Special Nutritional Needs
Feed Your Children Well: What Kids Need to Eat and How You Can Get Them to Eat It

Beyond These Walls: Stress in Our Families

What Expectant Parents Can Expect
Toddlers with Working Parents: Hints for the Latter
    About the Former
Kids Staying Home Sick from School: When, Why, and
    How?
Surviving Your Adolescent's Adolescence
Grandparenting Well
The Two-Career Couple

You and Your Aging Parent

Parenting Your Parent
Understanding Social Security
Community Resources for the Elderly
Making Decisions About Retirement/Nursing Homes

Workshops/Skills Training

In a workplace health promotion program, the purpose of any skills training intervention essentially is to teach people the skills they need to reach the goal of physical and psychological well-being. Areas for which workshops and training programs are appropriate include the traditional areas of risk behavior change such as weight control, stress management, smoking cessation, and cardiovascular fitness. Other appropriate areas, less obviously health related but no less important, include communications, management, decision making, and interpersonal skills. The objective of skills training offered by a health promotion program, no matter what the subject, should be to educate, motivate, and facilitate the acquisition of new health-related skills.

Once the area of training has been identified, there are a number of ways in which a health promotion skills training program can be conducted:

- Check to see whether some already-designated person or department in your organization delivers or can deliver such a program: for example, occupational nurses and physicians,

employee assistance counselors, some personnel officers or
employees, employees in training and development, and other
human resource specialists.

- If you are an expert, develop and deliver your own skills
training package(s).
- If having a consistent training program on any topic is important to you or your organization, you may consider hiring a consultant to develop materials and "lesson plans" for
you.
- Check with your local American Red Cross, American Cancer Society, American Heart Association, or American Lung
Association about the kinds of training they offer. Often,
such organizations are interested in training someone from
your organization to teach the skills. This person would then
be able to deliver programs whenever needed at no cost.
- You may wish to hire an outside vendor or consultant to deliver the training program.

No matter which option is most appropriate for your organization, keep in mind the following characteristics of good
skills training:

1. Make certain there is a solid, logical overall plan for the
   training, whether it takes place over the course of one half-
   hour, one half-day, or eight weeks at one hour per week.
2. Skills should be broken down into manageable units, each
   providing an opportunity for practice, feedback, and the
   experience of success.
3. The instructor should be able to provide you with a detailed lesson plan for each quarter hour.
4. The instructor should exhibit interpersonal competence,
   patience, and expertise and should present a generally
   healthy appearance. In other words, the selection of an instructor should include considerations of referrent power
   and credibility.
5. Keep in mind that the goal of skills training is to teach
   skills and motivate people to use those skills beyond the
   limits of the class. Programs that promote dependency of

individuals on group feedback for weight lost or on incentives such as T-shirts for miles run generally are effective only for as long as the "treat" is available. Sustained behavior change depends to a large extent on increasing self-efficacy and the intrinsic rewards of the new behaviors.

In the following section, generic health promotion topics are listed, along with the main objectives necessary to sustain healthy behavior.

Smoking Cessation

- identify physical, psychological, and environmental "triggers" for cigarettes
- identify the reinforcing consequences of smoking and develop alternative consequences
- identify, practice, and substitute the means of managing stress and managing weight by means other than smoking
- set a target quit date
- elicit and use social support

Weight Control

- set realistic and healthy goals for weight control (as opposed to loss)
- learn about the situations that elicit eating and the reinforcing consequences of eating
- develop appropriate substitute activities
- understand relevant basic physiological concepts such as metabolism, calories, and the role of exercise
- plan a safe and detailed menu
- plan and elicit support needed to maintain the plan
- develop and follow through on a safe and realistic exercise plan
- recognize personal feedback mechanisms other than scales
- evaluate shopping, eating out, and controlled eating on holidays

Blood Pressure Control

- understand the asymptomatic nature of high blood pressure (HBP)

- learn the behavioral controls thought to be associated with HBP (salt, smoking, physical exercise, and relaxation training)
- learn to self-monitor and/or develop a plan for short-term intensive monitoring to validate fluctuations (or lack thereof)
- develop a step-by-step program for control, including behavioral changes and monitoring
- comply with a physician's medical recommendations

Nutrition

- understand basic and personal nutritional needs
- understand the benefits of a low-fat, high-fiber diet
- learn sources of cholesterol, fiber, vitamin C, cruciferous vegetables, and other health-related foods and food components
- develop a long-term plan for gradual diet modification with a feedback mechanism such as weight change or cholesterol testing

Stress Management

- understand the definition and consequences of stress
- identify personal sources of stress and monitor stress reactions
- learn a variety of behavioral and cognitive strategies for coping and/or alleviating stress
- develop a plan for practice and the ongoing use of appropriate techniques
- define a method of monitoring oneself to see if the strategies are successful

Exercise

- learn the basic requirements of physical fitness
- develop a realistic and safe personal exercise plan in consultation with a physician or exercise physiologist
- define and implement a system of support for ongoing adherence to the plan

Cancer Detection and Prevention

- understand the behaviors associated with the primary prevention of cancer

- understand what are the early detection techniques and their recommended frequency of use
- identify where to get tests and how to perform a self-examination
- identify the barriers to adherence to recommended actions and plan solutions

Communication Skills

- recognize the importance of the various elements of communication (listening, responding, active listening, and so forth)
- experiment and collect feedback about strengths and weaknesses in communication
- practice new skills
- identify mnemonics or triggers to remind one about continued use

Other "workshop" or skills training topics might include:

Cardiopulmonary Resuscitation
First Aid
Decision Making
Parenting Skills
Conflict Resolution
Assertion Training
Healthy Cooking and Shopping
How to Use the Company Health Care Services/Benefits Package

Ongoing Programs

A fine line exists between the health promotion program being a continuing presence and becoming a part of the woodwork. For example, permanent literature displays fade into the same wasteland as fire extinguishers after about a week, as do ongoing weekly activities such as aerobic fitness. For this reason, consider setting time limits and goals for every activity sponsored by the program. Another strategy is to set up a permanent framework for ongoing activities but to divide it into shorter, manageable time units. For example, organize a six-week-long walking group whose goal is to walk the equivalent of the distance to the North Pole. Interested employees can sign up again after completion. As another example, organize a post-holiday weight control support group whose objective for the first eight weeks is to return to pre-holiday weight and for the second eight weeks is to get into shape for summer. Another possibility is to set up a permanent general structure for activities and continually make short-term changes in focus. One example of such an activity is a cafeteria nutrition awareness program that can focus on a different aspect of good nutrition every week.

The following are some other examples of ongoing programs you might want to consider:

Facilitate the organization of all kinds of fitness activities, for instance, walking during lunch hour, running, biking, swimming, or aerobics. The fact that you do not have fitness facilities available on-site should not deter you from exploring these options with the employee population and with the community. You may be able to work out a deal for your company's employees with the local YMCA or YWCA or arrange to use the shower facilities and gym of a nearby school. Make a map of safe walking streets around your workplace and include mileage and tips about walking safely for fitness (shoes, hats, pulse rate, and so on). Make public the accomplishment of goals set by such groups: It adds to their spirit and to the visibility of the health promotion program.

Set up a nutrition awareness program in the company cafeteria, lunchroom, or vending machine area to inform food-choice and decision making by employees. It is often possible to work with vendors and suppliers to find alternatives to at least some of their offerings, for example, skim milk or fruit juice in place of one or two sugary soft drinks. Often a number of healthy alternatives are already available but are not identified as such. Labeling foods with calories, cholesterol, fat, and sodium can be an onerous task without the whole-hearted cooperation of food service providers, but it can provide a valuable learning tool for the general public. When attempting any collaboration with an outside vendor or supplier, try to include them early in the planning process and take their real-world market-place constraints seriously. Many of the larger food service providers are developing their own nutrition programs as a marketing strategy and are pleased to find a receptive audience to share in both the labor and reward of organizing such a program.

Organize regularly scheduled public meetings to discuss a particular work-related topic with an executive or an expert. Such meetings primarily serve the function of keeping the health promotion program in the limelight.

Self-Help/Support Groups

Use of self-help or support groups is an approach that has been suggested for encouraging maintenance and support of health behavior changes in employee groups. Although the idea is a good one and seems like a cost-effective intervention, the realities of group dynamics and particularly those of leaderless groups are such that they are not an effective option for supporting the health behaviors traditionally targeted by health promotion efforts; that is, such groups have difficulty remaining task oriented and as a result, they are not useful in promoting behavior change. However, self-help groups are extremely useful in providing socioemotional support for health-related topics such as living with certain chronic diseases or conditions or dealing with someone who has a health problem that is difficult to manage. The sponsorship of such support groups at the workplace may be an important gesture toward the goal of the workplace as a caring community.

Referral

Because no workplace will ever serve all of the health and psychosocial needs of every employee, the health promotion program also must serve as a source of referrals to community groups and agencies such as health clubs, the YMCA and YWCA, university extension services, hospital screening clinics, and psychological counseling centers. The latter can be a sticky topic, particularly if your organization has no referral program for psychological or substance abuse services: In the absence of such a referral source, the health promotion program will be sought out, and it is a good idea to be prepared. Consider the following tips about referrals:

- The key is to give employees choices not endorsements of a person or program you think is effective.
- The process by which one person is referred by another to a service or organization is not the act of selling but rather of matching, that is, narrowing down a broad list to two or three options. If you have not had experience doing this, ask for some training: Remember to listen carefully to the person you are referring.
- If you decide that your program's approach to cardiovascular fitness will be to educate employees about the many resources the community has available, invest time in developing a complete and informative referral list and then extensively market the fact that you have this list. You may want to do more than merely market; you may want to provide some incentives for use of these community resources. For example, you may subsidize some fraction of the membership fee at a local fitness center.

You may wish to develop referral lists for such services as:

1. fitness or other health promotion activities that you may not offer or that may be offered more frequently or conveniently elsewhere
2. fitness facilities in hotels (and even airports) across the country, especially if your organization requires employees to travel extensively
3. hospitals or health agencies offering low-cost screening or other services related to employee health
4. counseling referral services including family, marital, substance abuse, and individual

Screening for Early Detection of Disease

Screening for the early detection of disease is an important health promotion service because it increases the probability that existing pathology will be detected at a point early enough to be able to reverse the process, manage the disease, or treat it while it is still a relatively minor problem. The cost-management implications are obvious: By detecting a disease early in its history, the likelihood of its leading to a more serious and costly outcome is reduced. Sponsorship of mass screening or early detection clinics by the health promotion program is another main area of intervention that, if handled properly, can be a fairly high-impact, low-cost service. However, screening should be offered on a regular basis for it to be effective. Screening only a single time for any disease or risk factor is rarely worth the time or energy. The mass screening technology has developed to the point that a number of tests can be conducted at the worksite itself. Others are more comfortably or appropriately offered through a local health facility.

The responsibilities of a health promotion program in relation to either type of screening are threefold. First, you must inform and educate the appropriate segment of the employee population about why the test is important, what the test can and cannot do, and at what intervals it should be repeated. Second, arrange with the internal medical department or local health agencies such as clinics and hospitals or voluntary agencies to supply the needed skills, expertise, and equipment required for the screening. Third, promote the screening so that significant numbers of employees participate. Last, be certain that arrangements are made for adequate reporting of results and follow-up. Because screening is definitely a medical activity, the use of your own company's medical department, person, or adviser is critical in planning. From the perspective of the health promotion professional, the same principles that apply to other health promotion activities also apply to screening: careful planning, targeting specific risk populations, enthusiastic and widespread publicity, and sensitivity to the norms and needs of your own workplace. When offering any screening program, you must be especially aware of the concerns associated with confidentiality. Information gathered in this way must remain absolutely confidential, available only to the individual employee and to the health promotion program and the medical department if appropriate. In the case of outside clinics or hospitals providing screening, the information needed by the health promotion program and medical department must be negotiated.

The following section presents some of the various types of early detection procedures currently available, along with a brief explanation of what each is and how each may be carried out in relation to the workplace.

High Blood Pressure Screening

Blood pressure is measured through the use of a sphygmomanometer, an inflatable cuff with pressure sensor and meter. Measurement takes about one to two minutes and should be administered by trained personnel. Because elevated blood pressure is a major risk factor for coronary heart disease (CHD) and stroke, hospitals and the American Heart Association are often willing to volunteer the services of nurses or paramedical staff to assist in workplace screening. During National High Blood Pressure Month (May), you can take advantage of free or low-cost publicity and materials by coordinating your activities with the local Heart Association.

Serum Cholesterol

Once the only way to determine serum cholesterol levels, another major risk factor for CHD, was to take a relatively large blood specimen, drawn by a nurse or trained phlebotomist, and analyze it in a laboratory. Now a number of finger-stick blood tests are available that require only a few drops of blood and provide immediate feedback on cholesterol and high density lipoprotein readings. The machines used to analyze the blood currently are fairly expensive, but they are expected to decrease in price and increase in reliability as the technology advances. Again, hospitals and the American Heart Association may be willing to assist with an on-site screening and may in fact have access to the latest equipment. If not, it may be possible to arrange with a local clinic or hospital to provide such a service.

Breast Cancer

There are three early detection procedures for breast cancer: mammography, clinical breast examination, and breast self-exam. Mammography is recommended yearly for all women over the age of forty. Because the mammography equipment is not portable nor likely to be something that even the largest companies have on-site, arrangements must be made to have women screened elsewhere. One of the main barriers to mammography is the expense. Many companies and organizations have contracted with hospitals and clinics for lower fees for women coming through their referral. Additionally, the American Cancer Society in some states (California and Minnesota) sets aside a month during which mammograms are offered at selected sites for a low fee. Again, coordination with your local health and voluntary agencies is critical.

Clinical breast examination is best done by a woman's own physician, but it also can be done by a trained health professional as part of the referral process for mammography. Breast self-examination is the third important component of breast cancer screening. It is a fairly simple skill for women to learn, and your local Cancer Society unit should be able to provide instructors or train employees to instruct others in the company.

Cervical Cancer

The Pap test for early detection of cervical cancer in women requires obtaining a sample of tissue from the cervix during a pelvic examination. Unless there is a medical clinic within your organization that insures privacy and confidentiality, these tests may be conducted better away from the workplace. Again, arrangements often can be made for referrals at a reduced fee.

Colorectal Cancer

Screening for this disease is quite simple, requiring only a guaiac slide test kit. Because this test requires three consecutive stool samples, people are given the kit, instructed on how to use it, and on completion, return the kit for processing at a laboratory. Relevant voluntary health agencies can help to plan and implement such a screening program and also can be helpful in promoting tactfully and effectively what some people consider a difficult or embarassing test procedure.

*Other Conditions for Which
Screening May Be Appropriate*

> Glaucoma
> Hearing loss
> Diabetes
> Vision problems

Screening Advantages and Disadvantages

Consider the following advantages and disadvantages of offering screening programs on-site or off-site: Screening programs offered at the workplace are certainly convenient and for this reason can attract many people. On the other hand, on-site facilities may not offer the kind of privacy necessary for people to feel comfortable or to allay their concerns about confidentiality of results. Concerns about privacy vary with the screening techniques. It is generally (but not always) less of an issue for blood pressure than for colorectal cancer. Screening programs off-site present people with an initial barrier, that is, they have to leave work and expend extra effort to participate. However, employees may feel less reluctant to talk about their medical concerns with recognized professionals who are unrelated to the company.

Health Risk Appraisals

A health risk appraisal (HRA) is, in the most general sense, a questionnaire that compares individual personal characteristics and behavior patterns with factors believed to increase the risk of disease, injury, or death. HRAs are considered one of the major tools of health promotion and are used in three ways: (1) to identify clusters of risk-producing behaviors in large populations, (2) to evaluate health promotion activities through administration at fixed intervals over time, and (3) to educate participants about the relationship between their behavior and health risks, thereby motivating behavior change. As health promotion has gained in popularity across the country, the development and marketing of new and more elaborate health risk appraisals have blossomed. At least sixty different HRAs are available, ranging from free, one-page self-scored quizzes to 300-question, full-color, computer-scored packages, available for upwards of $40.00 each. Faced with this plethora of products and related services, the decisions of whether to use an HRA, how to use it, and which one to choose becomes difficult. We have already touched on the topic of health risk appraisals in Chapter Five. Because there is a good deal more to say, Resource E is devoted to this topic. The resource will help you to understand more precisely what HRAs are, what they can do, and what they cannot do, so that should you decide to use one for any reason, the choice of the actual product will best meet your program's specific needs.

Conclusion

In this chapter, we have presented and discussed in considerable detail a lengthy collection of tools of the health promotion specialist. This list is certainly not exhaustive: Other tools are available. Which tools you use will depend on (1) the type of program you envision, (2) the resources available to you, and (3) the individual characteristics of your organization. Organizations with limited resources undoubtedly will want to use the least expensive of these tools. Better endowed organizations will have a greater range from which to select.

Another criterion for selection of tools is the nature of the employee population. In a manufacturing operation, for example, audio-visual materials are likely to be superior to microcomputer-based approaches. In a white-collar research and development organization, however, the opposite may be true. When using print materials, carefully consider the target population and its level of literacy. Illiteracy is a serious problem in the United States. Programs using print materials over the head of the general audience are not likely to succeed.

Similarly, recognize that the use of authority figures and upper-level management as endorsements of the program will have different appeal to different groups. In an organization characterized by harmonious relationships between management and staff, endorsement by upper management may be of value. In an organization in which there is widespread distrust and animosity toward management, such an approach will be counterproductive.

Whatever you do, make certain that you select as wide a variety of tools as possible. The wider the variety, the less likely the program will become part of the woodwork. Health promotion programs that are innovative in their selection of tools will be better received by management and employee participants. One of your most fundamental responsibilities as program coordinator is to maintain a high level of interest in the program. Using a variety of tools will contribute to this end.

Finally, recognize that the use of these tools has at least two purposes: (1) to encourage awareness of the health promotion program and participation in it and (2) to promote incremental changes in the organization's norms regarding health. Each time the program stages an event, it has an impact on the way health is regarded. Properly conducted and promoted events contribute to increasing the awareness that health is an appropriate concern in the workplace.

10

Running the Program: Internal Organization, Marketing, and Selection of Vendors

As your health promotion program moves from the planning stage toward implementation, attention should be paid to five general topics to facilitate a smooth transition between the two modes of operation:

- organization of the program
- the development of an employee health promotion committee
- using existing divisions within the organization
- marketing
- selection of vendors and consultants

Regardless of the size or form of the program you have planned, these topics should be addressed seriously.

Organization of the Program

Organizational Structure

The organizational structure of the health promotion program varies directly with the amount of formal investment of resources. Where there are few resources, organizational planning may mean negotiating secretarial time, storage space, phone use, and photocopy billing procedures; for a larger investment of resources, it may mean setting up an office, writing preliminary job descriptions, acquiring equipment, hiring staff, and so on. Whatever size operation you plan to run, you should get the basic housekeeping tasks done as much as possible during the planning phase.

Organizational Location of the Program

Although we have touched on this issue already, it merits further consideration. Since we conceive of workplace health promotion as a broad undertaking, in the manner of organization development, it encompasses numerous activities relevant to already existing organizational functions. Because it has implications for medical care expenses, it is relevant to the benefits department. Since health promotion serves a preventive medicine function, a medical or employee health department shares some of its concerns. The health education aspect of programs makes a training and development department a natural ally. Other natural organizational divisions are employee relations or human resources. Because in many organizations all of these functions are subsumed under personnel, this may be an appropriate department for the health promotion program. And, of course, since the program has financial implications, both in incurring expenses and in potential for cost savings, there may be justification for locating it in the finance department.

There is no single, proper organizational location for a workplace health promotion program. Location depends on many factors, among them the kind of program you develop and the nature of the overall organization. For example, if your program is limited to education only instead of broader attempts to encourage risk behavior change or policy change, the training department may be an appropriate location. Alternatively, if your program calls for intensive screening for medical conditions, the medical or employee health department may be a better choice.

Characteristics of the organization and intraorganizational

departments also will influence program location. In many
Swedish industries, for example, the nature of the medical departments is quite different from their American counterparts.
At Volvo, for example (this case is discussed in greater detail in
Chapter Thirteen), the medical department is involved heavily
in examination and modification of the psychosocial aspects of
the workplace. In different organizations, the same departments
may have completely different functions or responsibilities.
Some of this information should come to light in the course of
your organizational analysis.

Other aspects of the organization also will have an effect
on the location of the health promotion program. In a small organization, for example, many functions are gathered in a single
department, for example, personnel. In fact, a single person
may be entrusted with these responsibilities. Such organizations
have fewer considerations in regard to organizational location.

Another issue regarding location is that, in any organization, different departments have different reputations and im-
ages. These reputations, positive, negative, or neutral, derive not
only from the departmental functions but also from the person-
alities of those in charge. Whatever their character, they will
have an effect on the health promotion program and its capacity to attract interest, participants, and organizational support.
The image of *your* program will be influenced by the departmental function with which it is affiliated. Therefore, it is *essential* to be aware of these reputations in considering the location
of the program.

You may be surprised to discover that those in charge of
departments with questionable reputations often are well aware
of their image in the workplace. We were contacted by a state
organization interested in developing some smoking and weight
control programs for employees. The department nominally in
charge of program development was personnel, the director of
which was fully aware of the punitive reputation of her department. (She, not so incidentally, was new on the job and therefore was not responsible for the development of this image.)
She was confident enough to relinquish full control of program
development and to share it with representatives of the union.
Thus, the program became a joint enterprise, sponsored by

each. Through this arrangement, the program profited from the positive reputation of the union but still was seen by upper management as under adequate organizational scrutiny and control. Its success was greatly enhanced by reducing its association to the personnel department.

Central to the success of any workplace health promotion is the creation of a positive image that connotes freshness, health, energy, enthusiasm, novelty, and competence. Affiliating with an organizational department that is known to lack these qualities or, even worse, to epitomize their opposites, can jeopardize opportunities for success. Factors beyond departmental image operate in selecting the organizational location of the health promotion program. Ultimately, a decision regarding location will be a compromise among these many factors. In negotiating this compromise, the program manager must not lose sight of the importance of program image.

Establishing a Health Promotion Committee

In the initial planning stages, it is desirable to establish a health promotion committee to provide guidance and to confer legitimacy on the program. Individuals, especially those occupying positions of authority in the organization, can benefit from the information of others. An axiom of organization development, a field which has much to offer to the designer of a workplace health promotion program, is that decisions regarding organizational changes are best made by people closest to the data. The employees for whom the program is designed are rich sources of information relevant to program development. For this reason, responsibility must be shared, no matter how small the company. The committee's function is to provide you with input and feedback at various points in the design and implementation process.

Committee Composition

Who should participate on the committee? Several factors should be considered. First, recognize that committees serve multiple functions. The most fundamental function, in this case, is to provide advice and direction. A second, and more subtle, function is political: Committee composition sends a message, especially to those constituencies excluded. The message is that this program will be (or will not be) designed with the needs and ideas of the excluded constituencies in mind.

Management and Nonmanagement. Attempt to have all levels of management and nonmanagement employees on the committee. Having representation from upper management enhances the program's credibility and the members' commitment. However, it is equally important to have representatives of employees at other organizational levels. Organizational level is not the only criterion for committee membership. Try to encourage the participation of some of the organization's real enthusiasts as well as some "enablers"—that is, people who are well connected and who as advocates of the program can ease your way.

Encourage Feelings of "Authorship" of the Program. Feelings of "authorship" of a health promotion program will contribute heavily to its success. Active participation in the planning of the health promotion program promotes feelings of ownership in the program. The probability that the program will be taken seriously is enhanced greatly by such feelings of ownership. If the program is created by an elite group of upper-level managers having little contact with the rest of the workforce, for whom it is designed, the opportunity for resentment arises. As indicated, those employees who ultimately will use the program can tell us a great deal about how it should be developed. We have seen many cases of well-meaning managers who provide direction without proper consultation. You can refer to Sashkin (1984) for further discussion of the effect of participation. We cannot overemphasize the importance of encouraging widespread involvement in starting off on the right foot.

Consider, for example, the case of a small West Coast company that decided unilaterally that the most important program that could be offered with smoking cessation. Although it was true that smoking was a serious problem in this workplace, a more serious problem, from the perspective of the employees, was their periodic exposure to toxic substances. Needless to say, the success of the smoking program was hampered seriously by the failure to consider the opinions of the employees involved.

Currently we are working with a state government program designed to improve the work environment of a class of mental health workers. In the absence of consultation with representatives of these employees, the administration of a local state institution decided to enhance that environment by providing weight control and smoking programs. Spending only a few moments with representatives of the mental health workers, we discovered that they were much more concerned with what they perceived to be their dead-end jobs. The last thing they wanted was a weight control or smoking program.

We mention these examples because it is absolutely essential, in program development, to make a serious effort to involve representatives of the employee populations for whom the program will be designed. Concern about dead-end jobs is not something for which a health promotion program is an appropriate resolution. In fact, it is quite certain that this pervasive concern on the part of the mental health workers would doom any weight control or smoking cessation program. Implementation in the face of this concern would be worse than the mere failure of two programs; it would suggest (quite correctly) that management, however well-intentioned, is insensitive to the concerns of these employees. This is precisely the consequence to be avoided. One of the primary justifications for organizations' interest in workplace health promotion programs is that such programs often are seen as evidence that management is providing something of value to employees.

Solicit Representation from Other Relevant Departments. For smaller companies, this may not be a real issue. However, if your organization has other relevant departments, for example, personnel, benefits, human relations, training and development, health and safety, or medical, it is likely that there will be interdepartmental competition of one sort or another for input in program development. The competition may result in multiple requests to locate the program in specific departments or, conversely, multiple expressions of lack of interest, due, perhaps, to feelings of being overwhelmed with other work. Each organization will differ in this regard, but it is likely that such turf issues will arise from the outset. Be prepared.

Optimal Committee Size.   Finally, to have a functional and effective committee, consider how many members you want. At a minimum, there should be four members; at a maximum, there should be nine. Consider having members serve for a finite time period, for example, one year, and stagger their terms so that you will not be confronted with the retirement of an entire committee at the same time. Maintaining continuity of the committee is important. You will want to be able to add new members as enthusiasm and interest in the program grow. Having a finite time limit for committee membership will help keep members' motivation high.

Committee Meetings

Like all meetings, the employee health promotion committee meetings should be carefully planned. Have a formal agenda and stick to it. If you have done your homework in regard to committee composition, this will be especially important since members will differ greatly in background and organizational position. Work with the committee to define its role—what are individual members ready, willing, and able to do both immediately and over time?

Meet at least once per month in the beginning. Once the program is up and running, consider meeting less frequently, depending on committee interest and enthusiasm and your own needs for the committee's help and support. End every meeting with each member having a clear assignment for the next meeting, even if it is only to ask colleagues about an idea. (For instance, would you be interested in hearing a speaker talk about being a working parent?)

Because you have a committee with representation from diverse levels of the organization, be sensitive to the group dynamics, both overt and hidden, that may arise in such meetings.

Be careful not to let the meetings dissolve into counterproductive bickering between different constituencies.

Suggestions for Committee Activities

- Develop the logo and mission statement for the program or sponsor an employee contest to do this.
- Conduct informal surveys—for example, have members ask their immediate workgroup if there is interest in a before-work aerobics class.
- Provide feedback on ongoing projects—for example, is anyone buying the fresh fruit in the vending machines?
- Brainstorm ideas—for instance, how can we build a community consensus that there should be no smoking in this building?
- Sponsor or help with labor-intensive activities—for example, a family picnic and fun run.
- Problem solve—for example, what should be our strategy for getting a bigger budget next year?

Using Existing Divisions Within the Organization

Do you have any of the following divisions or functions in your organization?

- organizational effectiveness (OE)
- organization development (OD)
- employee assistance program (EAP)
- unions
- safety
- quality of worklife (QWL) circles
- human resources development/management training
- medical

An effective health promotion program should work closely with each of these other areas in the company for three reasons:

1. The broader the program's base of support within the organization, the better integrated it will be into the daily concerns of all employees.
2. The broader the affiliations of the program, the less likely it is to take on the stereotypes and associated stigmas of the parent department.
3. The broader the cooperation, the higher the likelihood of enlisting the skills, ideas, and expertise that already exist at the workplace.

Each of these groups has a set of skills and concerns and can, when "sold" on the idea of health promotion, bring these to bear on the task of finding new and creative solutions to problems health promotion attempts to solve. Formally involve representatives from these departments in the program. Negotiate ongoing support and contributions from each group. This kind of interdepartmental cooperation can be the source of marvelous support.

In addition to providing help in planning, the various groups might take on a number of tasks relevant to the health promotion program.

OE or OD groups might be able to offer seminars on such topics as time management, management training, or negotiating skills. Although such programs appear not to be related directly to health, they do have an effect on the quality of life at work. As we have indicated, the focus of workplace health promotion should be broad.

Employee assistance programs typically offer short-term counseling and referral for emotional troubles that can affect all employees. Other EAP activities include handling substance abuse problems. Both of these areas have direct relevance for the workplace health promotion program and can be seen as a part of the overall effort.

Unions often are willing to be of assistance to your program. They are usually good sources of information about employee concerns and interests. In addition, they may have their own media, such as newspapers, magazines, or letters, which can augment your own efforts to promote the program. Also, unions are a source of high credibility with many employees.

The safety department may perceive the health promotion program as an intruder or competitor for limited resources and may be resistant to working with you for that reason. However, many of the concerns of health promotion are related to those of safety, and cooperative gestures strengthen the efforts of each group.

QWL circles often have limited time for contributions beyond their charge, but they are good sources of information and feedback about the needs and perceptions of the employees. They also often have the ear of upper-level management and can support a health promotion program through this channel.

Human resources development departments often sponsor activities that are important to a well-rounded health promotion program, for example, assertiveness training, conflict resolution, participative management, and so on. They typically are familiar with local consultants who can provide health promotion services, and they can help the program to train or evaluate facilitators for various health skills workshops.

The medical department is another entity that may feel that health promotion falls within its domain. If the program is located elsewhere, the relationship between these two groups must be negotiated carefully so that employees are not confused by differing messages and sources of expertise about health issues. Most occupational medical departments pay little attention to prevention except in the case of occupational injuries. This, however, is changing in some companies. Investing time in building a cooperative relationship or at least a clear definition of differential tasks and goals of the health promotion program and the medical department is time well-spent.

Concerns about program relationships with other intraorganizational divisions pertain even to smaller companies. Every organization, no matter how small, has multiple divisions. The better the relationship with each division, the greater the program's likelihood of success.

Marketing

Conceiving of and developing an excellent workplace health promotion program, although satisfying, is not sufficient. Most especially, it is not identical to having an effective program. Unless the program is sought by employees, it will be an abysmal failure, no matter how clever it is. Accordingly, one of your foremost responsibilities is to market the program.

Until quite recently, the concepts of marketing and health belonged to different universes. Selling health behavior in the same way that cars or shampoos are sold was quite repellent to health professionals. However, as the link between personal behavior and environmental events, on the one hand, and physical health, on the other, became more apparent, the social marketing of health correspondingly became more accepted. In this chapter, we can address marketing strategies only briefly. Resource B contains several recent references that cover the topic in considerably greater detail.

General Marketing Theory

The Four P's.   Professional marketing specialists often refer to the four *P*'s of *p*roduct, *p*rice, *p*romotion, and *p*lace. Products, according to Kotler (1975), have five dimensions: durability, complexity, visibility, risk, and familiarity. In selecting and marketing your health promotion products, consider these dimensions and develop your marketing strategy so that you can maximize their appeal. Consider, for example, two contrasting smoking cessation products: (1) a ten-week behavioral program that emphasizes gradual smoking reduction, intensive monitoring of cigarette smoking, examination of both the situations that provoke smoking and the consequences that follow it, and the development of alternative behaviors or (2) a medical program that offers a short-term treatment based on the administration of a prescription drug. The latter approach is considerably less complex, an advantage over the former. However, it is also more risky and less familiar. Understanding your target market and the five product dimensions will help you to identify the most appropriate products.

One other aspect of the product merits examination, specifically in relation to the marketing of health behavior. The use of threatening messages generally is not effective in encouraging risk behavior change. Focus your campaign on the positive aspects of the product. For example, in regard to weight loss, emphasize the benefits of feeling better, looking better, having greater self-esteem, having more energy, and so on, instead of reducing the risk of heart disease. We cannot emphasize strongly enough that the entire approach of your health promotion program must be up-beat and positive, highlighting the benefits that people really want. Health does not "sell" as well as other values such as appearance.

The price of the product is an equally important consideration. Price, of course, refers to more than financial cost. It includes psychological costs and the time and effort required to attain the product. Even if the two alternative smoking programs already mentioned are equal in financial cost (either to the individual employee or to the organization), they differ in the time and effort required. The behavioral program requires more of both.

Place refers to product accessibility: how you will make your health promotion products available to the target market. Offering programs at the workplace itself makes them much more accessible than if they are offered off-site, for example, at local community facilities. It should be recognized, however, that "place" refers to physical location only very generally as one of many ways in which product accessibility can be maximized. Offering programs in healthy nutrition and diet may be enhanced if you collaborate with the company food vendor to identify low-calorie, low-fat entrees on the menu. In so doing, you maximize the likelihood that the product, eating behavior change, will be adopted.

A similar issue arises in any workplace health promotion that offers its services on company time: the willingness of managers to release their employees to participate. If a desirable product is inaccessible, it will not "sell." Some of our recent research (Sloan and Gruman, 1987) has indicated that supportiveness of the manager is as important a determinant of participation in a workplace health promotion program as the traditional health factors of perceived vulnerability to disease, satisfaction with health, age, and sex.

Finally, promotion refers to the tools of persuasive communication: advertising, personal appeals by prestigious people, incentives, and so on, all designed to "sell the product."

Problem Definition. A critical aspect of any marketing strategy is to specify precisely what problem is to be addressed. Kotler (1984) has pointed out that early attempts to address the smoking problem in the United States focused on increasing awareness of the relationship between smoking and disease. However, it became apparent that merely increasing awareness of this relationship was not sufficient. Most smokers, as surveys have indicated, would like to quit but do not know how to do so. Therefore, although the national efforts to increase awareness of the dangers of smoking have been enormously successful, the problem at hand goes well beyond awareness: It requires attention to behavior change, too.

A similar situation exists in the case of social marketing for a low-fat, low-cholesterol diet. Many workplaces offer programs in such "heart-healthy" diets. Although it is highly desirable to promote such eating habits, you always must consider a potential impediment to implementation of such a diet: Are the people who come to the program the same ones who actually shop and cook in their families? If not, then the problem is different: You must convince the husbands or wives who do the shopping and cooking (as well as the employees themselves) of the virtue of such a diet.

Identify and Understand the Target Market. This suggests another important aspect of social marketing of health promotion: segmentation and identification of the target markets and analysis of each different market. Within a workplace, especially a large one, many different subpopulations exist, each with different characteristics, interests, and health habits. Blue-collar and white-collar employees differ from each other in regard to many health behaviors—for example, smoking is more prevalent among blue-collar workers. And different ethnic groups have different dietary habits, some of which are less healthy than others.

In marketing a health promotion program in the workplace, it is important to understand these differences and plan accordingly. To encourage healthy behaviors, you must understand the different attitudes and beliefs that underlie poor health habits. The health promotion program must provide viable alternative behaviors that address these attitudes and beliefs. Thus, it becomes necessary to know what products will appeal to your target audience. An example from the automobile industry underscores this issue: Prior to serving as secretary of defense in the Kennedy administration, Robert McNamara was the chief executive officer at Ford Motor Company. In his tenure there, McNamara was said to have favored advertising the impressive safety features of their cars. In contrast, General Motors' advertising strategy focused on the flashy qualities of GM cars. As people have said of these respective strategies, "McNamara was selling safety and Chevy was selling cars." The moral: Know your target populations and what each wants.

In this regard, your organizational analysis should provide you with information relevant to marketing your program. Specifically, the survey of employee health habits and program preferences will direct your activities appropriately.

Marketing Activities

General Marketing Considerations. Marketing, as this section demonstrates, is more than mere advertising. It refers to identification and analysis of the target populations, examination of those factors that both facilitate and impede acceptance of the product, development of a strategy to "sell" the product, and finally, an evaluation to determine the effectiveness of the strategy.

The organizational analysis described in Chapter Five is similar to market research in that it attempts to describe the target audience as completely as possible relative to the health-related products to be sold. Using the information from the analysis as well as your own knowledge of how the organization operates, your overall objective is to "position your product," that is, to envision how the health promotion program can best excite the interests and meet the perceived needs of its consumers so that they will want to participate in it. As you formulate your plans, consider some of the following:

- For many people, "health at work" and "wellness" basically mean exercise or smoking activities. If your program includes more than these two elements, ways of presenting a more-rounded picture will be important.
- Every organization has its own tolerance for humor. Safeway Bakery Division's "Buns on the Run" program may not be considered acceptable at a more staid organization. The use of humor may be important in the creation of an energetic, fun image for the program, but it cannot (1) violate the prevailing cultural norms of the organization or (2) undermine the seriousness of the health issue and the referent power of the program.
- The level of formality in written health promotion communications also should be considered. Because any individual behavior change is a personal matter, the tendency is to adopt a tone that is less formal than that normally used in a workplace setting. Being sensitive to the limits of the informality is as important as being informal in the first place.
- Depending on the size of your program and the number of people who will be working on marketing the program, you may want to develop written guidelines to ensure consistency over time.

Talks About the Health Promotion Program.   Once you have designed the program, have a timeline for activities, and have all the participation details worked out, it is time to begin program outreach. Basically, this means that you (and your staff, if you have one) begin to inform all appropriate people of the program. One of the most efficient ways to do this is to (1) develop a concise, effective, spoken presentation of the program's most important points, including its rationale and structure; and (2) search out as many opportunities as possible to present this talk to groups. From the point of view of your own good public relations, it is preferable to arrange for space on the agendas of upper-management meetings first, both to inform and to elicit support, and work your way through other groups with a high degree of referent power, for example, unions, QWL organizations, finally reaching employee groups in general. If your presentation is concise, there is no need to call a meeting specifically for it; in fact, presenting the program at a regular work-group meeting gives a message that the health promotion program is an integral part of the work environment.

The following is a sample outline for a fifteen-minute presentation that, with modifications in emphasis, is appropriate for any group in the workplace.

I. Introduce yourself and your relation to the program.
II. Define idea of "wellness" and its active relationship to health.
    A. The margin of health that is affected by behavior/workplace climate
    B. Actions that promote or reduce health and health risk
III. The economics of health at work—Why here?
    A. Cost of poor health to the company and its effect on profits, which affect all employees
    B. Mention prominent upper-management (and union, if appropriate) supporters and why they are supporters.
VI. Overall structure of program
    A. What are the best offerings? How does the program work?
    B. Available to whom? When? Under what circumstances?
VII. Specific details
    A. Schedule of planned events, and so forth
    B. Questions

Talks like these eat up your time and may become boring, particularly if you have a large employee population and must give the same talk thirty or forty times. However, your interest, enthusiasm, and assurance that the program will be valuable for employees is essential for the kind of participation a program requires to be well-received and useful in the long run. In this capacity, you are a salesperson.

Developing a Program Logo.   The early stage of marketing is the time during which you need to create a name and a symbol for the program. A health promotion program needs a visible, identifiable, and compelling symbol that will (1) provide visible continuity between the diverse health promotion activities and (2) increase in potency over time as health concerns increase in their legitimacy in the work environment. Developing the symbol/title at this point may seem like putting the cart before the horse, but it is important that any health promotion initiative be launched with the intent of continuity and stability that a logo symbolizes.

We already have suggested some ways to create the name and symbol:

1.   sponsor an all-employee contest
2.   have the Employee Health Promotion Committee develop it
3.   involve an internal or external creative/graphic/art department

The logo should be clear and reproducible and should reflect the spirit of your program. Once the logo has been chosen, get a print rendering and have camera-ready copy made in a number of sizes. Be prepared to have the logo appear on every piece of print material related to the program.

Using the Media.   After using this information to develop a marketing plan for the health promotion program, it is time to consider how to get the word out. You should have compiled a list of all internal organs of publicity (union newsletter, bulletin boards, company paper, weekly newsletter of announcements, public address announcements, and so forth) during the analysis phase. Take time now to investigate each one of the resources on your list. You need to know how to get things printed or announced by each, who needs to approve the copy, what the deadlines are, how long notices can stay on bulletin boards, building policies for posting of signs of various sorts, and any other relevant policies. Since you will be using each of these avenues of publicity for promoting the program, you will have to meet their deadlines and follow their procedures. If you have not done so already, add the local community newspapers to your list and plan to send them information about your program whenever appropriate. Investigate company policies on this matter. Many companies carefully scrutinize material released to the general public.

Selection of Vendors and Consultants

Workplace health promotion programs can make use of the services of many different types of vendors and consultants. First, consultants can be hired to assist in overall program development. Consultants who specialize in program evaluation may also be required. Finally, you may wish to hire vendors to deliver specific program components, for example, a stress management training program or a heart-healthy eating course.

Hiring of outside vendors for services is not an organizational exigency that has arisen only for health promotion programs. Organizations are accustomed to seeking outside help in such diverse areas as computer systems, finance, marketing, management training, and facilities development. The criteria used for selection of vendors in these areas should be employed in selection of vendors for health promotion services.

Seek Multiple Bids

Solicit bids from many area vendors. Many such vendors will make themselves known to you, but others can be found through hospitals, local health agencies, community colleges, and university extension services. You should be sure that you have a wide choice about the appropriate person for the job.

Previous Experience

Obviously, you will want to know about a vendor's previous experience specifically related to the delivery of the services you wish. If, for example, you want to hire someone either to de-velop and/or deliver programs in stress management, ask for a list of the vendor's previous clients. Do not hesitate to contact some of these clients to ask about their impressions of the ven-dor and the quality of the program delivered. You will discover that some vendors' reputations on paper may not match their reputations among clients. You may discover that the client list includes entries with whom the vendor has had only fleeting contact. A colleague of ours, the director of training at a metro-politan New York public service organization, has complained that virtually every vendor he sees claims as former clients both IBM and AT&T. When you see such huge organizations on a vendor's client list, find out precisely what services were deliv-ered and who actually delivered them. You may discover that the vendor's relationship with the client was quite tangential.

Don't hesitate to ask hard questions: "What would you do if half the class dropped out after the second session?" "How will you handle absenteeism?" "We have a number of 'resident experts' on this topic; how will you handle them in class?" "What would you do about someone who came to class reli-giously but never followed instructions or did assignments?" "What is your philosophy about how people learn?"

Professional Training

Look at the consultant's professional training. It is not neces-sary to have a graduate degree from a major university to be a competent vendor of health promotion services, but it may re-quire more than an undergraduate degree in physical education. Of course, even those with advanced and appropriate degrees from prestigious institutions may be miserable consultants, just as those with few impressive professional credentials may be ter-rific. Nevertheless, you should ask for information on training and experience; evaluate it in combination with reports from previous clients.

Also recognize that having a degree in a specific field re-lated to health promotion does not necessarily mean that the vendor is qualified in other areas. Having a degree in exercise physiology may mean that a vendor is qualified to conduct an exercise fitness program. It does not automatically mean the vendor is qualified to run an entire health promotion program. Many companies, erroneously identifying health promotion with physical fitness, have hired people with such qualifications to do just this. Health promotion is an organizational activity, and it requires skills and expertise beyond the physiology of exercise.

Conclusion

The management of a workplace health promotion program is not fundamentally different from that of any other innovation in an organization. Having a successful marketing strategy, an effective health promotion committee, and a well-functioning organization will enhance the likelihood of success. Program awareness within the organization is likely to increase incrementally, with each successive activity contributing. Since the program will depend on employee participation, it is essential that the program's image be attractive, compelling, and visible. Both your marketing strategy and health promotion committee will have a hand in this process.

A key aspect of your program management is sensitivity. Success will depend on the program's acceptance by the workplace population. Acceptance, in turn, will come only if the employees feel that the program addresses their real concerns.

11

Helping Individuals Change Their Behavior

Health promotion programs designed to encourage positive health behavior change among individuals have been, throughout the relatively brief history of the field, the most common type of interventions practiced in the workplace. In Chapter Three, we suggested that this approach imposes limitations on the effectiveness of reaching larger health promotion goals. Nevertheless, encouraging changes in the health behavior of employees is important and should remain part of workplace health promotion program plans. Frequently, however, programs that address this level of intervention are designed without consideration of how people learn and change behaviors that are bound firmly by habit and tradition (for example, eating patterns, smoking, levels of physical activity, and so on). This has resulted in wasted effort and money. The program fails twice: Little behavior change occurs and the program receives poor publicity.

In this chapter, a basic model of health behavior change in individuals is described. Although each aspect of this model is accompanied by examples, please recognize that many of the tools presented in Chapter Nine are appropriate to this level of workplace health promotion. For example, the discussion of workshops and skills training or of ongoing programs refers to activities undertaken to promote individual health behavior change. The same is true of the use of print and other materials. The framework we present here provides the rationale for use of these tools.

This chapter presents a discussion of workplace health promotion as it is practiced most typically in the United States. It can serve an orienting function for practitioners and represents the first of three different levels of workplace health promotion. (Chapters Twelve and Thirteen address the other two levels.)

Health Promotion Goals for Individuals

The goals of workplace health promotion can be served best when both risk-related behaviors *and* illness behaviors are considered appropriate targets for intervention. Determinants of these behaviors fall into two categories: (1) those over which individuals have some control, for example, smoking, weight control, and learning coping skills for stress management and (2) those over which individuals can exercise relatively little control such as aspects of the physical and psychosocial work environment. The universe of health promotion activities directed toward individuals should include only the former.

With this as the arena for intervention, the health promotion goals for individuals are simply that individuals (1) recognize the extent and limits of responsibility for their own health and (2) that they practice the recommended behaviors within those limits. These two goals are deceptively simple; arriving at point 1 is a major undertaking and is a necessary precursor to moving from point 1 to point 2, a process that is a major topic of inquiry in the social sciences. A number of theoretical models have been proposed to explain how this process takes place, among them the Health Belief Model (Rosenstock, 1974), Social Learning Theory (Rotter, Chance, and Phares, 1972), attitude-behavior theory as articulated by Fishbein (Fishbein and Ajzen, 1975), and Triandis's theory of social behavior (Triandis, 1977, 1980). Each of these models has its own strengths and weaknesses, and none is markedly more adequate than the others in explaining the process of promoting individual health behavior change in the workplace. Nevertheless, each model has something to offer to workplace health promotion. What follows is a description of an optimal process for facilitating individual behavior change, distilled from some of the most useful elements of each model. This process begins with establishing a framework of information and ideas within which the individual finds behavior change an interesting and meaningful consideration. It then moves toward the acquisition of new and personally relevant information and skills and continues, hopefully, indefinitely in the maintenance of the new behavior(s). The process can be explained by considering the cognitive tasks to be accomplished by the individual at each stage. From the individual's point of view, these stages are:

1. "I understand the general relationship between people's behavior and their health."
2. "There are things that I do that affect my health negatively and positively."
3. "I want to become healthier, and I have a plan that will help me to do so over time."
4. "I know how to make the changes in my behavior that will help me to reach my goal."
5. "The changes I have made are a normal part of my life."

Recognizing That Behavior Influences Health

Addressing this first step is often overlooked in the health promotion process, probably because it is one of the central assumptions of the process and, as such, is taken for granted. In fact, current trends in the media and the public interest in health have made this relationship more salient in recent years, but it is still not a widely endorsed belief in many communities. Nor do many individuals have an accurate understanding of the relationship between behavior and health. The importance of introducing this idea as the first step in behavior change lies in the establishment of a causal framework in which it makes sense to be concerned about your own behavior and to seek further information.

At this first point in the process, people need to understand that there are both positive and negative health consequences of their behavior and that those consequences can occur now as well as in the future. Encouraging understanding of the generic link, as opposed to the specifics of what each individual should do about it, is the program's initial objective. It is also important for the limitations of this link to be clearly delineated: There are many determinants of health over which an individual has little or no control and failure to recognize them sets the stage for self-blame and victim-blaming.

Part of any discussion of this idea involves the introduction of the concept of risk, since the relevant poor health behaviors do not *cause* disease but only confer increased risk of future disease. Although we discuss this issue in relation to health risk appraisals, we raise it here because of its relevance to behavior change. For the most part, people do not understand probability very well and therefore find it difficult to grasp complex presentations of risk, risk factors, and risk behaviors. Nevertheless, since there must be some understanding of the assumptions of risk to understand the relationship between your own behavior and health, the simplest presentation of this idea will be the most compelling and effective.

The introduction of this idea to the workplace population is the first step in the implementation of any health promotion program emphasizing behavior change. Without it, the program will be attractive only to the already committed, those employees who already understand and act on the relationship between health and behavior. The most straightforward way of introducing the idea is to make it an important piece of the initial marketing plan for the program: Publicize not only what the new program is but also, more importantly, what the rationale behind it is. This basic idea should occupy a substantial part of any newspaper articles, information pamphlets, and promotional talks to both management and employees. It should be a part of any public relations activity of the program and should be repeated in brief during all employee contacts with the program. The following are some examples of how different companies have introduced this idea:

- Scherer Brothers Lumber Company, whose innovative programs we have discussed previously, conducted a four-week educational exercise throughout the organization to explain the idea of wellness and the process of health promotion and to assess the needs and interests of the population. This was accomplished through handouts and surveys and introduced the individual health risk appraisals to the employees.
- Participation in AT&T's Total Life Concept begins with an hour-and-a-half presentation orienting employees to the idea of health promotion. During this meeting, which is held on work time, members of the health promotion staff present different aspects of health promotion, and a twenty-minute videotape is shown. This videotape features participants who have been active in the program speaking about their experiences in making long-term behavioral changes. In addition, the TLC program uses two pamphlets for internal publicity. The first pamphlet introduces the ideas of health promotion and establishes a rationale for concern about the relationship between health and behavior in the workplace. The second pamphlet describes the program. Both pamphlets are used extensively in the initial presentation of TLC to new employee groups and managers.

Personalizing the Link Between Behavior and Health

The second stage of moving individuals toward behavior change is to facilitate the personalizing of the idea that there is a relationship between health and behavior. Each individual thus develops a picture of personal modifiable and unmodifiable risk factors and discovers what actions can be taken to reduce or control these risks. One of the most efficient ways of reaching this stage is through the use of some form of health risk appraisal. Although we have been critical of HRAs, these instruments, if used appropriately and with professional guidance, can be helpful in illustrating the connection between specific behaviors and health. For more information, refer to Resource E.

As a supplement to the administration of a health risk appraisal, many health promotion programs provide biometric measurement of such health indicators as height and weight, blood pressure and heart rate, and serum cholesterol and trigly- cerides. By collecting this biometric information, the relation- ship between each individual's health behavior and health char- acteristics is personalized even further. Some of the variations in what part HRAs play in the program are listed:

- There are differences in how employees are channeled into the risk appraisal process, for example, as a requirement be- fore participating in other health promotion activities (Pills- bury's "Be Your Best," AT&T Communications' "Total Life Concept"), through annual or semi-annual medical examinations that are considered part of the program (Blue Cross and Blue Shield of Indiana), or through choosing to complete a health risk appraisal as one of a number of differ- ent health promotion activities available through a program (Prudential Insurance Company).
- There are major differences between companies in the extent of biometric testing that accompanies or supports the admin- istration of the HRA. In companies where there is an on-site medical facility, extensive screening is often a part of the process. For example, at Kimberly-Clark, the screening in- cludes a computerized medical history, hypertension, glau- coma, hearing and vision screening, back strength and flexi- bility, and laboratory tests to measure hemoglobin, blood sugar, cholesterol, triglycerides, liver function, pulmonary function, and body density. In smaller companies and in companies where the health promotion program is located in a department other than the medical department, minimal screening is often a part of the process (height, weight, and blood pressure), and the emphasis is placed on behavioral self-assessment.

Creating a Plan

During this stage of the individual health promotion process, the goal is to guide individuals to use the information about their own personal risk factors, as well as their knowledge and experience of themselves, to create a long-range plan for good health. Once again, this step is frequently overlooked in the health promotion process, but it is one that is critical (1) to maximize the value of the information and ideas presented to this point, (2) to maximize the probability that the action taken in response to this information will be substantive and sustained, (3) to differentiate this attempt to change health behaviors from other less formal attempts, (4) to help individuals to monitor their progress in reaching their larger goals, and (5) to highlight personally relevant health information.

Questions an individual will need to consider when formulating this long-term plan are as follows:

- What changes do I need to make in my behavior?
- How urgent are these changes? What is the most important thing I can do? What is the second most important?
- How willing am I to make these changes? What is my personal history with trying to make these changes?
- What are the obstacles to my success? What factors contribute to the probability of my success?
- What new skills and information do I need to acquire to make each change?
- What kind of support will I have from my family, friends, and work community in sustaining these changes?

The plan that results from the consideration of these questions should direct the individual to attempt one major behavioral change at a time, with each major change divided into more manageable tasks that can yield short-term successes and, as a result, increased confidence in the ability to make behavior change. The ability to succeed in health-related behavior change is critical and every effort should be made to maximize the individual's likelihood of success. Here are some organizational examples of this phase of the process:

- At the Pillsbury Company, once employees have received the results of the initial screening and risk assessment, they attend a workshop on motivation and goal setting. This workshop is followed by workshops on other health topics.

- At Johnson & Johnson companies, on completion of the company health screen, employees are scheduled for a life-style seminar during which the "Live for Life" program is introduced. The results of the health screen provide the basis for taking action through participation in program activities. The three-hour seminar is offered on company time to groups of fifty employees each.
- The Phillips Petroleum "Livingwell" program includes an initial interview for all new employees to develop a personal health profile. Employees, spouses, dependents, and retirees are all eligible for membership in the program.
- The "Good Life" program at Southwestern Bell places heavy emphasis on these first three stages of the individual behavior change process, with particular attention to self-assessment and planning. Participants undergo minimal biometric measurement to enable accurate completion of a simple risk assessment instrument as part of a carefully designed workbook that takes a step-by-step approach to motivation for behavior change, goal setting, and specific planning.

Initiating Behavior Change

This fourth stage is the most familiar one in the traditional health promotion process. In this stage, individuals are given the encouragement and/or opportunity to act on their personal health promotion plan. Through the planning process, individuals have identified discrete and manageable tasks. The health promotion program must recognize the need for incremental learning to accomplish these tasks and for presenting opportunities to learn new skills, to practice them, and to receive feedback on the degree of success. Additionally, attention should be paid to teaching participants to monitor their own progress. Examples of how different programs have approached this issue on a programwide basis are presented below:

- General Mills uses outside organizations to present activities or to train General Mills staff to deliver their own programs. Some examples include using the American Cancer Society's

Quit Smoking program and the American Heart Association's Heart Saver program for basic life support.

- Safeco's Health Action Plan for Everyone (SHAPE) provides an organized informational program without any seminars or classes. Following the completion of a health quality profile, self-assessment questionnaire, and a how-to notebook on lifestyle change, participants receive a monthly newsletter that offers tips and encouragement on health-related topics.

- A different and unusual approach to individual behavior change was taken by three banks in the Williamsport, Pennsylvania, area (Williamsport National Bank, Northern Central Bank, and the Commonwealth Bank). With assistance from specialists from the University of Pennsylvania, a twelve-week weight-loss competition among the three banks was organized. The combined weight loss for the employees of each bank was displayed and updated on a weekly basis on a thermometer-like chart placed prominently in each workplace to increase the public incentive value of weight loss. So vigorous was the competition that some good-natured subversion was practiced: Toward the end of the contest, the organizer of one bank's efforts ordered dozens of doughnuts to be delivered to the two competitors! This highly innovative weight-loss competition proved to be as cost effective as it was innovative: At an extremely low cost, considerable weight was lost by employees in each of the participating banks. Of course, losing weight is only important if the weight loss is maintained, and research is continuing to monitor maintenance.

- The Bakery Division of Safeway Stores has combined programmatic efforts with modifications in company policies. Health promotion activities include the building and managing of a fitness facility; fitness assessments and prescriptions; a "laugh clinic" designed to get employees to take things (including themselves) less seriously and in so doing, to manage stress; classes in nutrition, weight training, and sports injuries; creation of a policy through which profits from cigarette machines in the smokers' lunch area paid for a color television in the nonsmokers' lunch area (the smokers have only a black and white TV).

A Healthy Lifestyle

The final step of the individual change process is for the individuals to build the new behaviors and attitudes into their daily routine. It is at this point that the individually directed efforts of health promotion most directly intersect with the other levels of intervention (organization and policy change). As we have pointed out before, it is unrealistic to expect that individuals will maintain new and positive health behaviors in an environment where these behaviors are neither practiced regularly nor supported by authority figures and policy. This point of intersection between the individual and organizational change efforts is critical to the success of any health promotion program that encourages health behavior change. Consider the following examples of how this has been done in companies across the country:

- Blue Cross and Blue Shield of Indiana provides maintenance and follow-up sessions that continue for a year beyond the initial entry into the program. Participants are telephoned periodically to check on progress and to encourage continued change, groups are encouraged to meet on their own, and some participants are rescreened at six-month and yearly intervals.
- In the Pillsbury "Be Your Best" program, action teams are formed by alumni of specific health promotion programs who wish to stay involved with others in the pursuit of continued lifestyle change. Typically, teams form around activities, such as the walking team, the weight control team, and so on.

Conclusion

The design of health promotion interventions directed at individuals has a great deal to do with the kind of management support and level of resources available. The more there is of each, the greater the access is to the employees, and the wider is the range of tools with which to reach them. However, the design of the individual behavior change interventions should be carefully matched to the prevailing workplace cultures and attitudes.

Always remember that individual health behavior change is best accomplished with a "soft-sell" approach. It is never permissible to force an employee to join a weight control or stress reduction group. Management concern with individual health behavior can be seen just as easily by employees as intrusive, patronizing, and violating privacy as it can be seen as supportive, positive, and affirmative. Inasmuch as the health promotion program is a true expression of these latter concerns, efforts must be made to infuse each of these stages of the individual change process with a strong sense of the individual employee's privacy, autonomy, and integrity.

12

Changing the Organization's Health-Related Policies

The thrust of this book has been to demonstrate that workplace health promotion, at its best, is an organizationwide effort. It involves not only individual health behavior change on the part of employees but also normative and cultural changes at the organizational level. Nevertheless, many or even most programs take a more limited approach and attempt to promote health in the organization only by encouraging individual employees, their spouses and dependents, and retirees to make health behavior changes. Characteristic of this approach is the need for the individual employee to be sufficiently motivated to make the necessary lifestyle changes. Success of programs depends on their ability to generate such motivation.

This dependence of traditional health promotion on individual behavior change leads to certain limitations. Because of the reliance on individual motivation, attrition rates tend to be higher than we would like: People often tend to lose interest in health promotion programs and drop out. Changing old health habits and developing and maintaining new ones is difficult and requires sustained motivation.

These facts pertain, of course, only to those people who actually are sufficiently interested to participate in the first place. A large fraction of the workplace population will never participate at all, often because they are not sufficiently moti-vated to take even the first step of enrollment in a program. Of course, since workplace health promotion involves not only the delivery of programs but also efforts to change the organiza-tional culture in regard to health, even nonparticipants will be exposed. Nevertheless, one of the most serious problems en-countered in establishing an effective workplace health promo-tion program is the development and sustaining of interest and motivation in the education and behavior change programs that constitute a major fraction of the health promotion program. This is a formidable problem.

Many organizations, recognizing the magnitude of this problem, have attempted to supplement their health promotion programs with approaches that depend less heavily on individual motivation to make health behavior changes. These alternatives involve changes in organizational policies. Their focus, although organizational, is still on changing the health behaviors of the individual employees, but the way in which they attempt to do this differs from the ways we have discussed so far.

Table 1 presents a conceptual organization of these ap-proaches. The table describes a continuum of workplace health promotion activities, from programs that depend almost entire-ly on individual motivation (the traditional programs of behav-ior change) to policies regulating behavior (but still depending, to a certain degree, on motivation to comply with policy), to policies that call for the elimination of certain things from the

Table 1. Continuum of the Reliance of Workplace Health Promotion Programs on Individual Motivation.

Traditional workplace health promotion	Policies mandating or prohibiting certain be-haviors	Policies that control risk behavior by eliminating things from workplace
High	Moderate	Low

Dependence on individual motivation

workplace environment, for example, foods from the cafeteria that are associated with risks to health. The latter approach relies on the least amount of individual motivation for health behavior change.

As this continuum suggests, supplemental approaches to traditional workplace health promotion programs move away from reliance on individual motivation. Policy change is a first step in this direction. Another step, organizational change, is the topic of Chapter Thirteen.

The Role of the Health Promotion Manager

Organizational health policy change, by definition, is an activity that transcends the domain of the health promotion manager. Ultimately, policy decisions will be made by upper management. However, the health promotion manager, by virtue of knowledge of the dynamics of health behavior change, has expertise to lend to policy development. Accordingly, the manager's role is somewhat different in this arena.

Policy change should never be the product of a single individual. A primary responsibility of the health promotion manager, then, is to provide advice to those who ultimately will make decisions on the need for new policy and on how to develop and implement it. A related responsibility is to serve on the policymaking body and to serve as an advocate for change. The following sections are written with this in mind.

Policies Regulating Health-Related Behavior

One obvious solution to the problems associated with reliance on individual motivation is to create policies making certain health behaviors either mandatory or unacceptable. In the health promotion literature, such approaches are referred to as "active control of health behavior." Although the phrase "control of behavior" may seem ominous, most organizations exercise this control already through their safety departments. One typical example of such regulations is the requirement that employees wear protective masks or clothing in hazardous areas of the workplace. Such policies have been around for a long time, well before the advent of health promotion programs. Although these requirements may seem burdensome, there is general agreement regarding their appropriateness. Rarely are objections to such examples of "controlling health behavior" raised.

More recently, many organizations have implemented other regulatory health promotion policies in which a desirable health behavior is made mandatory while at work, for instance, requiring the use of safety belts during all driving on company time. As an example of the prohibition of an unacceptable health behavior, many companies recently have issued a variety of workplace smoking policies. These policies range from outright prohibition of smoking to restrictions of smoking to certain areas of a facility.

Note that these policies still deal with health-related behavior change. The problems associated with loss of interest and motivation are dealt with, not through the establishment of activities designed to sustain involvement and interest, but rather through regulations mandating change. Although this strategy may eliminate some problems, it may raise others. One such problem is the monitoring of the required or prohibited behavior. Another is the treatment of violators of the policy. A third, and possibly the most serious, is the limitation of such a strategy. Although it is relatively easy to conceive of regulations requiring the performance of certain health behaviors such as using safety belts or the prohibition of such behaviors as smoking, other health behaviors are less amenable to regulatory control. For example, modification of diet, control of stress, and increasing regular exercise are all difficult to manage through policies that directly regulate behavior. Finally, such policies may raise ethical questions regarding constraints on freedom and violations of privacy. We have dealt with these ethical issues previously.

Such considerations suggest that implementation of new policies in the workplace, in areas of health and elsewhere, be handled with great sensitivity and care. In contrast to a traditional program that offers to employees courses in interesting issues and is perceived as a desirable addition to their work environment, a policy change mandating certain behaviors or restricting others may be perceived as undesirable since it is restrictive and coercive. Responses to the recent passage of seat-belt laws in many states suggest just this resistance. Even though the behavior change mandated by these laws was perceived by the sponsors and state legislatures as desirable because it contributes to the health of drivers and passengers, a substantial fraction of the population in these states has actively resisted, complaining about infringements on personal freedom. So great has some of this resistance been that two states were forced to rescind their recently enacted seat-belt laws.

Considerations for Policies Regulating Health Behaviors in the Workplace

Interest in development of policies regulating health behaviors in the workplace should arise from the same broad concerns from which conventional health promotion programs arise: interest in improving the health of the organization and its workforce and through this improvement, enhancing the organization's productivity and cost efficiency. Accordingly, policy change should have a clear mandate from upper-level management.

   Implementation of new organizational policies that restrict the behavior of employees represents a major organizational change. Changes of this sort have long been the province of the field of organization development (OD), which has a great deal to say on the matter. Beckhard's work (1969) suggests that four conditions must be met when OD principles are applied to workplace health promotion:

1.   First, no policy change is possible without full commitment of the top management of the organization.
2.   The change must be planned, involve the entire system, and be based on a careful assessment.
3.   The change must be related to the mission of the health promotion effort and to the overall organization's mission.

4.   The policy change should be the product of a long-term effort.

   Drawing on Beckhard's work in OD and on the experience of many organizations in health promotion policy development, we present case examples that illustrate the major considerations. Because one of the greatest opportunities for policy change lies in the area of smoking, the cases we present are about smoking policy.

Development of a Model Smoking Policy. On average, one-third of adult Americans smoke cigarettes. Many of these smokers have tried to quit and have failed. Many others would like to quit, but fear that they will fail. Surveys repeatedly indicate that a high fraction of smokers expresses the desire to quit. Even though this is the case, the development of a smoking policy that imposes restrictions on smokers will be met with resistance. All efforts toward policy development must recognize that this resistance will surface and, in fact, should encourage expression of this resistance. For this reason, policy development and implementation is affected by certain considerations:

1.   As Beckhard and others have suggested, there must be a mandate from top management. Without such a mandate, the policy is doomed to failure.
2.   Smoking policy development and implementation should be the responsibility of a committee. Representatives should be selected from different levels and divisions within the organization. Most importantly, the committee should include both smokers and nonsmokers. Nothing is likely to provoke greater resistance to policy implementation than a smoking committee composed entirely of nonsmokers. Whenever possible, include employees with stature among others in the whole organization or at least in a specific division of the organization. Policies developed by those who do not command the respect of others are likely to fail.
3.   The implementation of an organizationwide policy may

be enhanced if it is preceded by an ongoing media and education campaign aimed at changing the health norms of the organization. This campaign may be specific to smoking or more general and include smoking as one of many health behaviors as its focus. Approaches to such campaigns have been examined in Chapter Nine.

4. You may want to have the health promotion committee survey the employee population on smoking at work. Ask for opinions about restrictions on smoking in general and in regard to specific areas in the workplace. Also ask about the extent to which employees are bothered by the smoke of others. Of course, you should ask about the smoking status of the employee. Use this opportunity to ask smokers of their interest in smoking cessation information and programs and how they would respond to restrictions on smoking. Information gathered in this way, like all health promotion data from individual employees, must be strictly confidential.

5. Consult the union leadership from the beginning. Failure to do this can condemn the policy even before it is implemented. Although unions may express concerns about the imposition of restrictive policies on their members, they are concerned also about the spiraling cost of health care and the part that smoking plays in that spiral. Unions should be regarded as assets, not impediments, in the development of a smoking policy.

6. Recognize that policy change is a long-term effort. In fact, the committee may decide that the policy should be phased in. Although the ultimate goal is a "smoke-free" workplace, there may be intermediate stages in which smoking still will be permitted in restricted form. Set a time-line for policy development and implementation.

7. Properly prepare the organization for the coming change. Develop a schedule of communications for conveying information on the policy to employees. Include posters and signs in your communications effort. Make certain that supervisors know what will be expected of them in policy implementation. This requirement will be easier to

fulfill if supervisors have been represented on the policy committee.

8. Always provide some kind of opportunity to help smokers stop in combination with the development of a smoking policy. You may provide smoking education seminars, distribute hints on how to stop smoking, list smoking cessation clinics in the area, or offer a smoking cessation program in-house. The goal of such a policy is to encourage employees to stop smoking, not merely to move it from the workplace to the parking lot. Many employees who smoke will welcome the implementation of a smoking policy; it will help them in developing further resolve to quit. Accordingly, the moment for smoking cessation programs is propitious.

9. Consistent with the overall emphasis of health promotion on changing the organizational culture in regard to health and work, recognize *nonsmoking* as the norm.

10. Be prepared for conflicts between smokers and nonsmokers. Have procedural guidelines for written submission of complaints from employees. Management should empower some division within the organization to resolve such conflicts. This may be the personnel department, the medical department, or it may be the responsibility of the individual manager(s) of the disputants. Remember, however, that since the objective of a smoking policy is to make nonsmoking the norm, the preferences of the nonsmoking employees should take precedence over those of the smokers if a dispute cannot be resolved.

11. Determine what existing laws and regulations already exist in your local area. Many states, counties, and municipalities have ordinances regarding smoking.

12. The policy should be accompanied by statements regarding enforcement.

13. The policy's intent, to create a healthier, smoke-free workplace, should be clearly stated, but the policy should be sufficiently flexible to permit modification for unique situations.

14. Consider using some kind of incentives to encourage em-

ployees to quit smoking. Such incentives may include money (Speedcall Corporation), gym clothing (Johnson & Johnson), time off from work to participate in the cessation program (AT&T Communications), reductions in life insurance premiums (Provident Indemnity Life Insurance Company), and lottery tickets for each month of abstinence (Dow Chemical). Other incentives include certificates, coffee mugs, tee shirts, and so on.

Because each organization is different, the shape of the smoking policy will differ from company to company. But these general considerations will pertain for organizations of all types: large or small, high tech or manufacturing, established or developing. Whether your company's policy prohibits smoking in the workplace altogether or restricts it only in certain areas depends on the physical structure of the workplace, the desires of the employees, the resolve of management, and interest of the health promotion committee. The following are some examples of smoking policies.

Case Example of Smoking Policy 1: The Boeing Company.   "After careful review and consideration of all available information, The Boeing Company has decided to take additional positive steps toward providing a smoke-free working environment for all employees. While no absolute date has yet been set for establishing a total prohibition on employee smoking, it is the intent of the Company ultimately to do so and in the meantime to implement the following:

The following areas are designated as no-smoking areas:

a. restrooms
b. lobbies
c. classrooms
d. auditoriums
e. hallways and stairways
f. medical facilities
g. elevators
h. libraries

i. computer rooms
j. areas in which smoking is prohibited for safety reasons or for protection of equipment

Employees in an office workplace may designate their assigned 'immediate workplace' as a no-smoking area and post it with an appropriate sign provided by the Company.

Provisions will be made for a contiguous no-smoking area of not less than two-thirds of the seating capacity and floor space in cafeterias and lunchrooms.

All prospective new hires will be informed of our ultimate no-smoking policy.

All smokers who wish to quit by enrolling in a Company-sponsored off-hour 'stop smoking' program in the next year may do so free of charge. A partial cost reimbursement program will also be made available soon for employees who may wish to attend one of the several other commercial types of 'stop smoking' programs.

Supervisors have a responsibility to see that the spirit and intent of this policy are complied with and to enlist the cooperation of employees in accomplishing this objective recognizing the needs and problems of both smokers and non-smokers. Supervisors should be alert to smoking problems and make every reasonable effort to minimize the effects of smoking on their employees such as may arise in the use of conference and meeting rooms."

Case Example of Smoking Policy 2: McGraw-Hill. **"What Is the Basic Policy?** To encourage employees not to smoke on company premises in order to reduce potential health hazards to smokers and nonsmokers.

What Are the Health Hazards of Tobacco Smoking? The United States Surgeon General states that the use of tobacco is harmful to smokers and nonsmokers and is a large factor in producing heart attacks, strokes, high blood pressure, emphysema, and several forms of cancer. According to the Surgeon General and other health authorities, nonsmokers can be affected by breathing the toxic products added to the air by smokers. Some employees are allergic or sensitive to smoke or find the odor objectionable.

What Procedures Does the Company Implement to Reduce Tobacco Smoking on Company Premises?

1. The company encourages no smoking in conference rooms, waiting rooms, and reception areas at all times, and in all business or group meetings.
2. The company encourages smokers to reduce tobacco smoking as much as possible.
3. Appropriate company signs encouraging employees not to smoke are prominently displayed in conference and meeting rooms and waiting and reception areas.
4. The company provides assistance to smokers to help them reduce or quit smoking.

What Procedures Should Managers Follow to Reduce Tobacco Smoking on Company Premises?

1. Managers should request that employees not smoke in conference rooms and other meeting places before, during, and after meetings.
2. Managers should make every attempt to separate nonsmokers from smokers when requested to the extent feasible.
3. Managers should encourage employees who smoke to attend smoking cessation programs.
4. If pipe or cigar smoke becomes objectionable to other employees, the manager must require the smoker to refrain from smoking cigars or pipes during working hours.
5. The manager should contact the medical director in New York or the personnel administrator if any problems arise relating to tobacco smoking.

What Procedures Does the Medical Department Implement to Reduce Tobacco Smoking on Company Premises? The Medical Department plans and conducts smoking cessation programs for smokers who want to quit and will conduct an educational program on the deleterious effects on health as stated by the United States Surgeon General and other health authorities."

Case Example of Smoking Policy 3: Provident Indemnity Life Insurance Company. "Provident Indemnity, in 1982, instituted a smoking cessation campaign to encourage employees to stop smoking. At that time, we added a statement to our employment application forms advising applicants that we have taken a strong stand against smoking.

We are a health care provider and originator of a nonsmoker reduced-premium life product. Our employees have received information from the American Council of Life Insurance and the Health Insurance Association of America Joint Council indicating a concerted effort in 1983 to eliminate smoking from the workplace of all health care providers and their client companies. Statistics have proven that, not only is smoking a health hazard to smokers and those around them but also is extremely costly to any employer in terms of absenteeism and productivity.

Smoking is not permitted in our buildings or on our grounds. Enrollment in our group insurance includes a signed statement that the employee is a smoker or a nonsmoker. Smokers are charged $5.77 weekly for group insurance, or the difference in premium between a smoker and a nonsmoker. We are proud of our health lifestyle theme and of being a leader among companies in the United States for our nonsmoking policy."

General Considerations Regarding Regulatory Policies

We have discussed the development of a company smoking policy in great detail, not because we believe that this is the most important policy change one can initiate, but rather because it illustrates most of the important points to consider in the development and implementation of any health-related policy change. Many of the same points discussed pertain to the development of an automobile safety-belt policy as well. Other health policies, perhaps developed by your organization's safety department, will have the same characteristics.

Passive Influence of Health-Related Behavior

Unlike policies that seek to promote health through active regulation of health behaviors, passive strategies seek to eliminate the conditions that permit unhealthy behaviors to emerge, to provide conditions that encourage healthy behavior, or both. Among the best examples of these strategies are elimination of cigarette vending machines from an organization's premises and modification of the offerings in the company cafeteria and vending machines or canteens. These changes greatly reduce the possibility that employees can engage in unhealthy behavior and they do so without relying on individual motivation to change behavior or to comply with regulations mandating behavior change. Note, however, that these passive approaches still deal with health promotion through modification of risk factor behavior. By eliminating cigarettes or heavily sugared foods from vending machines, it is probable that risk behaviors associated with these temptations are less likely to occur.

Passive strategies appear to have real but limited value in workplace health promotion programs. Many organizations have arranged with food service companies to modify significantly the quality of the food available through the company cafeteria and vending machines. If low-fat, low-cholesterol meals and snacks are the rule rather than the exception in company food facilities, it becomes easier to have an effect on the health behaviors of employees. Employees are less likely to behave in unhealthy ways because the conditions of the workplace make it difficult to do so.

Where else can the work environment be modified to make unhealthy behaviors less likely? Clearly, the elimination of cigarette vending machines is one step to take. In a different vein, not reimbursing out-of-pocket expenses for alcohol purchased for organizational functions is a modification of an aspect of work that can have a profound health effect.

Other policy changes that have an effect on health behavior of employees operate not by eliminating aspects of the environment associated with risk behaviors but, conversely, by adding things to the environment to make healthy behaviors more likely. One example of such a policy approach is the providing of showers and lockers for the use of employees who wish to participate in physical exercise programs or exercise on their own during the workday. Millard Manufacturing Company of Omaha, Nebraska, offers a morning snack of juice and muffins for its employees who have no unexcused absences for a week. This policy has had the effect of providing healthy snacks for employees and has produced the additional benefit of reduced absenteeism. The Boeing Company offers daily nutrition specials at prices 25 percent below the cost of the regular cafeteria fare. Incidentally, making available healthy choices in the company cafeteria can not only provide health benefits to employees, but it also can have a significant impact on the cafeteria's bottom line: When the Memorial Sloan-Kettering Cancer Center in New York introduced such a program, cafeteria business increased markedly.

Other health promotion policy changes are worthy of mention. Scherer Brothers Lumber Company has replaced its "sick day" policy with a "wellness pay" plan: By not being absent or late, employees can earn extra money. For example, yard employees can earn "$100 if no injuries require clinical attention; $100 if no injuries result in loss of company time; and a $100 bonus for each yard person if the company as a whole has a better claims experience than the year before" (Boal, 1984, p. 7). Developing a flex-time arrangement so that employees can make use of health promotion activities is another example of how a policy change can encourage healthy behaviors. A different kind of supplement to the work environment is to provide biomechanically sound chairs and other furniture to reduce the likelihood of musculoskeletal injuries. Policies such as these have their health promotion impact through encouragement of healthy behavior with no restrictions imposed on employees.

Although these passive approaches are powerful, they are also limited. You can distinguish between health behaviors of excess or deficit. The former involve behaviors in which something unhealthy is involved, for example, cigarettes. The latter involve the omission of a healthy behavior. Passive approaches are generally more effective in the case of health behaviors of excess, when the unhealthy aspect of the behavioral environment can be eliminated. In health behaviors of deficit, for instance, leading a sedentary life and failing to exercise, there is nothing unhealthy that can be removed from the behavioral environment. Therefore, the passive approach essentially operates either by providing incentives for healthy behavior or by removing impediments.

Passive approaches do not suffer from some of the drawbacks of more active attempts to regulate health behavior. The latter often arouse resistance because they are perceived to restrict the personal freedom of employees. In addition, they may arouse concerns of privacy and incursions by the company into areas that should be "off-limits." Passive approaches typically do not provoke such resistance. Elimination of cigarette vending machines from the workplace may arouse protests, but they will be muted compared to those directed at a new and restrictive automobile safety-belt policy. Removal of impediments to healthy behavior is often welcomed by employees.

This does not mean, however, that less care need be taken in the development and implementation of passive health policies. The same procedures as listed for active approaches should be followed. It is critical that the policy not be viewed as the idiosyncratic product of a single individual who does not represent the best interests of the workforce.

Policy Change in the Smaller Company

Throughout this book, we have focused on the case of the smaller company. As the example of the smoking policy of Provident Indemnity Life Insurance demonstrates, policy change is a vehicle for health promotion that is not limited by an organization's size. In fact, you might make the case that policy change is more likely to succeed in the smaller organization precisely because of its size: Many small companies are characterized by a "family" feeling among employees, and this feeling makes the establishment of an organizationwide policy easier. Moreover, adherence to new policies in such organizations is likely to be greater. One reason for this is that successful implementation of policy change requires, as indicated, that employees feel that they have been included in the development process. In Chapter Ten, we raised the importance of feelings of "authorship" in connection with program development. In the smaller company, the likelihood of employees having this feeling of authorship or empowerment is significantly greater. Many of the smaller companies we have been in contact with over the past several years have suggested just this.

Conclusion

Policy change is a powerful vehicle for promoting health behavior at work. But just as it is powerful, it has its limits and some of those limits are directly related to that power. Employees are understandably sensitive to restrictions on their activities, especially when they appear to be arbitrary, unilateral, and related to aspects of their private lives. Accordingly, the use of policy change as an approach to health behavior change must be tempered with sensitivity to these issues and most definitely should be embedded in a larger workplace health promotion effort that has the endorsement of the largest fraction of the workforce. This means that policy change should accompany the traditional behavior change approaches described in Chapter Eleven, increasing acceptance of policy change and demonstrating that the organization is broadly committed to a healthy workforce.

13

Beyond the Individual: Health Promotion Through Organizational Change

As is obvious, we are quite enthusiastic about the progress of workplace health promotion in organizations around the country. We expect that this emerging interest will continue to grow and that the confidence in workplace health promotion will prove to be justified in light of the benefits such programs ultimately will produce. Our enthusism is not without some qualification, however. When new programs of any sort become popular, there is a tendency for program development to rigidify as a single, accepted form of the program becomes established. Our concern is that as workplace health promotion becomes more and more popular, such a restricted vision of how these programs ought to operate will arise. In fact, we believe that this restriction has already begun to take place and, as a consequence, further evolution will be stunted.

Chapter Three presented a larger view of the problem addressed by workplace health promotion. Programs addressing this larger view are scarce. In this chapter, we will discuss how an established view of the field has evolved and how that view restricts further development and, consequently, restricts still greater benefits.

As it is typically implemented, workplace health promotion focuses on the development of a variety of programs all

characterized by a central assumption: that the way to reduce
the high incidence of costly disease among employees of an organization is to reduce the individual employee's risks for disease through modification of health behaviors. Reducing the
risk for coronary heart disease, for example, may be accomplished by changing the way we eat: by reducing consumption
of saturated fats and cholesterol-rich foods. Similarly, to reduce
the risk of cancer, the individual employee is trained to stop
smoking.

Thus, the focus of workplace health promotion programs
has been almost exclusively on the modification of individual
risk behavior. This, of course, makes perfect sense in light of
evidence presented earlier in the book. As stated, a sizable fraction of the incidence of chronic disease in the twentieth century
is attributable to the lifestyles of individuals. Therefore, by
modifying our lifestyles, we can reduce the incidence of disease.
We do not dispute this for a moment. What we question is
whether we should be satisfied with a set of programs that implicitly assumes that this is the *only* way in which risk of disease
can be reduced. Notice that the data indicate that a sizable fraction of the incidence of chronic disease is attributable to lifestyles such as getting too little exercise, eating improperly, not
managing stress well, and smoking. The data do not indicate
that *all* of the incidence of chronic disease is attributable to lifestyle. Our point is that workplace health promotion programs,
smug with success (although success has not been fully demonstrated yet), generally have not gone beyond attempts to modify the behavior of individuals in pursuit of still further reductions of chronic and costly disease.

Although the approaches discussed in the previous two
chapters are significantly different from each other in their reliance on individual motivation to promote behavior change,
most are still characterized by interest in modifications of the
traditional risk factor behaviors, whether by encouraging individuals to change health behaviors through education or by
regulation of health behaviors through policy change. Even policy change generally deals with modification of individual health
behavior. What we discuss in this chapter comes from an entirely

different domain, with no particular concern for control of traditional risk factors, whether behavioral or otherwise. We examine instead organizational factors that have an effect on health. At the outset, we must indicate that many of the issues raised may be familiar to those with experience in human resources management. What is novel is that these issues, in general, have not been discussed in relation to workplace health promotion.

The Effect of Organizational Factors on Employee Health

We propose that workplace health promotion can succeed most completely by going beyond programs that rely on the modification of health behaviors of individuals to examine and ultimately to modify organizational structures that also have been demonstrated to have a significant effect on employee health. Such an approach is consistent with the analysis presented in Chapter Three. To continue exclusive reliance on individually oriented approaches is especially striking in view of persuasive evidence linking such health outcomes as coronary heart disease, gastrointestinal disorders, and stress to organizational antecedents such as participation in decision making (Jackson, 1983), social interaction and support (House, 1981), pace of work and work overload (Frankenhaeuser and Gardell, 1976), and responsibility for others (Cobb, 1974). Failure to consider this alternative takes on even greater importance in light of the fact that virtually all behavioral methods of health promotion suffer from the problems described in Chapter Twelve: reduced motivation of participants, attrition, and maintenance of behavior change in the long term. Precisely because the modification of organizational work design or climate does not rely on individual motivation and/or health-related behavior change, it appears to be a promising supplement to the existing array of behaviorally oriented health promotion programs delivered in the workplace.

These considerations suggest an addition to Table 1 presented in Chapter Twelve. That table described the dependence on individual motivation of health promotion programs based on health behavior change and policy change in relation to health behavior. But all of the activities along this continuum, from traditional workplace health promotion to policy change that controls risk by eliminating things from the environment, still rely on health behavior change to reduce risk of illness. Modifications of the work environment bypass health behavior altogether and, as such, are completely independent of individual motivation. Table 1 describes this addition.

Table 1.   Continuum of the Reliance of Workplace Health
            Promotion Programs on Individual Motivation (amended).

Traditional workplace health promotion	Policies mandating or prohibiting certain behaviors	Policies that control risk behavior by eliminating things from workplace	Organizational and work design changes that promote health
High	Moderate	Low	None

Dependence on individual motivation

To clarify this position, consider by analogy the work of Dubos (1959), who has written that our society has overestimated, by a considerable degree, the effect of traditional medicine on the great advances in health over the past several centuries. Dubos asserts convincingly that these advances are due instead to changes in public health practice, for example, sanitation, sewage removal, water treatment, immunization, and so on. That is to say, the effectiveness of medicine, which treats individuals, is much more limited than the corresponding effectiveness of public health actions, which have their impact on society as a whole. This in no way diminishes the brilliance of the medical advances of the past century. It only suggests that the broad effect of these brilliant discoveries has been limited relative to the much wider effect of public health activities. Such approaches, for example, fluoridation of water or pasteurization of milk, protect individuals automatically and without their involvement in contrast to approaches requiring action on the part of an individual such as taking medication, getting exercise, or avoiding fatty foods. By modifying, in a sense, "the structure of the society," the reliance on individual motivation for these health actions is limited. And as seen in previous chapters, one of the most difficult tasks for workplace health promotion programs is to encourage individuals to maintain healthy behavior, regardless of how good it is for them.

In this spirit, we suggest that the currently popular approach organizations take to promote the health of employees, however successful, is limited. By making modifications of the organization's design, management structures, remuneration systems, and other organizational-level features, the incidence of disease and consequently health care costs also will be reduced. Our suggestion is not merely theoretical; considerable evidence exists that it is also practical.

We recognize that by issuing this challenge to workplace health promotion, we are addressing concerns that are typically well beyond the authority of the health promotion manager. One of our goals throughout this book is to encourage you to think about health promotion in both accepted and novel ways, especially if novel approaches can realize program objectives. This approach requires recognizing the existence of concerns common to workplace health promotion and existing organizational enterprises, for example, human resources development, quality of worklife groups, and so on, and to recognize further that to be most successful, health promotion at work must become part of business as usual. Although the ultimate decisions will more than likely be made at a level above the health promotion program manager, it is nevertheless desirable to appreciate these issues. The individual health promotion manager probably may not be able to address or influence directly aspects of organizational climate or remuneration systems. However, the manager can cooperate with other organizational activities or entities more closely associated with such matters and, in relation to upper management, can be an informed and persuasive advocate for the kind of changes that will support a healthier workforce.

The Concept of Organizational "Climate"

In the workplace, just as there is a physical environment, so there is a psychological one. The collection of employees' perceptions and experiences in the workplace is often referred to as organizational "climate." Although the concept of climate has appeared in the literature for over twenty years, disputes still rage about precisely what it means. Although different views exist, most hold that climate refers to several categories of factors:

1. aspects of the structure of tasks in the workplace such as clarity of responsibilities or workload
2. interpersonal relationships on the job
3. recognition and reward for performance
4. autonomy, for example, control over work or participation in decision making

Organizational Climate and Health Outcomes

Twenty years of research in the area of organizational climate has demonstrated that the psychological environment or climate also has an effect on organizational outcomes. In fact, as suggested earlier, many of these outcomes are precisely the same as those of workplace health promotion programs: reductions in absenteeism, increases in productivity, operating more efficiently by containing unnecessary costs, increases in morale, and so on. Moreover, there is considerable evidence that aspects of organizational climate have a direct influence on health outcomes of individual employees, and those health outcomes influence organizational outcomes. In this context, it is worth presenting Figure 2 from Chapter Three again (p. 239).

Note again that this figure suggests that aspects of work climate have a direct effect on the physical health of employees. Although we will demonstrate that this is the case, we should anticipate briefly the conclusion: since psychological work climate influences the physical health of employees and through physical health, the organizational outcomes of medical care

Figure 1.   A Social-Psychological Model of Workplace Health
              Promotion (Figure 3.2).

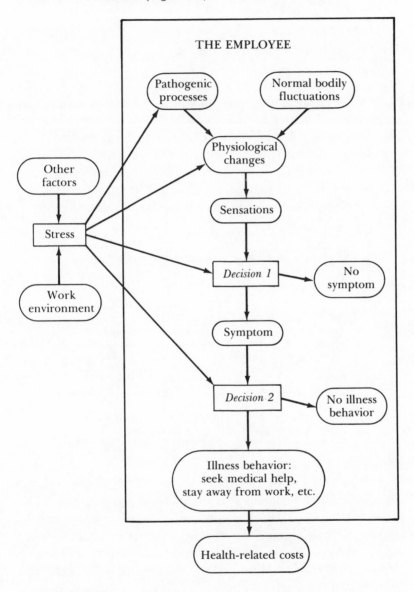

THE EMPLOYEE

costs, absenteeism, turnover, tardiness, reduced productivity,
and lower morale, a complete workplace health promotion pro-

gram must address psychological work climate in addition to those factors that reside within the individual employee, that is, motivation, health habits, and so forth.

Job Demands and Control over Work

Many in the industrial and research community have identified specific organizational determinants of workplace stress and demonstrated their relationship to health outcomes. For example, Karasek and his associates (Karasek and others, 1982) have underscored how the importance of the factors of job demands and control over the work process interact to determine stress-related disease to a significant degree. Figure 2 presents their model of how these two job-related factors influence health.

Figure 2.   The Relationship Among Job Demands, Control, and Strain.

Psychological job demands

		Low	High
Decision latitude (control)	High	Low strain	Active
	Low	Passive	High strain

The figure indicates that job demands and control over work interact to generate four distinct job profiles. The model predicts that when job demands are high *and* control over work is low (the "high strain" condition), a variety of negative health outcomes are the result. These outcomes include depression, sleeping problems, exhaustion, and consumption of medication. In addition, the combination of high job demand and low control is associated with significantly higher rates of coronary heart disease. The profile of high job demand and high control is not associated with higher rates of CHD. Testing in both the American and the Swedish workplace has confirmed these predictions. Thus, aspects of work design have been demonstrated to influence the health of the workforce. One solution to this problem, therefore, would be the modification of work design.

Physiological Effects of Work Design

Levi, Frankenhaeuser, and Gardell (1982) also have reported on evidence linking a number of properties of system design and job content to job satisfaction and to health. Such factors include quantitative work overload and underload, lack of control, and lack of social support. Assembly-line work, for example, provides little opportunity for the experience of control over the flow of work or the way in which the work is conducted. Moreover, such work provides little opportunity for social interaction. Examination of a Swedish sawmill (Frankenhaeuser and Gardell, 1976) provides a case in point. Increasing automation of sawmills has decreased the amount of personal control over much of the work process. Two groups of workers at the same mill were compared: (1) those whose work was closely tied to the machine and thus was characterized by high restriction of social interaction and movement, extreme repetitiveness, and high vigilance and (2) those with considerably fewer restrictions associated with the machine system and correspondingly greater control over the pace of their work. The stress hormones of adrenalin and noradrenalin were measured in these two groups of workers over the course of an eight-hour day. Not only did the low control group have generally higher levels of stress hormones but the time pattern of the differences also was quite striking: Hormone output generally decreased as the day progressed for the high control group but increased for the low control group. In addition, interview data suggested, as we might expect from the hormone data, that the low control group experienced greater difficulty in relaxing after work as well as greater absenteeism and psychosomatic symptoms. Note that although these studies involve sophisticated medical laboratory analyses, they nevertheless were conducted on real working populations, not collections of college students who come into a laboratory to work for an hour or two.

Some other examples shed more light on this issue. The physiological effects of piecework payment schedules and assembly-line work were examined in a study of Italian male workers (Timio and Gentili, 1976). In the examination of the effects of piecework, all workers performed the same tasks and were exposed to a schedule of piecework, then salaried work, then piecework again, or to the opposite schedule (salary, piecework, salary). Similar comparisons were made for two groups exposed to assembly-line work in contrast to nonassembly-line work. Piecework produced significantly higher levels of adrenalin and noradrenalin than salaried work did. Assembly-line work similarly produced higher levels than nonassembly-line work. When workers were switched from piecework to salary or from assembly-line work to nonassembly-line work, the levels of these stress hormones decreased.

These findings relating the production of adrenalin and noradrenalin and aspects of work are of great interest in light of the goal of workplace health promotion programs: reduction of disease risk and ultimately of medical care costs. There is considerable evidence that excess adrenalin and noradrenalin production appears to be an important contributor to the development of heart and blood vessel disease (Williams, 1978; Manuck, Kaplan, and Clarkson, 1983). To the extent that changes in the design of organizations and work processes produce reductions in adrenalin and noradrenalin, the risk of heart disease is reduced. Thus, there exists a real, physiological link between processes of work and health.

Limitations of Individual Behavior Change Approaches

The implications of this evidence are even greater when one considers that the effect of traditional individual behavior change programs in the workplace may be less effective than organizational programs that go beyond the modification of individuals' behavior. The case of a traditional stress management program delivered to employees in a Nebraska-based public agency

(Ganster, Mayes, Sime, and Tharp, 1982) makes this point. Participants in the program were taught to recognize and modify their interpretations of stressful events at work and to practice relaxation techniques; that is, the focus of this program was to train individual employees in the development of skills to cope with existing stressors in the workplace. Outcome measures of the program included measurements of adrenalin and noradrenalin. Although this stress management program produced significant reductions in these stress hormones, indicating that the program was effective, these reductions were smaller than those produced by manipulation of pay systems and assembly-line work in the Italian research; that is, the magnitude of stress reduction produced by changing the design of the work arrangements was greater than that produced by training individuals to manage stress. When we consider that for an individual stress management program, the long-term effect depends on continued motivation and practice, whereas for the organizational alternative, no such dependence exists, the difference between approaches becomes even greater. The developers of the individual stress management program concluded that because their "program is one that attempts to alter the reactions of employees to presumed noxious and stressful organization, task, and role characteristics . . . [and] does not . . . remove objective stressors from the employee's organizational environment" (Ganster, Mayes, Sime, and Tharp, 1982, p. 541), it should be regarded as a *supplement* to an organizational change program.

There are certain working conditions for which stress management programs designed to train individuals in compensatory coping skills are doomed to failure. The following example will help to make this point. We recently were contacted by a major utility company in the Northwest in connection with the stresses that their control room operators experienced. Work in a control room of a power plant is in many ways similar to the work of air traffic controllers, a group known to suffer from excessive stress, resultant disease, and excessive use of the health care system. Both groups of workers have tremendous responsibility. Failure to monitor and guide an aircraft accurately in take-off and landing can result in disaster. In the power station control room, responsibility is also great. Failure to close down a malfunctioning unit properly can result in risk to life of employees. Equipment failure may require split-second decisions, often made on the basis of only limited information, which may have a tremendous effect on the company's capacity to provide power to its customers and on the well-being of the equipment. Additional stressors include the extreme unpredictability of the work, the lack of control over their jobs, shiftwork, and relative isolation from other employees.

The utility company requested that we develop personal stress management programs for the control room operators; that is, we were asked to develop a program to train these operators on how to cope successfully with the stressors at work. A much more effective approach, the one we recommended, involved modifying the stress-producing aspects of the workplace. Without this environmental modification, reducing the stresses of the operators would have been impossible. Providing a personal stress management program was, unfortunately, mostly palliative.

Effect of Different Remuneration Systems

Other aspects of work design have been demonstrated to have an effect on health. We have already referred to remuneration systems in relationship to stress. Other health effects of remuneration systems exist. Although piece-wage systems may increase employee motivation to work, evidence exists that they also may promote increases in workplace accidents, thus increasing medical care costs. Kronlund and Kjellgren (1974 and 1975, respectively, both cited by Levi, Frankenhaeuser, and Gardell, 1982) demonstrated that the change from piece-wages to fixed salary produced a large decline in severe accidents accompanied by an increase in minor ones. The increase in minor accidents was attributed to the fact that workers, no longer on piece-wages, could seek medical care without loss of income associated with time away from work. In one of these two studies, the change was also accompanied by a decline in productivity. The extent to which the decline in productivity was offset by reduced medical care costs was not known.

Shift-Work

Finally, shift-work has been implicated in increased risk for many health problems. Most obviously, shift-workers suffer from sleep-wake disorders much more often than day-workers do. For example, American food-processing workers who worked on rotating shifts had greater difficulty in falling asleep, staying asleep, and staying awake at work (Smith, Colligan, and Tasto, 1982). As one might expect from these data, use of sleeping pills is greater among shift-workers. Another serious problem is the increased likelihood of falling asleep at work. According to Martin Moore-Ede and Gary Richardson (1985), sleep physiologists at the Harvard Medical School, a confidential survey of industrial plants indicated that between one-third and two-thirds of shift-workers fall asleep *at least once per week while on the job.* This problem occurs during the day and evening shifts as well as during the night shift. Thus, even when they are awake, shift-workers' sleep–wake rhythms may be so disrupted that they are at increased risk for accidents, both at work and at home.

Gastrointestinal disorders, from general discomfort to documented peptic ulcers, are also considerably more common among shift-workers than among day-workers. Evidence suggests that risk of ulcer disease increases as exposure to shift-work increases; that is, the disease tends to become apparent only after considerable time on the shift-work schedule.

The third category of health problems associated with shift-work is cardiovascular disease. Studies of both American and Swedish industry indicate an increased risk of myocardial infarction among shift-workers. Other risk behaviors associated with shift-work include greater smoking and alcohol consumption (Moore-Ede and Richardson, 1985).

These reports and experiences, and the many others like them, suggest that systemwide changes in work design can have a significant impact on employee health and the consequent medical care costs. Yet the typical workplace health promotion program excludes these types of changes from consideration. Of course, such changes in work design have long been the province of organization development, and the effectiveness of these changes, measured by other standards, has been established. But the link between organization development and workplace health promotion has never really been established, at least in the United States.

In the Scandinavian countries, however, this expanded view of workplace health promotion has been applied most extensively. More limited applications exist in the United States. Some of our research in the workplace, still in progress, also indicates the close interrelationship between aspects of work design and health.

Organizational Interventions and Health: Case Studies

An Automobile Manufacturing Company

At Volvo, the main responsibility of the company health service is to prevent illness, not to treat already existing illness. According to Corporate Medical Director Leif Wallin, the health service historically focused on aspects of the physical environment and its relation to health. In recent years, however, the focus has been on the psychosocial work environment and health. Recent work (Wallin and Wright, 1986) at Volvo has demonstrated the relationship between various aspects of the psychosocial work environment and outcomes of medical symptoms, psychological stress, and job satisfaction. For example, people with a high degree of influence over their work report that they enjoy going to work and that their work is interesting. Those reporting low influence show the opposite effects and, in addition, report significantly more medical symptoms, more psychological stress, and lower job satisfaction.

These findings led to a company effort to modify aspects of both the physical and psychosocial work environment. Changes in the physical environment are not our concern here, but the changes in the psychosocial environment most definitely are. The general changes included:

• changing of individual work-tasks
• more job training

- job rotation
- reorganization and restructuring of jobs
- reorganization of work groups

The case of a group of white-collar workers provides a specific example. Data from the initial assessment led to eight specific recommendations:

"1. rebuilding and changing of the layout of both the office and the workshop
2. replacement of the supervisor
3. change of management style
4. change of trade union attitude toward members and managers
5. introduction of computer aids to improve work efficiency
6. change of organization, resulting in more personal contact between customers and employees
7. introduction of teamwork
8. antismoking campaigns" (Wallin and Wright, 1986, p. 387)

Note that these changes included not only modification of the physical workplace but also of aspects of the psychosocial work environment: management style, teamwork, organizational change, and replacement of the supervisor. Even the introduction of an antismoking campaign constitutes an organizational-level change. Two years after the implementation of these changes, there was "a dramatic drop in the incidence of psychosomatic symptoms such as depression and headache; a marked reduction in gastrointestinal symptoms; a decrease in the incidence of psychological problems; a virtual cessation of smoking; and a reduction in work stress" (Wallin and Wright, 1986, p. 387). In addition, there were improvements in workload, pace of work, and dealing with customer demands. Most importantly for those interested in bottom-line considerations, overall motivation improved and profits increased.

From our perspective, this evaluation indicates that modifications of the workplace climate or psychosocial environment can have a direct effect on the outcomes of a health promotion program and through these effects, on the organization's bottom line. As Wallin and Wright (1986) put it, "the members of the health care team [must] act as agents of change [in the organization]" (p. 387).

This effort at Volvo represents one of the few in the world that shows that health outcomes are the products of aspects of the organization's psychosocial climate *and* that modifying this climate will produce improvements in health and productivity and reductions in medical care costs. The results of this evaluation underscore the model we presented in Chapter Three: that a larger view of workplace health promotion is called for and that this larger view must recognize that health outcomes are determined by multiple factors. Although the list of these determinants includes the health habits of individual employees, it must also include aspects of the organization's design and structure.

A Hospital Outpatient Facility

Application of this organizational approach to the concerns addressed by workplace health promotion programs has also been successful in an outpatient facility affiliated with a university hospital (Jackson, 1983). The approach taken in this facility was to determine the effect of implementing participative decision making in some groups within the organization. This was operationalized by increasing the number of scheduled staff meetings from one or fewer per month to two or more per month. The implementation involved a two-day training workshop in which unit heads were trained in the use of the Delphi method for conducting meetings (Delbecq, Van de Ven, and Gustafson, 1975). This method, developed by specialists in organization development, involves group problem solving to generate greater quantity and quality of ideas. To make this process specific to the needs of the organization, unit heads were provided with a list of potential topics and encouraged to discuss these meaningful issues in their staff meetings. After six months of the intervention, increased participation was shown to have numerous positive consequences: reduced role conflict and ambiguity, reduced emotional strain, increased job satisfaction, and reduced absenteeism and intention to leave the job. These outcomes fit nicely the model depicted in Figure 1.

A Mining Company

One final example will present a different health-related problem that was addressed by an organizational intervention. At the Great Salt Lake Minerals and Chemicals Corporation in Ogden, Utah, weekly work shifts were rotated every seven days to the preceding eight-hour shift, that is, from the night shift (midnight to 8 A.M.) to the evening shift (4 P.M. to midnight) to the day shift (8 A.M. to 4 P.M.). This rotation pattern was associated with greater insomnia and a greater likelihood of falling asleep at work compared to nonrotating groups. To address these problems, some of these shift workers were placed on a new schedule that was different in two ways: (1) shifts were rotated only every twenty-one days and (2) the shifts rotated in the opposite direction. The basis for these changes was the research on the circadian timing system, which controls basic biological rhythms. The consequences of this change in work schedule were significant. First, employees clearly preferred it to the previous schedule. In addition, and most relevant to workplace health promotion, employee health improved, turnover decreased, and productivity increased (Czeisler, Moore-Ede, and Coleman, 1982). These benefits arose from a modification of the work design that was independent of the health behaviors of the employees.

Conclusion

As indicated, it is difficult enough for human resources professionals to secure the organizational support necessary to begin a *traditional* workplace health promotion program. To suggest to top management that the way to reduce health care costs and absenteeism while simultaneously improving employee morale and job satisfaction is to redesign the organization and revamp the systems of remuneration is not likely to meet with squeals of joy. Few organizations are willing to undertake wholesale organizational change unless faced with a crisis of extreme proportions. Nevertheless, such crises do occur, and on occasion organizations consider large changes in their operations under less extreme circumstances. Armed with a broader view of workplace health promotion, one not restricted simply to encouraging individuals to change their health behavior, the health promotion manager may be in a position to move the organization toward a broader approach to improvements in employee health and associated reductions in health care costs. This broader approach will include both programs designed to help individuals *and* the organization change.

14

Conclusion: Observations on the Healthy Workplace

In Chapter One, we called attention to the difference between the treatment people and machines receive. We suggested that it was strange that there was widespread recognition of the need to take machines out of service periodically for preventive maintenance but that people were assumed to be sufficiently resilient that such "maintenance" was unnecessary. It is our hope that this book has demonstrated not only that such treatment of people is necessary but also that it is in the best interests, financial and otherwise, of the organizations that employ them.

Some may object to this comparison between people and machines, fearing a return to the days in which employees were treated as if they were machines. Although this concern may be justified in other contexts, it is not consistent with the spirit of our analogy. In Taylor's scientific management view, treatment of employees need be no better than the treatment of machines. Implicit in this view is the fact that "unscientific" managers treated workers better than machines and that this was unnecessary and counterproductive. Our comparison suggests quite the opposite: that under certain circumstances, it is the machines, not the people, that receive superior treatment.

Recently published works are in some ways consistent with this comparison. "Human capital is the combination of in-

nate talent, knowledge, skill, and experience that makes each
human a valuable contributor to economic production" (Perelman, 1984, p. 1). Seen in this way, employees are a vital resource, central to the optimal functioning of any organization.
Accordingly, it is in the best interest of any organization that
this "capital" be maximized. Current health care statistics suggest that this position is not widely endorsed and, moreover,
that the failure of organizations to treat this capital appropriately is very expensive:

- "Corporate expenses for health care are rising at such a fast
  rate that, if unchecked, in eight years they will eliminate all
  profits for the average Fortune '500' company and the largest 250 nonindustrials" (Herzlinger and Schwartz, 1985, p.
  69).
- "Corporations spent $104.6 billion in health insurance pre-
  miums and an average of $2,560 per employee for health-
  related costs in 1985" ("Employers Pay $2,600 per Em-
  ployee for Health Costs," 1986).
- Cardiovascular disease alone in 1984 cost $64.4 billion in
  treatment and lost output (Herzlinger and Calkins, 1986).
- Total economic cost of musculoskeletal injuries was over
  $59 billion in 1982, second only to cardiovascular disease
  (National Institute of Arthritis, Diabetes, and Digestive and
  Kidney Diseases, 1984).
- "In 1984, health care expenditures in the United States to-
  taled $387.4 billion, an average of $1,580 per person, and
  comprised 10.6 percent of the gross national product" (U.S.
  Department of Health and Human Services, 1985).

Statistics such as these are presented with increasing regu-
larity in the news media. We presented some other examples in
Chapter One. There is no question but that health care costs in
the United States are increasing exponentially and that although
some evidence may exist that the trajectory of this increase may
fall slightly, the upward direction will continue. Employers,
who provide health care benefits in the form of medical insurance and who bear all of the indirect costs of ill health, pay for
a substantial fraction of these increasing health care expenses.

Why Workplace Health Promotion Programs
Are Likely to Grow in Importance

Demographic Changes in the United States

The rate of increase in health care expenses has moderated slightly in the past year or two. This is the good news. The bad news comes in the form of demographic changes in the United States population. In 1980, there were about 3 million people over the age of 65 in the United States. Forecasts indicate that by the year 2,010, people over age 65 will number approximately 5 million. Whether these people remain in the workforce, thus increasing average workforce age, or choose to retire, it is highly likely that organizations will continue to bear the cost of this older group's medical expenses, either because they are still employed or through retiree benefits. Since the risk of disease increases with age, the increase in the number of elderly in the population will bring with it increasing upward pressure on health care costs. These demographic changes, along with the steadily increasing cost of medical care, will generate greater interest in health promotion, at the workplace and elsewhere.

"Compression of Morbidity"

Fries (1980) has argued that the human life span has a relatively fixed limit of approximately 85 to 100 years. Throughout the history of medicine and public health, we can see increases in average life expectancy as health problems are conquered. Today, it is the chronic diseases of lifestyle that cause death before the fixed limit Fries has suggested. Since these diseases are influenced heavily by behavioral and environmental changes, it should be possible to delay their onset through health promotion activities. The implication of this view is that since there is a relatively fixed human life span, by compressing morbidity toward the end of this span, the number of years during which medical care expenses are great will be reduced. Correspondingly, overall medical expenses will decrease.

The view that there is a fixed human life span and that morbidity can be compressed toward the end of this span is controversial. Critics have contested the idea that the human life span is fixed and have reasoned that if it is not fixed, health promotion will simply postpone, not compress, morbidity. Although there is no resolution to this controversy, the possibility that Fries may be correct justifies further interest in health promotion.

Delayed Effects of Corporate "Downsizing"

In 1985 and 1986, AT&T eliminated over 35,000 jobs. Union Carbide Corporation, through restructuring, eliminated about 4,000 white-collar jobs. Many other organizations around the country (and elsewhere) are "downsizing" or actively seeking to reduce the number of employees to cut back on expenditures. In many cases, however, these reductions in workforce do not come with parallel reductions in organizational workload. The consequence, of course, is that there will be fewer and fewer people to perform the same amount of work.

In Chapter Thirteen, we discussed the health consequences of such organizational climate factors as workload and control over work. According to a survey of readers of *Training* magazine, these reductions in workforce are starting to have the predicted effect (Zemke, 1986). *Training* readers, who typically are human resources professionals, report that middle managers in their organizations routinely came in to work on weekends twice as often in 1986 as in 1985. Predictably, middle managers now appear more stressed than they did one year before. Compared to a similar survey in 1985, twice as many readers in 1986 report that managers seem to be tired all of the time. One-third believe that a significant number of middle managers are close to burnout.

Such findings are entirely predictable. Reductions in staff with no reductions in the organization's total workload require that fewer people do more work. In the short term, this may appear to be cost effective. Even if this appearance is correct, whether it will remain so in the future is debatable. One certain outcome is that organizational stress will increase and with it, the negative health consequences. As more and more companies adopt this strategy, the more widespread the problem will become. In such an environment, the demand for workplace health promotion will grow.

Greater Interest in Medical Self-Care

Conventional medicine, as previously indicated, holds the central premise that disease is a function of the presence of a specific pathogen. This premise assumes that only when sick does one engage in health-related behavior and that the only appropriate action in these circumstances is to see a physician. In opposition to this premise is an increasing interest on the part of the general public to become more involved in matters of health. As a result of nationwide campaigns regarding the dangers of smoking and the benefits of exercise, we have seen marked changes in the health behavior of large segments of the population. Cigarette smoking, for example, has been reduced significantly in the past twenty years. More adults than ever are getting significant amounts of exercise. Other changes are also apparent: In the area of nutrition, there is increasing interest in low-fat, low-salt diets. These health behavior changes are the consequences of increased interest in self-management of health.

This increasing interest in involvement in health matters is fertile soil for workplace health promotion programs. Employers, seeking new ways to make their companies or organizations more attractive to candidates and to retain current employees have and will continue to capitalize on this interest through the development of health promotion programs at work.

The Effect of Health Information Technologies

Every generation is shaped by the development and spread of new technology. In health care, recent technological advances and new developments on the horizon are likely to increase the tendency toward greater personal involvement in health. A case in point is the decade-long nationwide effort to increase awareness and control of hypertension. The technological advances in this case are not major but the distribution of blood pressure monitoring devices has increased greatly, permitting individuals to assume greater control over their health in this area. This national effort and the ready availability of monitoring technology has increased greatly the number of patients with hypertension under control. Flush with this success, the National Institutes of Health have embarked on cholesterol control as their next major initiative.

In regard to cholesterol control, the impact of health information technologies will be profound. Until quite recently, serum cholesterol measurement required specimen analysis in a medical laboratory. For these analyses, relatively large specimens of blood were necessary. Within the past several years, desktop-sized analysis machines, using only minute amounts of blood from a finger prick, have become commercially available. Within another several years, it is likely that litmus paper–type cholesterol tests, using only a drop of blood from the end of the finger, will be widely distributed.

One consequence of such advancing medical technology is the increasing personalization of medical care. Such devices will permit individuals to monitor their health care in a way that simply was not feasible in the past. Thus, it will become increasingly possible and interesting to become more personally involved in self-health care. These changes are likely to increase interest in workplace health promotion programs.

Increasing Interest in "Expressive" Values

Over the past several decades, sociologists and demographers have been monitoring fundamental changes in American values, especially as they relate to work. Yankelovich and others (1983) have called these new values "expressive." Among their central aspects are the pursuit of autonomy, inner growth, self-expression, rejection of authority, and participation in decision making. So entrenched are these new values that they have a direct effect on employees' behavior in the work setting. Although management may lament these changes, Yankelovich argues that they are here to stay and that it is management, not the workforce, that must adapt. One direction in which this adaptation can develop is to modify the work environment and structure to satisfy these expressive values. Many of these new values, for example, rejection of (medical) authority, participation in decision making, and the pursuit of autonomy, are consistent with the themes of health promotion.

Organizations as Interdependent Systems

All organizations function as systems of interrelated components. Some of those components are the physical aspects of the organization: equipment, facilities, and so forth. Other components are procedures, policies, and organizational structures that govern operations. Finally, there are employees who act (usually) in accordance with the procedures and structures and who make use of the organization's physical aspects. It should come as no surprise that when a building roof collapses, the organization as a system is disrupted. Most of us believe that such an event should not occur, that it should be preventable. Similarly, during policy and procedural changes such as those that occur during relocation or retrenchment, the functioning of the organization is influenced, and at least initially, for the worst. In such cases, most organizations attempt to prevent the most serious consequences of these disruptions. But when employees fall prey to disease, most organizations feel satisfied that they have provided the means—that is, medical benefits, by which the afflicted individuals can recover. Rarely is it considered that such disruptions in the organization might be avoidable. We have made the case here that this is a mistake, and a costly one at that.

The workplace has seen many innovations that, although controversial at first, have become part of the accepted view of work. You no longer ask about whether it is appropriate to offer vacations to employees or to provide medical benefits. The eight-hour workday, once revolutionary, now is fully accepted, even viewed by some as antiquated. The same is true of the five-day workweek. Similarly, for most organizations, the purchase of computers and other advanced information technologies no longer seems an extravagance, the way it did only several years ago. What is accepted as part of the normal course of operations for organizations changes, sometimes incrementally and sometimes drastically.

Investing in employee health is an idea whose time has arrived. The creation of a healthy workplace in which the norms, culture, organizational structure, and behavior are conducive to health is no longer a luxury to be endorsed only by the largest and wealthiest of companies. It has the potential to become as central to the optimal functioning of an organization as any other component, not only because it is good for individual employees but also because it is just as good for the organization and its bottom line: productivity, cost efficiency, stability, and competitiveness. Organizations that ignore the opportunity to promote health at work do so at their own risk.

A

Alternative Strategies for Managing Health Care Costs

Investing in Employee Health discusses how workplace health promotion programs can help organizations manage health care costs and such related considerations as absenteeism and turnover. Of course, there are many other ways to manage health care costs; in this section, we briefly discuss some alternatives. For clarity's sake, we have organized these alternatives into four categories: benefit redesign, reducing usage, increasing efficiency, and health maintenance organizations (HMOs). For more detailed information on these and other cost-management approaches, we recommend Fielding (1984).

Benefit Redesign

The strategy of redesigning health care benefits typically attempts to control costs through two approaches: (1) cost sharing and (2) offering flexible benefits. It seems obvious that sharing the costs of health care with employees will encourage them to use the benefit system more carefully. *(Of course, this assumes that a fundamental cause of high health care costs is poor consumer behavior on the part of employees.)*

Cost Sharing

Cost sharing generally takes one or more of the following forms: paying for a portion of the premium, deductibles and coinsurance, and establishing an annual out-of-pocket maximum. Contributions to the cost of health care coverage, through, for example, a payroll deduction, saves the company considerable money. However, it provides no encouragement for employees to make more prudent use of the health care system since their payments are independent of usage. Deductibles and coinsurance are, on the other hand, more likely to provide some disincentive to excessive use, with the deductible having a greater effect. In fact, some studies have demonstrated just this. Some organizations have experimented, with some success, with a variable deductible based on the employee's income. Many companies have out-of-pocket maximums over which the employee no longer contributes.

Changes in employee payments in any of these three categories are regarded as effective means of health care cost management. The assumption justifying these approaches is that as long as employees have a blank check, they will not exercise caution in their health care consumption. Of course, manipulations of contributions to premiums, deductibles and copayments, and out-of-pocket maximums will have different effects and must be carefully considered before implementation. In addition, there is concern that benefit redesign may do little more than shift health care costs from the employer to the employee. As a consequence, there may be increased pressure for higher salaries to offset these shifted costs.

Flexible Benefits

Flexible plans permit employees (1) to select from various benefit plans, each with different characteristics (for example, different copayment schedules or deductibles); (2) to allocate employers' benefit contributions among multiple options, for example, vacations, day care, health care, or deferred compensation; or (3) incentive systems designed to provide employees with compensation, deferred or otherwise, if they reduce health care spending. Such flexible plans encourage coordination of benefits. For example, a working husband and wife do not each need family health care coverage. Flexible plans have a positive impact on employee morale, too.

In considering flexible plans, remember that they may have tax implications. Some of the options from which employees select may be taxable, others may not be.

Mechanisms to Reduce Use of the Health Care System

Strategies to reduce use of the health care system generally fall into two categories: those that seek to limit unnecessary use and those that encourage the delivery of medical services outside of a hospital.

Discouraging Unnecessary Use

Second Opinions. The most well-known of these mechanisms is the requirement for a second medical opinion for certain nonemergency services. Typically in such policies, reimbursement for procedures undertaken without a second opinion are paid at a lower rate than when a second opinion was obtained. The rationale behind this approach is that providers may recommend unnecessary medical procedures, thus increasing the burden on the health care system. Although evidence supports the effectiveness of a second-opinion program as a cost-management strategy, there is also evidence that it may produce *increases* in surgery. When confronted with *two* opinions calling for a procedure, people may be more inclined to undertake that procedure than if only one opinion had been obtained.

Utilization Reviews. Preadmission review requires that outside experts examine cases to determine the necessity and appropriateness of hospitalization before patients are admitted. Without agreement from this panel, reimbursement is provided but only at a lower rate.

Concurrent review monitors the care of patients in the

hospital. This kind of review typically concerns itself with length of stay, the need for admission, and the appropriateness of some medical procedures.

Retrospective review calls for examination of provider bills after the fact to determine their validity. If, for example, a bill has been submitted for a mastectomy for a man, then the claim can be disallowed. Typically, retrospective review is conducted by the company or the insurance carrier. In so doing, the user of the medical services—the employee—is not involved in the process. Some companies have attempted to encourage employee involvement in examining health care claims by providers by sharing a fraction of the unnecessary charge with the employee.

Ambulatory Care.   Because the cost of hospital care is so great, benefits policies that encourage conducting procedures outside the hospital whenever medically feasible have the potential to reduce health care costs. One way to encourage ambulatory care is to structure the benefit package to reimburse at a lower rate for inpatient procedures that could be performed on an outpatient basis.

As is the case for all of these cost management strategies, there is a potential downside. Encouraging ambulatory care will result in reductions in hospital use. To compensate for this reduction, hospitals may be inclined to increase the rates they charge for the remaining services. Therefore, although the company may pay less for certain procedures performed outside the hospital or by the hospital on an outpatient basis, it may pay more for inpatient procedures.

Increasing the Efficiency of Health Care Providers

Another approach to health care cost management is to encourage the providers—physicians and hospitals—to be more efficient. Some companies have tried to accomplish this by joining the local hospital's board of directors. Currently, the most common approach is through a "preferred provider organization" (PPO). PPOs are groups of health care providers who agree to reduce their professional fees in exchange for a guarantee of a certain number of patients. Although PPOs appear, on the surface, to be effective means of reducing health care costs, closer examination reveals some potential problems. For example, although a PPO may agree to reduce the fee for certain services, individual members may compensate for this reduced income by providing more of these services than would be otherwise necessary.

Health Maintenance Organizations

Health maintenance organizations (HMOs) serve two distinct health care functions: They are simultaneously providers and insurers. HMOs receive a fixed payment for every individual subscriber. Since their rate of pay is fixed, no incentive exists to provide unnecessary services. Accordingly, HMOs have lower rates of hospitalization than other benefit plans. However, there are many reasons why this may be so. It may be due to increased emphasis on the delivery of preventive services. It may be the consequence of a greater emphasis on ambulatory care. Or it may be that people who enroll in HMOs are different, perhaps younger and therefore healthier, than those who opt for other benefit packages. If the latter is true, then the apparent advantage of HMOs disappears, especially as they enroll more unhealthy subscribers who select the HMO as an alternative to the company's newly redesigned benefit package with higher deductibles and copayment.

The moral is that health care services must be managed in a comprehensive manner. Selecting only one approach may reduce costs in one area while inflating them in another.

B

Publications for Health Promotion Professionals

Action

A membership publication of:
Association for Employee
  Health and Fitness
965 Hope Street
Stamford, CT 06907

American Journal of Health Promotion

PO Box 1287
Royal Oak, MI 48068-1287

American Journal of Public Health

American Public Health Association
1015 15th Street, NW
Washington, DC 20037
202-789-5666

Building a Healthier Company

Available from your local Blue
  Cross and Blue Shield Association

Business and Health

Washington Business Group on
  Health
229 1/2 Pennsylvania Avenue, SE
Washington, DC 20003

Cardiovascular Primer for the Workplace

High Blood Pressure Information Center
120/80 National Institutes of Health
PO Box WS
Bethesda, MD 20205

Coalition Report

Clearinghouse on Business
Coalitions for Health Action
1615 "H" Street, NW
Washington, DC 20062

Corporate Commentary

Washington Business Group on
Health
229 1/2 Pennsylvania Avenue,
SE
Washington, DC 20003

Corporate Health Management
by Jonathan E. Fielding, M.D.

Addison-Wesley Publishing
Co., Inc.
South Street
Reading, MA 01867

*A Decision-Maker's Guide to
Reducing Smoking at the
Workplace*

National Health Information
Clearinghouse
PO Box 1133
Washington, DC 20013–1133

*Design of Workplace Health
Promotion Programs* by
Michael P. O'Donnell

Health Insurance Association
of America
1850 "K" Street, NW
Washington, DC 20006

*Developing an Occupational
Drug Abuse Program:
Considerations and
Approaches*

Government Printing Office,
Superintendent of Docu-
ments, Stock No.
017-024-00757-9,
Washington, DC 20402

*The EAP Manual: A Practical,
Step-by-Step Guide to
Establishing an Effective
Employee Alcoholism/
Assistance Program*

Publications Department
National Council on
Alcoholism
733 Third Avenue
New York, NY 10017

*Education for Health:
The Selective Guide*

National Center for Health
Education
30 East 29th Street
New York, NY 10016

*Employee Health and
Fitness*

American Health Consultants,
Inc.
67 Peachtree Park Drive, NE
Atlanta, GA 30309

Employee Health Promotion:
A Guide for Starting Programs
at the Workplace

Health Works Northwest
Puget Sound Health Systems
   Agency
601 Valley Street
Seattle, WA 98109

Employer's Guide to Health
Promotion in the Workplace

Minnesota Coalition on Health
   Care Costs
Suite 400
Health Associations Center
2221 University Avenue, SE
Minneapolis, MN 55414

Good Health Is Good Business
(on health habits and
   pregnancy)

Supply Division
March of Dimes Birth Defects
   Foundation
1275 Mamaroneck Avenue
White Plains, NY 10605

A Handbook for Worksite
Blood Pressure Programs
by Michael Alderman, Ph.D.

Available from:
New York State Health
   Department
Division of Health Education
Empire Street Plaza
Tower Building
Albany, NY 12237

Health Education Quarterly

John Wiley and Sons, Inc.
605 Third Avenue
New York, NY 10158

Health and Industry: A
Behavioral Medicine
Perspective by Michael F.
Cataldo and Thomas J. Coates

John Wiley and Sons, Inc.
605 Third Avenue
New York, NY 10158

Health Promotion and
Business Coalitions: Current
Activities and Prospects
for the Future

National Health Information
   Clearinghouse
PO Box 1133
Washington, DC 20013-1133

Health Promotion in the
Workplace by Michael P.
O'Donnell and Thomas
   Ainsworth

Wiley Medical
John Wiley and Sons, Inc.
605 Third Avenue
New York, NY 10158

HealthLink

National Center for Health
   Education
30 East 29th Street
New York, NY 10016

Helping Your Employees to Protect Themselves Against Cancer

Available from your local American Cancer Society

How to Develop a Company Fitness Program

Developed by the President's Council on Physical Fitness and Sports
Available from:
Universal
PO Box 1270
Cedar Rapids, IA 52406

Journal of Fitness in Business

Williams and Wilkins Company
428 East Preston Street
Baltimore, MD 21202

Journal of Occupational Medicine

Williams and Wilkins Company
428 East Preston Street
Baltimore, MD 21202

Medical Benefits

410 East Water Street
Charlottesville, VA 22901

Medical Care

J. B. Lippincott Company
East Washington Square
Philadelphia, PA 19105

Nonsmoking in the Workplace: A Guide for Employers

Health Insurance Association of America
1850 "K" Street, NW
Washington, DC 20006

Occupational Health Promotion: Health Behavior in the Workplace by George S. Everly and Robert H. L. Feldman

John Wiley and Sons, Inc.
605 Third Avenue
New York, NY 10158

A Practical Planning Guide for Employee Health Promotion Programs

Health Planning Council, Inc.
995 Applegate Road
Madison, WI 53713

The Profit in Safety Belts: An Introduction to an Employer's Program and Guidelines for Conducting Employers Safety Belt Workshops

U.S. Department of Transportation
NHTSA
400 7th Street, SW
NTS-10
Washington, DC 20590

*Reducing Smoking at the
Workplace*

National Health Information
   Clearinghouse
PO Box 1133
Washington, DC 20013-1133

*Small Businesses and Health
Promotion: The Prospects
Look Good*

National Health Information
   Clearinghouse
PO Box 1133
Washington, DC 20013-1133

Smoking and Health Reporter

National Interagency Council
   on Smoking and Health
c/o American Lung Association
1740 Broadway
New York, NY 10019

*State and Local Programs on
Smoking and Health*

Office on Smoking and Health
Stop 1-10
Park Building
5600 Fishers Lane
Rockville, MD 20857

*Staying Healthy: A
Bibliography of Health
Promotion Materials*

National Health Information
   Clearinghouse
PO Box 1133
Washington, DC 20013-1133

*Strategies for Promoting
Health for Specific
Populations*

National Health Information
   Clearinghouse
PO Box 1133
Washington, DC 20013-1133

Taking Executive Action
(smoking policy in the
workplace)

Available from your local
   American Lung Associa-
   tion

*Wellness and Health
Promotion for Elders*

Special Issue of *The Journal of
the Western Gerontological
Society*, 1983, Volume 7.
Available from:
Western Gerontological
   Society
833 Market Street,
   Room 516
San Francisco, CA 94103

*Wellness at Work:
A Report on Health and
Fitness Programs for
Employees of Business
and Industry* by
Robert Cunningham, Jr.

Available from your local
   Blue Cross and Blue Shield
   Association

*Work to Be Well: A Small
Business Guide to Wellness
at the Workplace*

Health Projects Office
Health Systems Agency of
  Western Lake Superior
202 Ordean Building
424 West Superior Street
Duluth, MN 55802

*Worksite Health Promotion:
A Bibliography of Selected
Resources*

Office of Disease Prevention
  and Health Promotion
Room 2132, Switzer Building
330 "C" Street, NW
Washington, DC 20201

*Worksite Nutrition:
A Decision-Maker's Guide*

The American Dietetic Asso-
  ciation
Sales Order Department
PO Box 10960
Chicago, IL 60610-0960

Worksite Wellness Works

Health Insurance Association
  of America
1850 "K" Street, NW
Washington, DC 20006-2284

C

Organizations Providing
Health Promotion
Information

Throughout the country, many organizations provide valuable assistance to the managers of workplace health promotion programs. Their assistance can come in a variety of forms. Many of the organizations listed here provide topical health promotion literature including flyers, films, audio- and videotapes, and computer software. Some are a source of valuable health statistics useful in the program planning phase or during evaluation. Many have direct expertise in the planning, development, and implementation of workplace health promotion programs. Because the field is developing so rapidly, the precise nature of assistance and advice each organization can offer is constantly changing. Do not hesitate to contact any of them for information of any sort.

Also, remember that this resource can provide only a partial list of organizations that may be of use to you. In virtually every community, there are local sources of information and assistance: colleges and universities, medical societies, business groups, local offices of national organizations, unions, and other groups to which you can turn. Do not hesitate to seek them out, too.

Action on Smoking and
  Health
2013 "H" Street, NW
Washington, DC 20006
202-659-4310

American Cancer Society
90 Park Avenue
New York, NY 10016
212-736-3030
or your local ACS office

American Council of Life
  Insurance
1850 "K" Street, NW
Washington, DC 20006
202-862-4124

American Dietetic Association
Division of Practice
430 North Michigan Avenue
Chicago, IL 60611
312-280-5000
or contact your state or local
  chapter

American Health Foundation
320 East 43rd Street
New York, NY 10001
212-953-1900

American Health Planning
  Association
1110 Vermont Avenue, NW,
  Suite 950
Washington, DC 20005
202-861-1200

American Heart Association
7320 Greenville Avenue
Dallas, TX 75231
214-750-5300

American Hospital Association
840 North Lake Shore Drive
Chicago, IL 60611
312-280-6000

American Institute of Stress
124 Park Avenue
Yonkers, NY 10703
914-963-1200

American Lung Association
1740 Broadway
New York, NY 10019
212-315-8700

American Occupational
  Medical Association
2340 South Arlington Heights
  Road
Arlington Heights, IL 60005
312-228-6850

American Public Health
  Association
1015 15th Street, NW
Washington, DC 20037
202-789-5600

American Red Cross
17th and "D" Streets, NW
Washington, DC 20006
202-737-8300

Association for Employee
   Health and Fitness
965 Hope Street
Stamford, CT 06907
203-359-2188

Association for Health
   Services Research
2233 Wisconsin Avenue, NW,
   Suite 525
Washington, DC 20007
202-223-2477

Behavioral Medicine Program
Box 427
Columbia-Presbyterian
   Medical Center
622 West 168th Street
New York, NY 10032
212-305-9985

Blue Cross and Blue Shield
   Associations
676 Saint Clair Street
Chicago, IL 60611
312-440-6000

The Business Roundtable
200 Park Avenue, Suite 2222
New York, NY 10166
212-628-6370

The Center for Health
   Promotion
Box 114
Teachers College, Columbia
   University
525 West 120th Street
New York, NY 10027
212-678-3961

Clearinghouse on Business
   Coalitions for Health Action
U.S. Chamber of Commerce
1615 "H" Street, NW
Washington, DC 20062
202-463-5970

Coalition on Smoking OR
   Health
1607 New Hampshire Avenue,
   NW
Washington, DC 20009
202-234-9375

Food and Nutrition
   Information Center
U.S. Department of Agriculture
National Agricultural Library
Room 304, 10301 Baltimore
   Boulevard
Beltsville, MD 20705
301-344-3719

Health Insurance Association
   of America
1025 Connecticut Avenue,
   NW, Suite 1200
Washington, DC 20036
202-267-8890

Home Economics and Human
   Nutrition
Extension Service
U.S. Department of Agriculture
Washington, DC 20250
202-447-3377
or contact your local Coopera-
   tive Extension Service, listed
   under "State and Local
   Government"

Institute for Aerobics
Research
12330 Preston Road
Dallas, TX 75230
214-661-3374

March of Dimes
Director of Business Health
Programs
1275 Mamaroneck Avenue
White Plains, NY 10605
914-428-7100

National Association of Health
Data Organizations
229 1/2 Pennsylvania Avenue,
NW, Suite 595
Washington, DC 20006
202-638-0455

National Cancer Institute
Office of Cancer Communications
Building 31, Room 10A-18
9000 Rockville Pike
Bethesda, MD 20892
301-496-5583

National Center for Health
Education
39 East 29th Street
New York, NY 10016
212-689-1886

National Center for Health
Statistics
3700 East-West Highway
Hyattsville, MD 20782
301-436-8500

National Dairy Council
6300 North River Road
Rosemont, IL 60018
312-696-1020

National Health Information
Clearinghouse
Public Health Service
PO Box 1133
Washington, DC 20013-1133
800-336-4797

National High Blood Pressure
Education Program
120/80 National Institutes of
Health
Bethesda, MD 20892
301-496-1809

National Institute for
Occupational Safety and
Health
Centers for Disease Control
1600 Clifton Road, NE
Atlanta, GA 30333
404-331-2396

National Safety Council
444 North Michigan Avenue
Chicago, IL 60611
800-621-7619

The National Wellness
Institute
UW-SP Foundation
University of Wisconsin-
Stevens Point
Stevens Point, WI 54481
715-346-2172

Office of Disease Prevention
and Health Promotion
Health Information Center
1255 23rd Street, NW
Suite 275
Washington, DC 20037
800-336-4797

Office of Prevention,
Education, and Control
Workplace Activities
National Heart, Lung, and
Blood Institute
Building 31, Room 4A18
Bethesda, MD 20892
301-496-5437

Office of Smoking and Health
5600 Fishers Lane
Park Building, Room 116
Rockville, MD 20857
301-443-1575

Office of Technology
Assessment
United States Congress
600 Pennsylvania Avenue, SE
Washington, DC 20510
202-224-8713

President's Council on
Physical Fitness and Sports
450 Fifth Street, NW
Suite 7103
Washington, DC 20001
202-272-3430

Public Health Service
Hubert H. Humphrey Building
200 Independence Avenue,
SW
Washington, DC 20201
202-245-7694

State Health Department (in
any state)
Department of Public Health/
Health Education

U.S. Centers for Disease
Control
1600 Clifton Road, NW
Atlanta, GA 21207
404-329-3291

U.S. Chamber of Commerce
1615 "H" Street, NW
Washington, DC 20062
202-463-5970

U.S. Department of Labor
Bureau of Labor Statistics
200 Constitution Avenue,
NW
Washington, DC 20210
202-523-1221

Washington Business Group on
Health
229 1/2 Pennsylvania Avenue,
SE
Washington, DC 20003
202-547-6644

D

Sample Employee Health and Attitude Survey

Dear Fellow Employee:

All of us who work here at _____ depend on one another to do our jobs to the best of our ability to ensure that our company will continue to prosper and grow. This means we all need to be here at work, feeling our best, to get the job done right. We are all looking into ways to help employees maintain and improve their health and feel good about working at _____ and would like to hear what you think about it.

Please fill out the attached questionnaire and return it to the box outside the personnel office as soon as possible. This questionnaire is anonymous—don't put your name on it. It is designed to find out about the health practices and interests of the _____ community.

Signed,

Employee Health Survey

Please fill in this information about yourself:

Height: _____ feet, _____ inches tall.

Weight: _____ pounds.

Do you smoke?   _____ no

                 _____ yes, I smoke _____ cigarettes on a normal day.

                 _____ yes, I smoke _____ full pipes on a normal day.

                 _____ yes, I smoke _____ cigars on a normal day.

Have you had your blood pressure measured recently?

       _____ yes

       _____ no

If "yes," what was your blood pressure reading? _____

Have you ever been told by a nurse or physician that you have high blood pressure or hypertension?

       _____ yes

       _____ no

Have you ever taken medicine for high blood pressure?

       _____ yes

       _____ no

Have you ever been told by a nurse or physician that your serum cholesterol level is too high?

       _____ yes

       _____ no

How much work time have you missed in the past two years because of back pain? _____ work days

How many hours of vigorous exercise do you get in a week? _____ hours

How many times have you seen the dentist in the past year? _____ times

Please answer the following questions either true (T) or false (F).

_____ I plan to make changes in my health practices soon.

_____ I feel I have too much stress in my life.

_____ My job causes me to feel very stressed.

_____ My behavior affects my health.

_____ I always wear a seat belt when I ride in a car.

_____ I drink two or more drinks containing alcohol in a normal day.

_____ I am concerned that my work environment is not as safe as it should be.

_____ I have been told that I have a drug or drinking problem.

_____ My health affects my ability to do my job right.

_____ My company should be concerned with my health.

I would be interested in learning more about the following (Please check as many of the following as you wish.):

_____ weight control
_____ how to stop smoking
_____ how to use the benefits package
_____ how to control my blood pressure
_____ managing stress
_____ exercising safely and effectively
_____ how to prevent back problems
_____ cancer prevention and detection

I would be interested in the following activities here at work:

_____ workshops or classes on any of the topics in the preceding list
_____ films, videos, and lunchtime talks on the topics in the preceding list
_____ an employee committee to organize health-related activities

_____ special events, like a picnic, health fair, or family fun run
_____ having accurate information available to me about health
topics
_____ having my family join me in health-related activities here
at work

Is there anything that we need to know about you or about
your fellow workers that would help us to plan to meet the
needs of the _____ community better?

Do you have ideas or suggestions we should consider in our
planning? If so, please explain in the space below:

E

Health Risk Appraisals

The Public Health Service's Office of Disease Prevention and Health Promotion has classified health risk appraisals (HRAs) in three categories: (1) the self-scored questionnaire, (2) the microcomputer-scored questionnaire for use with a personal computer, and (3) computer-scored questionnaires that are processed at a central computer facility.

The self-scored questionnaire is a rather simple instrument. It consists of questions about behavior, for example, smoking, high-fat diet, and so forth, and personal and family medical history that have been related to the major risk factors for chronic disease. Individuals answer these questions and then add up points assigned to each answer to receive an overall score. Usually these instruments are fairly brief (one to three pages), and all include information about the desirable behavior ranges in relation to each risk factor.

The use of a microcomputer for HRAs can take a number of forms: An individual's data can either be entered from hardcopy questionnaires or can be entered directly by the individual in an interactive program. The data can be used to generate both an individual summary report and in most cases can be added to aggregate statistics for a given population to generate a report on the health risks of the group as a whole.

Computer-scored HRAs, the Cadillacs of the breed, often consist of 200–300 multiple-choice questions. Individuals complete the questionnaire, which then is sent to a central processing point for batch-scoring. A detailed, personalized report showing the impact of the individual's behavior and medical history on health risks is returned in a sealed envelope to the individual in a few weeks. Aggregated reports are also available.

Which Type of HRA?

Whether you use an HRA and how you decide to use it will depend on the overall goals of the program and the norms and requirements of the organization. In the following section, the three types of HRAs (self-scored, microcomputer-scored, and batch-scored) are evaluated in relation to the most common functions HRAs have served in workplace health promotion programs.

Diagnosis

The use of the HRA to "diagnose" risk-producing behaviors in a population prior to designing a program is a logical way to go about identifying the major risk-producing behaviors in a population. Clearly, to use an HRA for this purpose, it is necessary to use one of the two computer-scored questionnaires that will collect and aggregate data while simultaneously generating reports for individuals. It is important to note that the HRA administration and feedback process in and of itself has impact as a health promotion intervention.

A critical question about the use of HRAs as a diagnostic tool is whether they provide the appropriate information in the most efficient manner. If the goal of the organizational diagnosis simply is to identify the presence and quantity of specific risk behaviors, the more elaborate questionnaires may gather unnecessary information. The areas of modifiable risk behavior associated with premature death and disability are fairly well proscribed: smoking, hypertension, drinking/driving, cholesterol, back pain, obesity, exercise, and stress. A brief yes/no questionnaire distributed randomly throughout the organization can yield the information you need for planning at considerably less expense and administrative effort.

Program Evaluation

One of the primary functions of workplace health promotion programs is to reduce health care costs, disability, and absenteeism through reduction of risk-producing behavior (for example, smoking or obesity) and to increase such health-enhancing behavior as exercise or monitoring of hypertension. The impact of these behavior changes on disease outcomes are measurable only in the long term. However, by measuring how behavior changes in relation to risk, it is possible to extrapolate and project the cost savings over time due to reduced risks.

It is possible to use either microcomputer-scored or batch-scored HRAs for this kind of evaluation, analyzing changes in aggregated information over time. Again, however, one faces the question of efficiency: Is using a complex and time-consuming HRA for this purpose justified? Personal and family medical history both account for a large number of questions on the more elaborate HRAs, and these factors will not change over time. The only area in an HRA in which change due to the health promotion program may be expected is in behavior, not in history. Hence, a substantial fraction of the information collected at follow-up is not useful for program evaluation. A much more simple instrument will probably provide the same information.

The HRA as an Educational Intervention

HRAs also can serve a health education function: to inform individuals of the link between their own behavior and health histories and their resultant risk of premature disease and death. This recognition, that there is, in fact, a margin of our own health over which we have some control, and recognition of the limits of that margin, is one of the first steps in making changes in behavior in relation to health. The extent to which a health risk appraisal presents this information in a clear, concise, and compelling way predicts its overall usefulness. Ideally, an HRA can organize a previously unstructured body of facts, knowledge, opinions, and attitudes into a compact, causal model. Most people know, for example, that in general, smoking, drinking, and obesity are not good for your health. Understanding the differential impact of each of these behaviors on health, relative to other risk behaviors, should make it easier for people to see the total picture of their health and then to plan to make changes.

Regrettably, there are a number of fundamental problems with the use of an HRA as a health education tool. The first and most important problem is that HRAs, as their name states, are based on the assumptions of risk, that is, the *probability* that, given X and Y behavior, a person will die of Z disease. However, with the exception of those who are involved intimately with physical/social science statistics and/or horse racing, the majority of Americans do not seem to understand the concepts of risk/probability. Moreover, evidence also exists that even when people *do* understand probability, they maintain a significant optimistic bias (Weinstein, 1982), essentially denying that the laws of probability apply to them. This lack of understanding renders meaningless much of the specific information produced by HRAs' complex algorithmic calculations (the accuracy of which is a major marketing claim of many of the larger HRAs). Frequently, you hear statements indicating confusion regarding the HRA report, for example, "I'm going to live 1.8 years longer than the guy sitting next to me because I don't smoke" (understanding a statement of probability as a statement of fact). Or, "My serum cholesterol level is normal for my age" (confusing the concept of "norm" with ideal). The lack of understanding of probability leads us to question whether the time-consuming, costly process of data collection and calculation of a "highly accurate" health risk is justified.

The other major limitation of HRAs as a health education tool is their format, which requires the user to be somewhat verbal, literate, able accurately to assess frequency/duration of different behaviors, and aware of family health history. In addition, the printed word must be valued as a source of authority and legitimate information. Although this may sound reasonable for most working populations, in this age of television, the written word is losing its power. In fact, the characteristics that give the computer-scored HRAs their apparent high impact, that is, the extensive range of questions, the personalization of risk, and the aura of high-tech analysis, are the same things that remove the concrete link between specific behaviors and health risk. Users of these HRAs may have no sense of how all of their personal information is combined to yield a final "health age" or "health risk." Users have no sense of the relative weights of their own behaviors and histories, and the final risk scores and suggestions for behavior change in the "personalized" report essentially are no different from those of a simple self-scored HRA.

In addition to these two main problems, you should consider other minor strengths and weaknesses when making a decision about whether to use an HRA. Keep in mind that all of the HRAs currently on the market should be used within the context of a larger program.

Self-Scored HRAs

Positive benefits are symbolized by "+" and drawbacks by "−."

+ Self-scored HRAs are the least expensive type. They involve only reproduction or printing costs, although some have a fee for rights.

+ Because of the brevity of most of these questionnaires, users can complete and score them in a single sitting, thereby providing immediate feedback.

+/− Because of the brevity of these HRAs, much of the general information about health risks should be supplied by the larger program in which the HRA is embedded.

+ Users score their own questionnaires, making for ease of group administration.

+ Users score their own questionnaires, increasing the probability of an accurate self-report. The problems of confidentiality of this kind of personal information go hand-in-hand with the honesty with which the questionnaire is completed. The self-scored HRA provides the most confidentiality of the genre.

+   Because users score their own HRAs, they know what factors are influencing their score negatively and positively and in most cases can see the relative impact of their behaviors.

—   The aura of computers is lacking; this may detract from the power attributed to the instrument.

+   Because the questionnaire is inexpensive, self-explanatory, and reproducible, it conceivably can be used by family members.

+   All self-scored HRAs collect adequate information to inform users in a general way about how their behavior is influencing their health risks.

—   Because they are self-scored, collection of aggregated data for group analysis is difficult.

Microcomputer-Scored HRAs

+   Although the packaging and format of the microcomputer-scored HRAs vary widely, these generally are considered to be the middle-priced option. However, the use of this type of HRA requires at least one microcomputer, and with a larger number of health promotion participants, perhaps more than one.

—   Interactive programs require each person to go through the entire HRA using the computer. Group administration, therefore, is highly impractical.

—   In this age of information, people are becoming more and more suspicious of how personal information will be used. As a result, people may be inclined to be less than accurate in their reporting of drinking, drug use, and physical symptoms when they complete this kind of HRA.

+   These HRAs have the capacity to give immediate and personalized feedback about behaviors and risks, thus providing a high-impact message.

+ The aura of computer technology can add salience to the message.

Batch-Scored HRAs

+ This kind of HRA has the capacity to provide the most complete and accurate picture of health risk available.
— The extensiveness of the questions is often experienced as extremely intrusive and often inappropriate in the context of the workplace.
— This perception leads to a lack of completeness of data and to inaccuracy of self-report, in spite of assurances of confidentiality. Data are linked by name and Social Security number in some computer, and the company is paying for storage. The result may be inaccurate input, which is then subjected to careful calculations yielding inaccurate assessments of risk.
— Because questionnaires must be shipped to some central point for processing, the time between questionnaire completion and receipt of report is often several weeks, during which time users forget what questions they were asked and how they answered them.
— This lag time may result in a user recognizing little or no overt connection between how questions were answered and the risks generated for the final report.
— These HRAs are the most expensive, and in many cases the charge is up-front; when you buy a copy of the questionnaire, you pay for the processing fee. Therefore, the organization is charged for questionnaires that are lost, not completed, or thrown away.
— Users are completely dependent on the goodwill and efficiency of (1) the mail service and (2) the HRA company's service department. As these new companies iron out their procedures and gear up for full production, this has become a real problem.

References

"A Catalog of Pain." *Forbes,* Nov. 18, 1985, p. 8.

Adams, J. D. *Understanding and Managing Stress.* San Diego, Calif.: University Associates, 1980.

Allegrante, J. P. "Potential Uses and Misuses of Education in Health Promotion and Disease Prevention." *Teachers College Record,* 1984, *86,* 359-373.

Allegrante, J. P., and Green, L. W. "When Health Policy Becomes Victim Blaming." *New England Journal of Medicine,* 1981, *306,* 1528-1529.

Allegrante, J. P., and Sloan, R. P. "Guest Editorial: Ethical Dilemmas in Workplace Health Promotion." *Preventive Medicine,* 1986, *15,* 313-320.

American Dietetic Association. *Worksite Nutrition: A Decision-Maker's Guide.* Chicago: The American Dietetic Association, 1986.

Beckhard, R. *Organization Development: Strategies and Models.* Reading, Mass.: Addison-Wesley, 1969.

Beehr, T. A., and Bhagat, R. S. "Introduction to Human Stress and Cognition in Organizations." In T. A. Beehr and R. S. Bhagat (eds.), *Human Stress and Cognition in Organizations.* New York: Wiley, 1985.

Bellingham, R., Johnson, D., and McCauley, M. "The AT&T

Communications Total Life Concept." *Corporate Commentary,* 1985, *1,* 1-13.

Berg, E. N. "Major Corporations Ask Workers to Pay More of Health Costs." *New York Times,* Sept. 12, 1983, p. 1.

Berkman, S. *Cancer News.* New York: American Cancer Society, Winter 1986.

Berry, C. *Good Health for Employees and Reduced Health Care Costs for Industry.* Washington, D.C.: Health Insurance Association of America, 1981.

Blair, S. N., Piserchia, P. V., Wilbur, C. S., and Crowder, J. H. "A Public Health Intervention Model for Work-Site Health Promotion." *JAMA,* 1986, *255,* 921-926.

Blair, S. N., and others. "Health Promotion for Educators: Impact on Absenteeism." *Preventive Medicine,* 1986, *15,* 166-175.

Bly, J. L., Jones, R. C., and Richardson, J. E. "Impact of Worksite Health Promotion on Health Care Costs and Utilization." *JAMA,* 1986, *256,* 3235-3240.

Boal, J. "It Pays to Stay Healthy." *Ozark Magazine,* Feb. 1984, pp. 7-8.

Bowne, D. W., and others. "Reduced Disability and Health Care Costs in an Industrial Fitness Program." *Journal of Occupational Medicine,* 1984, *26,* 809-816.

Brennan, A. "Worksite Health Promotion Can Be Cost-Effective." *Personnel Administrator,* April 1983, *28,* 39-42.

Bruno, R., and others. "Randomized Controlled Trial of a Nonpharmacologic Cholesterol Reduction Program at the Worksite." *Preventive Medicine,* 1983, *12,* 523-532.

Bylinsky, G. "The New Assault on Heart Attacks." *Fortune,* Mar. 31, 1986, pp. 80-89.

Califano, J. "Can We Afford One Trillion Dollars for Health Care?" Speech delivered to the Economic Club of Detroit, April 25, 1983.

Cantlon, A. *Corporate Commentary,* 1985, *1,* 53.

Chaves, M. A., Jennings, S. E., McKinlay, S. M., and McKinlay, J. B. "Cardiovascular Risk: Differences Among Health Hazard Appraisals." *20th Proceedings of the Society for Prospective Medicine,* 1984.

Cheloha, R. S., and Farr, J. L. "Absenteeism, Job Involvement, and Job Satisfaction in an Organizational Setting." *Journal of Applied Psychology*, 1980, *65*, 467-473.

Clearinghouse on Business Coalitions for Health Action. *A Guide to Sources of Health Care Data.* Washington, D.C.: United States Chamber of Commerce, 1986.

Cobb, S. "Role Responsibility: The Differentiation of a Concept." In A. McLean (ed.), *Occupational Stress.* Springfield, Ill.: Thomas, 1974.

Colacino, D. L., and Gulbronson, C. R. "New Perspectives on Pepsico's Fitness Participation." *Corporate Commentary*, 1984, *1*, 36.

Collings, G. H. "Health Care Management: A Review." New York Telephone document, 1982.

Cox, M., Shephard, R. J., and Corey, P. "Influence of an Employee Fitness Program Upon Fitness, Productivity, and Absenteeism." *Ergonomics*, 1981, *24*, 795-806.

Crawford, R. "Sickness as Sin." *Health Policy Advisory Center Bulletin*, 1978, *80*, 10-16.

Czeisler, C. A., Moore-Ede, M. C., and Coleman, R. M. "Rotating Shift Work Schedules That Disrupt Sleep Are Improved by Applying Circadian Principles." *Science*, 1982, *217*, 460-463.

Davis, M. F., and others. "Worksite Health Promotion in Colorado." *Public Health Reports*, 1984, *99*, 538-543.

Delbecq, A. L., Van de Ven, A. H., and Gustafson, D. H. *Group Techniques for Program Planning.* Glenview, Ill.: Scott, Foresman, 1975.

Dubos, R. *Mirage of Health.* New York: Harper & Row, 1959.

"Employers Pay $2,600 per Employee for Health Costs." *Coalition Report*, Oct. 1986, *5*, 1.

Fielding, J. P. *Corporate Health Management.* Reading, Mass.: Addison-Wesley, 1984.

Fishbein, M., and Ajzen, I. *Beliefs, Attitudes, Intention, and Behavior: An Introduction to Theory and Research.* Reading, Mass.: Addison-Wesley, 1975.

Frankenhaeuser, M., and Gardell, B. "Underload and Overload in Working Life: Outline of a Multidisciplinary Approach." *Journal of Human Stress*, 1976, *2*, 35-46.

Freeland, M., and Schendler, C. "Health Spending in the 1980s:

Integration of Clinical Practice Patterns with Management." *Health Care Financing Review,* Spring 1984, *5,* 1-68.

French, J. R. P., and Caplan, R. D. "Organizational Stress and Individual Strain." In A. J. Marrow (ed.), *The Failure of Success.* New York: AMACOM, 1972.

French, J. R. P., Caplan, R. D., and Harrison, R. V. *The Mechanisms of Job Stress and Strain.* New York: Wiley, 1982.

Fries, J. F. "Aging, Natural Death, and the Compression of Morbidity." *New England Journal of Medicine,* 1980, *303,* 130-135.

Galanter, R. B. "To the Victim Belongs the Flaws." *American Journal of Public Health,* 1977, *67,* 1025-1026.

Ganster, D., Mayes, B., Sime, W., and Tharp, G. "Managing Organizational Stress: A Field Experiment." *Journal of Applied Psychology,* 1982, *67,* 533-542.

Gibbs, J. O., and others. "Work-Site Health Promotion." *Journal of Occupational Medicine,* 1985, *27,* 826-830.

Glover, R. Speedcall Corporation internal documents, 1982.

Glover, R. "Exchange." *Corporate Commentary,* 1985, *2,* 52.

Gostin, L., and Curran, W. J. "AIDS Screening, Confidentiality, and the Duty to Warn." *American Journal of Public Health,* 1987, *77,* 361-365.

Green, L. W. "Individuals vs. Systems: An Artificial Classification That Divides and Distorts." *HealthLink,* Sept. 1986, pp. 29-30.

Green, L. W., and Gordon, N. P. "Productive Research Designs for Health Education Investigations." *Health Education,* 1982, *13,* 4-10.

Green, L. W., and Lewis, F. M. *Measurement and Evaluation in Health Education and Health Promotion.* Palo Alto, Calif.: Mayfield, 1986.

Gruman, J. C., and Sloan, R. P. "Disease as Justice: Perceptions of the Victims of Physical Illness." *Basic and Applied Social Psychology,* 1983, *4,* 39-46.

Hammer, T. J., Landau, J. C., and Stern, R. N. "Absenteeism When Workers Have a Voice: The Case of Employee Ownership." *Journal of Applied Psychology,* 1981, *66,* 561-573.

Haskel, W. L., and Blair, S. N. "The Physical Activity of Health Promotion in Occupational Settings." In R. S. Parkinson (ed.), *Managing Health Promotion in the Workplace.* Palo Alto, Calif.: Mayfield, 1982.

Herzberg, F. *Work and the Nature of Man.* New York: World Publishing Co., 1966.

Herzlinger, R., and Calkins, D. "How Companies Tackle Health Care Costs: Part III." *Harvard Business Review,* Jan.-Feb. 1986, pp. 70-80.

Herzlinger, R., and Schwartz, J. "How Companies Tackle Health Care Costs: Part I." *Harvard Business Review,* July-Aug. 1985, pp. 69-81.

Holmes, T. H., and Rahe, R. H. "The Social Readjustment Rating Scale." *Journal of Psychosomatic Research,* 1967, *11,* 213-218.

House, J. S. *Work Stress and Social Support.* Reading, Mass.: Addison-Wesley, 1981.

Ibold, K. "Safety First." *Gwinnett Daily News,* March 10, 1986, pp. 6D-7D.

Jackson, S. "Participation in Decision Making as a Strategy for Reducing Job-Related Strain." *Journal of Applied Psychology,* 1983, *68,* 3-19.

Kahn, R. *Work and Health.* New York: Wiley, 1981.

Kaplan, J. R., and others. "Social Stress and Atherosclerosis in Normocholesterolemic Monkeys." *Science,* 1983, *220,* 733-735.

Karasek, R. A., and others. "Job, Psychological Factors, and Coronary Heart Disease." *Advances in Cardiology,* 1982, *29,* 62-67.

Keyserling, W. M., and Chaffin, D. B. "Occupational Ergonomics." *Annual Review of Public Health,* 1986, *7,* 77-104.

King, J. "Exchange." *Corporate Commentary,* 1984, *1,* 60.

Knowles, J. "The Responsibility of the Individual." In J. H. Knowles (ed.), *Doing Better and Feeling Worse: Health in the U.S.* New York: Norton, 1977.

Kotler, P. *Marketing for Non-Profit Organizations.* Englewood Cliffs, N.J.: Prentice-Hall, 1975.

Kotler, P. "Social Marketing of Health Behavior." In L. W.

Fredericksen and K. A. Brehony (eds.), *Marketing Health Behavior.* New York: Plenum, 1984.

Kristein, M. "How Much Can Business Expect to Profit from Smoking Cessation?" *Preventive Medicine,* 1983, *12,* 358–381.

Lerner, M. J., and Miller, D. T. "Just World Research and the Attribution Process: Looking Back and Ahead." *Psychological Bulletin,* 1978, *85,* 1030–1051.

Levi, L., Frankenhaeuser, M., and Gardell, B. "Report on Work Stress Related to Social Structures and Processes." In G. R. Elliott and E. Eisdorfer (eds.), *Stress and Human Health.* New York: Springer, 1982.

Maccoby, N., and others. "Reducing the Risk of Cardiovascular Disease: Effects of a Community-Based Campaign on Knowledge and Behavior." *Journal of Community Health,* 1977, *3,* 100–114.

McKinlay, J. B., and McKinlay, S. M. "The Questionable Contribution of Medical Measures to the Decline of Mortality in the United States in the Twentieth Century." *Milbank Memorial Fund Quarterly/Health & Society,* 1977, *55,* 405–428.

McLeroy, K. R., Green, L. W., Mullen, K. D., and Foshee, V. "Assessing the Effects of Health Promotion in Worksites: A Review of the Stress Program Evaluations." *Health Education Quarterly,* 1984, *11,* 379–401.

Manuck, S., Kaplan, J., and Clarkson, T. "Behaviorally Induced Heart Rate Reactivity and Atherosclerosis in Cynomolgus Monkeys." *Psychosomatic Medicine,* 1983, *45,* 95–108.

Matarazzo, J. "Behavioral Health: A 1990 Challenge for the Health Sciences Professional." In J. Matarazzo and others (eds.), *Behavioral Health.* New York: Wiley, 1985.

Merrill, B. "Short-Term Evaluation in Worksite Health Promotion." *Corporate Commentary,* 1984, *1,* 9–15.

Mervis, J. "The Psychological Route to Cutting Costs." *New York Times,* Nov. 24, 1985, section F, p. 12.

Metropolitan Transit Authority and New York City Transit Authority Strategic Plan 1985–1989. Dec. 1984.

Michela, J. L., and Allegrante, J. P. "An Evaluation of the Impact and Process of a School-Based Workplace Health Promotion Program for Inner-City Teachers." (Rep. 86-1). New York: Center for Health Promotion, Teachers College, Columbia University, 1986.

Michela, J. L., and Wood, J. V. "Causal Attributions in Health and Illness." In P. C. Kendall (ed.), *Advances in Cognitive-Behavioral Research and Therapy.* Vol. 5. New York: Academic Press, 1986.

Minkler, M. "Ethical Issues in Community Organization." *Health Education Monographs,* 1978, 6, 198-210.

Moore-Ede, M., and Richardson, G. "Medical Implications of Shift-Work." *Annual Review of Medicine,* 1985, 36, 607-617.

Mowday, R. T., and Spencer, D. G. "The Influence of Task and Personality Characteristics on Employee Turnover and Absenteeism Incidents." *Academy of Management Journal,* 1981, 24, 634-642.

Mulvaney, D., Reed, R., Gibbs, J., and Henes, C. "Blue Cross and Blue Shield of Indiana: Five Year Payoff in Health Promotion." *Corporate Commentary,* 1985, 1, 1-7.

Murray, T. H. "Warning: Screening Workers for Genetic Risk." *Hastings Center Report,* 1983, 13, 5-8.

National Center for Health Statistics. "Annual Summary of Births, Deaths, Marriages, and Divorces: United States, 1983." *NCHS Monthly Vital Statistics Report,* Sept. 1984.

National Institute of Arthritis, Diabetes, and Digestive and Kidney Diseases, NIH pub. no. 84-109, 1984.

National Safety Council. *Accident Facts.* Chicago: National Safety Council, 1986.

Oliver, P. L., and Kirkpatrick, M. *Employee Health Enhancement.* Cambridge, Mass.: Arthur D. Little, 1982.

Pear, R. "Medical-Care Costs Rose 7.7% in '86, Counter to Trend." *New York Times,* Feb. 9, 1987, p. 1.

Pennebaker, J. W. *The Psychology of Physical Symptoms.* New York: Springer-Verlag, 1983.

Perelman, L. J. *The Learning Enterprise: Adult Learning Capital and Economic Development.* Washington, D.C.: The Council of State Planning Agencies, 1984.

Phillips, S. "Smoking Listed as New Ground for Losing Job." *New York Times,* Jan. 21, 1987, p. 16.

Quayle, D. "American Productivity: The Devastating Effect of Alcoholism and Drug Abuse." *American Psychologist,* 1983, *38,* 454–458.

Rosenstock, I. M. "The Health Belief Model and Preventive Health Behavior." *Health Education Monographs,* 1974, *2,* 354–386.

Rotter, J. B., Chance, J., and Phares, E. J. (eds.). *Applications of a Social Learning Theory of Personality.* New York: Holt, Rinehart & Winston, 1972.

Ryan, W. *Blaming the Victim.* New York: Vintage Books, 1976.

Sashkin, M. "Participative Management Is an Ethical Imperative." *Organizational Dynamics,* 1984, *12,* 5–22.

Sevelius, G. "Exchange." *Corporate Commentary,* 1984, *1,* 60.

Shephard, R. J., Corey, P., Renzland, P., and Cox, M. "The Influence of an Employee Fitness and Lifestyle Modification Program Upon Medical Care Costs." *Canadian Journal of Public Health,* 1982, *73,* 259–263.

Sloan, R. P. "Workplace Health Promotion: A Commentary on the Evolution of a Paradigm." *Health Education Quarterly,* 1987, *14,* 181–194.

Sloan, R. P., and Gruman, J. C. "Beliefs About Cancer, Heart Disease, and Their Victims." *Psychological Reports,* 1983, *52,* 415–424.

Sloan, R. P., and Gruman, J. C. "Participation in Workplace Health Promotion Programs: The Contribution of Health and Organizational Factors." Society for Behavioral Medicine Annual Meeting, Washington, D.C., March 1987.

Smith, M. J., Colligan, M. J., and Tasto, D. L. "Health and Safety Consequences of Shift-Work in the Food-Processing Industry." *Ergonomics,* 1982, *25,* 133–144.

Sontag, S. *Illness as Metaphor.* New York: Vintage Books, 1979.

Stone, G. "Health and the Health System: A Historical Overview and Conceptual Framework." In G. Stone, F. Cohen, and N. Adler (eds.), *Health Psychology: A Handbook.* San Francisco: Jossey-Bass, 1979.

Taylor, F. *The Principles of Scientific Management.* New York: Harper & Row, 1911.

Taylor, S. E., and Fiske, S. T. "Salience, Attention, and Attribution: Top of the Head Phenomenon." In L. Berkowitz (ed.), *Advances in Experimental Social Psychology*. Vol. 11. New York: Academic Press, 1978.

Thigpen, P. "Wellness in the Workplace: Its Role at Levi Strauss and Co." *OD Practitioner*, December 1984, p. 2.

Timio, M., and Gentili, S. "Adrenosympathetic Overactivity Under Conditions of Work." *British Journal of Preventive Social Medicine*, 1976, *30*, 262-265.

Tollin, G. "Lumber Company Pays Employees to Eat Properly and Stay Healthy." St. Paul, Minn., *Pioneer Press*, April 27, 1980, section 4, p. 15.

Triandis, H. C. *Interpersonal Behavior*. Monterey, Calif.: Brooks/ Cole, 1977.

Triandis, H. C. "Values, Attitudes, and Interpersonal Behavior." In M. M. Page (ed.), *1979 Nebraska Symposium on Motivation*. Lincoln: University of Nebraska Press, 1980.

U.S. Department of Health and Human Services. *Health United States 1985*. DHHS pub. no. (PHS) 86-1232. Hyattsville, Md.: 1985.

U.S. Department of Health and Human Services. *Vital and Health Statistics: Current Estimates from the National Health Interview Survey, United States 1985*. Washington, D.C.: U.S. Department of Health and Human Services, 1986.

Verbrugge, L. "Triggers of Symptoms and Health Care." *Social Science and Medicine*, 1985, *20*, 855-876.

Wallin, L., and Wright, I. "Psychosocial Aspects of the Work Environment." *Journal of Occupational Medicine*, 1986, *28*, 384-393.

Watson, C. J. "An Evaluation of Some Aspects of the Steers and Rhodes Model of Employee Attendance." *Journal of Applied Psychology*, 1981, *66*, 385-389.

Weinstein, N. D. "Unrealistic Optimism About Susceptibility to Health Problems." *Journal of Behavioral Medicine*, 1982, *5*, 441-460.

Weis, W. L. " 'No Ifs Ands or Butts'—Why Workplace Smoking Should Be Banned." *Management World*, Sept. 1981, pp. 39-44.

Weiss, C. H. *Evaluation Research: Methods of Assessing Program Effectiveness.* Englewood Cliffs, N.J.: Prentice-Hall, 1972.

Williams, R. "Psychophysiological Processes, the Coronary-Prone Behavior Patterns, and Coronary Heart Disease." In T. Dembroski and others (eds.), *Coronary-Prone Behavior.* New York: Springer-Verlag, 1978.

The Wyatt Company. "1984 Group Benefits Survey." New York: The Wyatt Company, 1984.

Yankelovich, D., and others. *Work and Human Values: An International Report on the Jobs in the 1980s and 1990s.* New York: Aspen Institute for Humanistic Studies, 1983.

Yenney, S. "Small Businesses and Health Promotion: The Prospects Look Good." New York: National Center for Health Education, 1984.

Zemke, R. "Delayed Effects of Corporate Downsizing." *Training,* Nov. 1986, *23,* 67-74.

Index

A

Absenteeism: and health promotion assumptions, 38; information for health analysis, 89-90; policies on, 40; and risk factors, 9-10
Accidents: and mortality, 18; and remuneration systems, 244; risk factors for, 22; work, 10
Adams, J. D., 42, 287
Ajzen, I., 207, 289
Alcohol abuse, cost of, 10. *See also* Risk factors
Allegrante, J. P., 9, 51, 139, 147, 287, 292
Alpha Corporation: analysis data from, 108; program proposal for, 113-114
Ambulatory care, 262
American Cancer Society, 25, 29, 96, 109-110, 159, 169, 173, 182, 213-214, 267, 271
American Diabetes Foundation, 25
American Dietetic Association, 9, 269, 271, 287
American Heart Association, 25, 29, 79, 96, 109, 113, 159, 173, 181, 214, 271

American Lung Association, 29, 79, 96, 110, 173, 271
American Red Cross, 96, 173, 271
Analysis(es), health, 78-79; examples of, 79-83; outline for, 83-96; qualifications on, 96-101
Arnold, C., 87
AT&T Communications, 204, 210, 211, 225, 254; analysis by, 79-80; mission statement of, 105; program of, 66-68
Attitude-behavior theory, 207
Audio-visual materials, 162-163

B

Barker, J., 5
Beckhard, R., 221, 222, 287
Beehr, T. A., 42, 287
Behavior: and health, 208, 211; and health promotion assumptions, 38; health-related, 219-222, 229-231; individual, 217-219, 242-244; initiating change in, 213-214; supporting changed, 30-31. *See also* Risk factors
Bellingham, R., 10, 67, 287
Benefits: flexible, 260-261; rede-

sign of, 259-261; reduced, 149-151
Berg, E. N., 149, 288
Berg Electronics, seat-belt policy of, 32
Berkman, S., 10, 288
Berry, C., 11, 288
Bertera, R., 10
Beta Hospital: analysis data from, 108-109; program proposal for, 114-115
Bhagat, R. S., 42, 287
Blackburn, H., 61
Blair, S. N., 12, 65, 132, 288
Blood pressure: program objectives for, 174-175; screening for high, 181. See also Hypertension
Blue Cross/Blue Shield, 9, 272
Blue Cross and Blue Shield of Indiana, 211; evaluation by, 133-134; follow-up by, 215; program of, 63-64
Bly, J. L., 66, 288
Boal, J., 40, 288
Bodolay-Pratt, 29
Boeing Company, 230; smoking policy of, 225-226
Bowne, D. W., 12, 288
Brennan, A., 11, 123, 288
Bruno, R., 140, 288
Budget, for workplace health promotion program, 119-121. See also Cost(s)
Burlington Industries, 11, 29
Business: financial effect of disease on, 9-10; health care cost for, 7-8
Business plan. See Plan
Bylinsky, G., 153, 288

C

Califano, J., 8, 288
California Biotechnology, 153
Calkins, D., 8, 252, 291
Campbell Soup, hypertension program of, 11, 29
Canada Fitness and Lifestyle Project, 68

Canada Life Assurance Company, 68-69
Cancer, 10; program objectives for, 175-176; risk factors for, 22; screening for, 182-183. See also Disease; Risk factors
Cantlon, A., 12, 288
Caplan, R. D., 42, 43, 290
Cardiovascular disease, 252. See also Disease; Heart disease; Risk factors
Chaffin, D. B., 9, 291
Chance, J., 207, 294
Change: behavior, 30-31, 213-214; environmental and policy, 31-32; organizational, 233-250; policy, 217-232; U.S. demographic, 253
Chaves, M. A., 152, 288
Cheloha, R. S., 40, 288
Cholesterol, screening for, 181
Chrysler Corporation, health care costs of, 8-9, 84
Clarkson, T., 242, 292
Clearinghouse on Business Coalitions for Health Action, 8, 289
Climate. See Organizational climate
Cobb, S., 235, 289
Colacino, D. L., 130, 289
Coleman, R. M., 249, 289
Colligan, M. J., 245, 294
Collings, G. H., 71, 289
Committee(s): activity suggestions, 193; composition, 189-192; as health promotion tool, 165-167; meetings, 192-193
Commonwealth Bank, 214
Communication, program objectives for, 176
Companies, small, 60; fitness programs of, 12-14; policy change in, 231-232. See also Organization(s); Speedcall Corporation
Computers, system maintenance of, 6. See also Microcomputers
Consultants, 203-205
Continental Bank, health seminars of, 27-28
Control Data Corporation, 130
Corey, P., 69, 289

Cost(s): direct and indirect, 7; health care, 7-8, 252; and risk factors, 9-10; potential to reduce, 59; savings, 11-12; sharing, 260; strategies for managing, 259-263. *See also* Budget
Cox, M., 69, 289
Crawford, R., 146, 289
Curran, W. J., 153, 290
Czeisler, C. A., 249, 289

D

Dallas Independent School District, fitness program of, 11
Davis, M. F., 58, 289
Death: causes of, 10; and risk factors, 22. *See also* Mortality
Delbecq, A. L., 248, 289
Diagnosis, and analysis, 78-79
Diagnosis-related groups (DRGs), 86
Disability, 38
Disease: blaming victim for, 145-147; chronic and infectious, 10, 17-18, 20; and health promotion, 24; and health promotion assumptions, 38; history of view of, 17-19; and risk factors, 9-14. *See also* Illness
Dow Chemical, 225
Drug abuse, cost of, 10. *See also* Risk factors
Du Pont Company, 10-11, 90
Dubos, R., 236, 289

E

Employee assistance program (EAP), 193, 194
Employees: coercion on, 147-148; on committees, 165-167, 190; as focus of health promotion, 146-147; information from, for health analysis, 93-95; and organizational climate, 238-246; and organizational factors, 235-237; sample survey for, 275-278; in scientific management view, 251;

unintended consequences for, 149-154. *See also* Individual(s); People
Equipment: maintenance of, 1-4, 5-6; views of, 4-5
Evaluation, 123-124, 141; designs for, 134-141; impact, 129, 131-132; outcome, 129, 132-134; process, 128-131
Events, health promotion, 168-169
Exercise, program objectives for, 175. *See also* Fitness

F

Failure, reasons for, 124-128
Farr, J. L., 40, 288
Federal Aviation Administration, maintenance viewpoint of, 5
Fielding, J. P., 259, 289
Fishbein, M., 207, 289
Fiske, S. T., 44, 295
Fitness: Canada Fitness and Lifestyle Project for, 68-69; lecture topics on, 171; programs of small companies, 12-14. *See also* Exercise
Flex time, 31
Ford Motor Company: evaluation by, 139; screening at, 151
Ford, H., 5
Frankenhaeuser, M., 235, 241, 244, 289, 292
Freeland, M., 8, 289
French, J. R. P., 42, 43, 290
Fries, J. F., 253, 254, 290

G

Galanter, R. B., 146, 290
Ganster, D., 243, 290
Gardell, B., 235, 241, 244, 289, 292
General Mills, 213-214
General Motors, 9, 29
Gentili, S., 242, 295
Gibbs, J. O., 64, 133, 290
Glover, R., 31, 69, 70, 290
Gordon, N. P., 129, 290

Gostin, L., 153, 290
Great American Smokeout, 25, 29, 110, 169
Great Salt Lake Minerals and Chemicals Corporation, 249
Green, L. W., 51, 128, 129, 134, 135, 138, 140, 287, 290
Gruman, J. C., 145, 197, 290, 294
Gulbronson, C. R., 130, 289
Gustafson, D. H., 248, 289

H

Hammer, T. J., 40, 290
Harrison, R. V., 43, 290
Hawaii, psychotherapy program in, 34, 62
Health: and behavior, 208-211; examples of organizational interventions and, 246-249; interaction of factors affecting, 21; meaning of, 16-17; and organizational climate, 238-246; risk factor view of, 20-23
Health Belief Model, 207
Health care: Chrysler Corporation's cost for, 8-9; cost of, 7-8; financial statistics on, 252; strategies for managing costs of, 259-263
Health insurance: and companies' profits, 8; and health promotion assumptions, 38; and risk factors, 10
Health maintenance organizations (HMOs): to reduce health care costs, 263; and workplace health promotion, 33-34
Health promotion: approaches to, 24; and "bottom line," 56; cost savings of programs for, 11-12; definition of, 23-24; goals for individuals, 207-208; history of, 16-20; and organization, 14-15; organizations providing information on, 270-274; percent of profits spent on, 8; publications for professionals in, 264-269; strategies for, 25-26. See also Health promotion program(s); Health promotion, workplace

Health promotion program(s): committee for, 189-193; evaluation of, 123-141; failure of, 124-128; marketing, 195-203; ongoing, 176-178; organization of, 186-189; using existing divisions for, 193-195; vendors and consultants for, 203-205. See also Health promotion; Health promotion, workplace
Health promotion, workplace, 26-27; analysis prior to, 78-101; assumptions of, 38, 39, 46, 48; behavior change in, 30-31; benefits of, 56-60; broader focus of, 48; environmental and policy change in, 31-32; ethical issues of, 142-148; evaluating, 123-141; examples of programs for, 63-71; goals of, 37; growing importance of, 253-257; implications of broader view of, 52-53; information programs in, 27-30; making case for, 71-76; models of, 39, 41, 239; organizations with information on, 270-274; planning for, 102-121; reasons for, 33-35; revised assumptions of, 46, 48, 51-52; time course of benefits of, 60-63; tools for, 156-185; unintended consequences of, 149-154. See also Health promotion; Health promotion program(s)
Health risk appraisals (HRAs), 97, 279-280; at AT&T, 66, 67; and behavior/health link, 210-211; as health promotion tool, 183-184; types of, 283-285; uses for, 280-283
Heart disease, 10, 22. See also Cardiovascular disease; Disease; Risk factors
Herzberg, F., 58, 291
Herzlinger, R., 8, 150, 252, 291
Holmes, T. H., 42, 291
House, J. S., 144, 235, 291
Hubbard Milling, fitness program of, 13
Human relations movement, 5

Human resources development, 193, 195

Hypertension: Campbell Soup program for, 11; New York Telephone Company program for, 70-71. *See also* Blood pressure; Disease; Risk factors

I

Ibold, K., 5, 291

Illinois Bell, employee assistance program of, 11

Illness: behaviors, 45, 47, 48; direct and indirect costs of, 7. *See also* Disease

Incentives: for nonsmoking, 224-225; to support behavior change, 30-31

Individual(s): behavior of, 208-211, 213-214, 242-244; creating plan for, 211-213; as focus of health promotion, 146-147; healthy lifestyle for, 215; health promotion goals for, 207-208; reliance on motivation of, 217-219, 233-234, 236; violating rights of, 151-153. *See also* Employees; People

Information: for health analysis, 83-96; from HRAs, 98; organizations providing health promotion, 270-274; programs, 27-30

Insurance. *See* Health insurance

International Business Machines (IBM), 116, 204

J

Jackson, S., 235, 248, 291

Johnson, D., 10, 67, 287

Johnson & Johnson, 225; creating individual plan at, 213; evaluation by, 131-132; mission statement of, 105-106; program of, 65-66

Jones, R. C., 66, 288

K

Kahn, R., 42, 291

Kaplan, J., 242, 292

Kaplan, J. R., 42, 291

Karasek, R. A., 240, 291

Keyserling, W. M., 9, 291

Kimberly-Clark Corporation, 30, 90, 211

King, J., 27-28, 291

Kirkpatrick, M., 9, 293

Kjellgren, 244

Knowles, J., 21, 291

Koch, R., 17

Kotler, P., 196, 198, 291

Kristein, M., 11, 292

Kronlund, 244

L

Landau, J. C., 40, 290

Lectures/talks, as health promotion tool, 169-172

Lerner, M. J., 145, 292

Levi, L., 241, 244, 292

Lewis, F. M., 128, 134, 135, 138, 140, 290

Lifestyle: and cause of death, 10; healthy, 215

Lockheed, health education activities of, 28

Loyalties, conflicting, 143-145

M

McCauley, M., 10, 67, 287

McGraw-Hill, smoking policy of, 226-228

McKinlay, J. B., 18, 292

McKinlay, S. M., 18, 292

McLeroy, K. R., 144, 292

McNamara, R., 199

Magic-bullet approach, 17

Maintenance, preventive, 1-6

Major diagnostic categories (MDCs), 86

Management: on health promotion committee, 190; as health promotion tool, 163-164; making case to, 55-63, 71-77

Manager, health promotion: conflicting loyalties for, 143-145; publications for, 264-269; role

of, in policy change, 219. *See also* Tools, for workplace health promotion
Manuck, S., 242, 292
Marketing, 195-196; activities, 199-203; general theory of, 196-198
Massachusetts Mutual Life Insurance Company, 29
Matarazzo, J., 21, 292
Mayo, E., 5
Media, for marketing, 202-203
Medical department, 193, 195
Medicare: companies' contribution to, 8; diagnostic categories of, 86
Melvin, W., 2
Memorial Sloan-Kettering Cancer Center, 230
Merrill, B., 130, 292
Mervis, J., 34, 62, 292
Metropolitan Life Insurance Company, 11
Metropolitan Transit Authority Strategic Plan 1985-1989, 2-3, 292
Michela, J. L., 42, 139, 292, 293
Microcomputer(s): as health promotion tool, 167-168; -scored HRAs, 284-285
Millard Manufacturing Company, 230
Miller, D. T., 145, 292
Minkler, M., 146, 293
Minnesota Heart Health Program, 61
Mission statements, for workplace health promotion programs, 103-106
Mood, and medical care, 44
Moore-Ede, M., 245, 293
Moore-Ede, M. C., 249, 289
Morbidity, compression of, 253-254
Mortality, causes of, 10, 17, 18, 20
Motivation, reliance on individual, 218, 236
Mowday, R. T., 40, 293
Mulvaney, D., 64, 293
Murray, T. H., 152, 293

N

National Center for Health Statistics, 22, 293
National High Blood Pressure Month, 25, 181
National Institute of Arthritis, Diabetes, and Digestive and Kidney Diseases, 252, 293
National Institutes of Health, 256
National Safety Council, 10, 293
New York City Transit Authority: deferred maintenance by, 2-3; Strategic Plan 1985-1989, 2, 292
New York Telephone: evaluation by, 140; hypertension control program of, 70-71; savings by, 11
North American Life Assurance Company, 68-69
Northern Central Bank, 214
Northern Telecom, Inc., fitness program of, 13
Nutrition: lecture topics on, 171; program objectives for, 175

O

Obesity, 9. *See also* Risk factors
Occupational Safety and Health Administration, 27
Oliver, P. L., 9, 293
Organization(s): changing policies of, 217-232; downsizing by, 254-255; employee health and factors in, 235-237; examples of cost savings by, 11-12; examples of interventions by, 246-249; health analysis by, 78-101; of health promotion program, 186-189; as interdependent systems, 257-258; preventive maintenance by, 1-6; providing health promotion information, 270-274; using existing divisions within, 193-195. *See also* Companies, small
Organizational climate: concept of, 238; and health outcomes, 238-246

Organizational development (OD), 193, 194; and policy change, 221-222; and work design, 245-246
Organizational effectiveness (OE), 193, 194

P

Pacific Bell, smoking policy of, 32
Parents, lecture topics on, 172
Pasteur, L., 17, 295
Pear, R., 84, 293
Pennebaker, J. W., 43, 293
People: myth of resiliency of, 6-9; views of, 4-5. See also Employees; Individual(s)
Pepsico, evaluation by, 130-131
Perelman, L. J., 252, 293
Phares, E. J., 207, 294
Phillips Petroleum Company, 90, 213
Phillips, S., 148, 293
Physical fitness. See Fitness
Pillsbury, 90, 211; creating individual plan at, 212; followup by, 215
Plan: business, 104, 107-118; individual, 211-213
Planning, 102-103, 121-122; to avoid unintended consequences, 149-154; budget in, 119-121; developing business plan in, 107-118; ethical issues in, 142-148; for evaluation, 123-124, 141; mission statement in, 103-106
Plaskolite, Inc., 29, 80
Policy(ies): change, 31-32, 218-219, 232; change in smaller companies, 231-232; examples of smoking, 225-228; and health promotion manager, 219; to influence behavior, 229-231; model smoking, 222-225; regulating behavior, 219-222
Preferred provider organization (PPO), 262-263
Print materials, 157-162. See also Publications

Programs. See Health promotion program(s)
Provident Indemnity Life Insurance Company, 13, 225, 228
Prudential Insurance Company, 211; fitness program of, 12
Psychotherapy, Hawaii federal employee program for, 34, 62
Publications, for health promotion professionals, 264-269. See also Print materials

Q

Quality of worklife (QWL) circles, 193, 195
Quayle, D., 10, 294

R

Rahe, R. H., 42, 291
Read, 9
Referral, as health promotion tool, 178-179
Remuneration systems, effect of different, 244
Resiliency, myth of, 6-9
Richardson, G., 245, 293
Richardson, J. E., 66, 288
Risk factors: and causes of death, 22; in contemporary view of health, 20-23; controllable and uncontrollable, 21-22; and disease, 9-14; and health promotion, 24. See also Behavior
Rosenstock, I. M., 207, 294
Rotter, J. B., 207, 294
Ryan, W., 145, 294

S

Safeco, 214
Safety department, 193, 195
Safeway Bakery Division, 14, 200, 214
Sashkin, M., 190, 294
Schendler, C., 8, 289
Scherer Brothers Lumber Company, 12, 210; absenteeism policy of,

40; environmental changes of, 31-32; health analysis by, 81-83; mission statement of, 106; "wellness pay" plan of, 230
Scherer, G., 12, 40
Schwartz, J., 8, 150, 252, 291
Scientific management, 4-5, 151
Screening: to accompany HRA, 211; for detection of disease, 29; as health promotion tool, 179-183. *See also* Testing
Seat belts, 32
Second opinions, 261
Self-care, 255
Self-help/support groups, as health promotion tool, 178
Sentry Life Insurance, 30
Sevelius, G., 28, 294
Shephard, R. J., 68, 69, 289, 294
Shift-work, 245-246
Simpson Timber Company, 28
Single etiology theory, 17
Sloan, R. P., 46, 51, 145, 147, 197, 287, 290, 294
Smith, M. J., 245, 294
Smoking: brainstorming ideas to discourage, 109-111; cost of, 9-10; development of model policy for, 222-225; examples of policies on, 225-228; objectives of program discouraging, 174; program banning, 148; savings due to programs for, 11; Speedcall program for, 30-31, 69-70, 225
Social behavior theory, 207
Social Learning Theory, 207
Sontag, S., 146, 294
Southern New England Telephone, 12
Southwestern Bell, 213
Speedcall Corporation, nonsmoking program of, 30-31, 69-70, 225
Spencer, D. G., 40, 293
Stern, R. N., 40, 290
Stone, G., 19, 294
Strategic Plan 1985-1989, of Metropolitan Transit Authority and New York City Transit Authority, 2-3, 292

Stress: and corporate downsizing, 254-255; lecture topics on, 172; limitations of programs to manage, 242-244; objectives of program for, 175; and work conditions, 240-241; in workplace, 42
Symptoms, and medical care, 44-45

T

Tasto, D. L., 245, 294
Taylor, F., 4, 151, 251, 294
Taylor, S. E., 44, 295
Teachers, 139
Technologies, health information, 255-256
Teletype Corporation of Arkansas, seat-belt policy of, 32
Tenneco, Inc., flex-time program of, 31
Testing, 151-153. *See also* Screening
Thigpen, P., 1, 295
Timio, M., 242, 295
Tollin, G., 12, 295
Tools, for workplace health promotion; audio-visual materials, 162-163; committees, 165-167; health promotion events, 168-169; health risk appraisals, 183-184; lectures/talks, 169-172; management, 163-164; microcomputer software, 167-168; ongoing programs, 176-178; print materials, 157-162; referral, 178-179; screening for disease, 179-183; self-help/support groups, 178; workshops/skills training, 172-176
Triandis, H. C., 207, 295

U

U.S. Center for Disease Control, 10
U.S. Chamber of Commerce, 7-8
U.S. Department of Health and Human Services, 12, 20, 21, 252, 295
Union Carbide Corporation, 254
Union Life Insurance Company, 13

Unions: for health promotion, 193, 194; as information source, 96
United Parcel Service (UPS), 2
United Storeworkers of America, 29, 96
Utilization reviews, 261-262

V

Values, 256-257
Van de Ven, A. H., 248, 289
Vendors, 203-205
Verbrugge, L., 44, 295
Victim, blaming, 145-147
Volvo, 188; illness prevention program of, 246-248

W

Wallin, L., 246, 247, 248, 295
Watson, C. J., 40, 295
Weight: loss program, 214; objectives of program to control, 174
Weis, W. L., 11, 295
Weiss, C. H., 124, 127, 296
Westlake Community Hospital, nonsmoking hiring policy of, 32

Williams, R., 242, 296
Williamsport National Bank, 214
Wood, J. V., 42, 293
Work design, physiological effects of, 241-242
Workplace: reasons for health promotion in, 33-35; stress in, 42, 240-241. *See also* Health promotion, workplace
Workshops/skills training, as health promotion tool, 172-176
World Health Organization, definition of disease, 19
Wright, I., 246, 247, 248, 295
Wyatt Company, 150, 296

Y

Yankelovich, D., 256, 296
Yenney, S., 60, 296
YMCA, 79, 96, 177, 178
YWCA, 177, 178

Z

Zemke, R., 254, 296